Guitar Chord Songbook

Contemporary Christian

ISBN 0-634-05602-6

7777 W. Bluemound Rd. P.O. Box 13819 Milwaukee, WI 53213

Contents

Abba

(Father)

Words and Music by Rebecca St. James,
Tedd Tjornholm and Otto Price

(Capo 1st fret)

D Gadd9 Bm7 Em7 Gmaj7 Cmaj7 B♭
A G A7sus4 F♯m7 Asus4 Cmaj9♯11

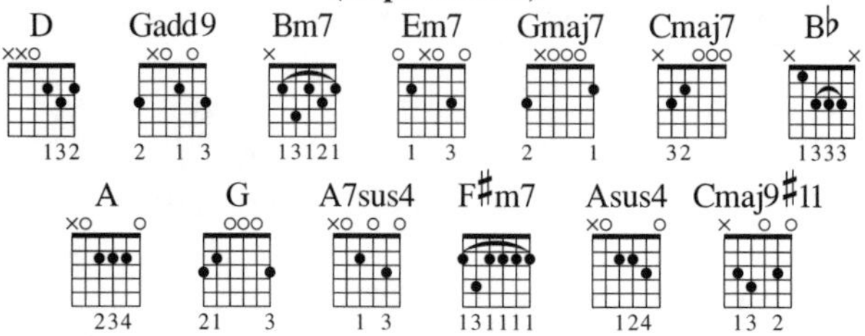

Intro

‖: **D** | **Gadd9** :‖ *Play 4 times*

‖: **Bm7** **Gadd9** | **Em7** :‖

Verse 1

Bm7 **Gadd9** **Em7**
I'm feeling like the eagle that rises,

Bm7 **Gadd9** **Em7**
Flies a-bove the earth and its troubles.

Bm7 **Gadd9** **Em7**
Oh, yes, he knows that there are valleys below,

Bm7 **Gadd9** **Em7**
But under __ his wings there's a stronger power.

Gmaj7 **Em7** **Cmaj7**
Oh, Fa - ther, You are ___my strength.

B♭ **A**
On You __ I wait upon.

Chorus 1

```
D                              Gadd9
  You make the road rise up        to meet me.
D                                  Gadd9
  You make the sunshine warm __ upon my face.
D                          Gadd9
  The wind is at my back       and the rain falls soft.
D
  God, I lift You high.
G    D Gadd9
You are my Abba.
```

Verse 2

```
Bm7            Gadd9 Em7
    Running in this race 'til the finish line,
Bm7        Gadd9          Em7
    The on - ly road for me is the narrow.
Bm7             Gadd9      Em7
    Not gonna stop or e - ven look to the side
          Bm7       Gadd9   Em7
When I __ fix my eyes on You, Jesus.
Gmaj7     Em7                Cmaj7
    Oh, Fa  -  ther, You are __ my strength,
     B♭               A
Now __ more than ev - er.
```

Chorus 2 *Repeat Chorus 1*

Chorus 3 *Repeat Chorus 1*

Bridge

```
Em7                    A7sus4
When you run too far,

                        Gadd9
(And the road is long,)
                  Can't walk another mile,

           F♯m
(He is wait - ing.)

Em7                 A7sus4
Hope in Him again.

(He'll renew you,)

     Gadd9
Then you will rise.

B♭             A
Gather up your wings and fly.
```

Guitar Solo *Repeat Chorus 1 (Instrumental)*

Chorus 4 *Repeat Chorus 1*

Chorus 5

```
D                                  Gadd9
  You make the road rise up          to meet me.
D                                     Gadd9
  You make the sunshine warm __ upon my face.
D                              Gadd9
  The wind is at my back       and the rain falls soft.
D
  God, I lift You high.
G    D  Em7   Cmaj9♯11
You are  my Ab-ba
```

Do you not know?

Have you not heard?

He gives strength to the weary,

To those who hope in Him.

They will soar like eagles.

Alive

Words and Music by
Sonny, Marcos, Traa and Wuv

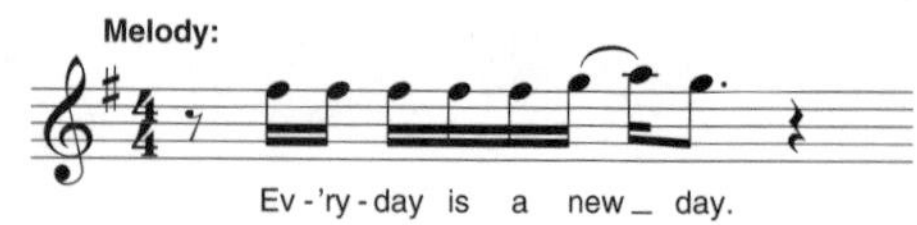

Drop D tuning, down 1 step:
(low to high) C–G–C–F–A–D

E5 D5 A5 C5 Esus2 Em

Intro

| E5 D5 E5 A5 C5 | G5 |
| E5 D5 E5 A5 C5 | G5 |

Verse 1

E5 D5 E5 A5 C5
Ev-'ry day is a new day.

G5
I'm thankful for ev'ry breath I take.

E5 D5 E5 A5 C5
I won't __ take it for grant-ed,
(I won't take it for granted.)

G5
So I learn from my mistakes.

E5 D5 E5
It's be - yond my control,

A5 C5
Sometimes it's best to let go.

G5
Whatever happens in this lifetime.

E5 D5 E5 A5 C5
So I trust in love. (So I trust in love.)

G5
You have given me peace of mind.

```
               C5        D5      E5
Chorus 1       I, I feel so __ alive
               Esus2                    G5
                 For the very first time

               I can't deny you.

               I feel so alive.
               C5        D5       E5              Esus2
               I, I feel so __ alive.   (I feel so a-live,)
                                     G5
               For the very first time.    (For the very first time.)

               And I think I can fly.

               E5   D5 E5           A5            C5
Verse 2          Sun  -  shine upon my face.
                                          (Sunshine __ upon my face.)
                                           G5
               A new song for me to sing.
               E5   D5  E5                  A5                    C5
                 Tell the world how I feel in-side
                                                  (Tell the world how I feel inside.)
                                                          G5
               Even though it might cost me ev'rything.
               E5 D5 E5              A5
                      Now that I know this,
                         C5
               So beyond, I can't hold this.
                                                   G5
               I could never turn my back away.
               E5 D5 E5             A5           C5
                      Now that I see you,
                                            (Now that I see you.)
                                         G5
               I could never look away.
```

Chorus 2 *Repeat Chorus 1*

Bridge | Em | | | |

And now that I know you,

I could never turn my back away.

And now that I see you,

I could never look away.

And now that I know you,

I could never turn my back away.

And now that I see you,

I believe no matter what they say.

Chorus 3 *Repeat Chorus 1*

C5 D5 E5 Esus2
Chorus 4 I, I feel so __ alive (I feel so a-live)
G5
For the very first time. (For the very first time.)
(For the very first time.)
N.C.
And I think I can fly.
C5 D5 E5 Esus2
I, I feel so __ alive (I feel so a-live)
G5
For the very first time. (For the very first time.)
N.C.
And I think I can fly.
E5 D5 E5
And I think I can fly.
D5 E5 D5 E5 D5 E5
And I think I can fly.
D5 E5 D5 E5
And I think I can fly.
| **D5 E5 D5 E5 D5 E5** | **D5 E5 D5 E5 D5 E5** |

Always Have, Always Will

Words and Music by Grant Cunningham,
Nick Gonzales and Toby McKeehan

Melody:

Part of me is the prod - i - gal,

C Am G Csus2 F B♭ Am7

Intro

| C | Am G | C | Am G |
| Csus2 G | Am | Csus2 G | Am |

Verse 1

```
C                        G
Part of me is the prodi-gal,
Am                       F
Part of me is the other brother.
C                           G
  But I think the heart of me is
Am                               F
Really somewhere between them.
C                           G
  Some days I'm running wild,
Am                          F
  Some days we're recon-ciled.
C                             G
  But I wonder all the while __
Am                          F
Why you put up with me, when
G         Am
I wrestle most days
   B♭
To find ways to do as I please.
```

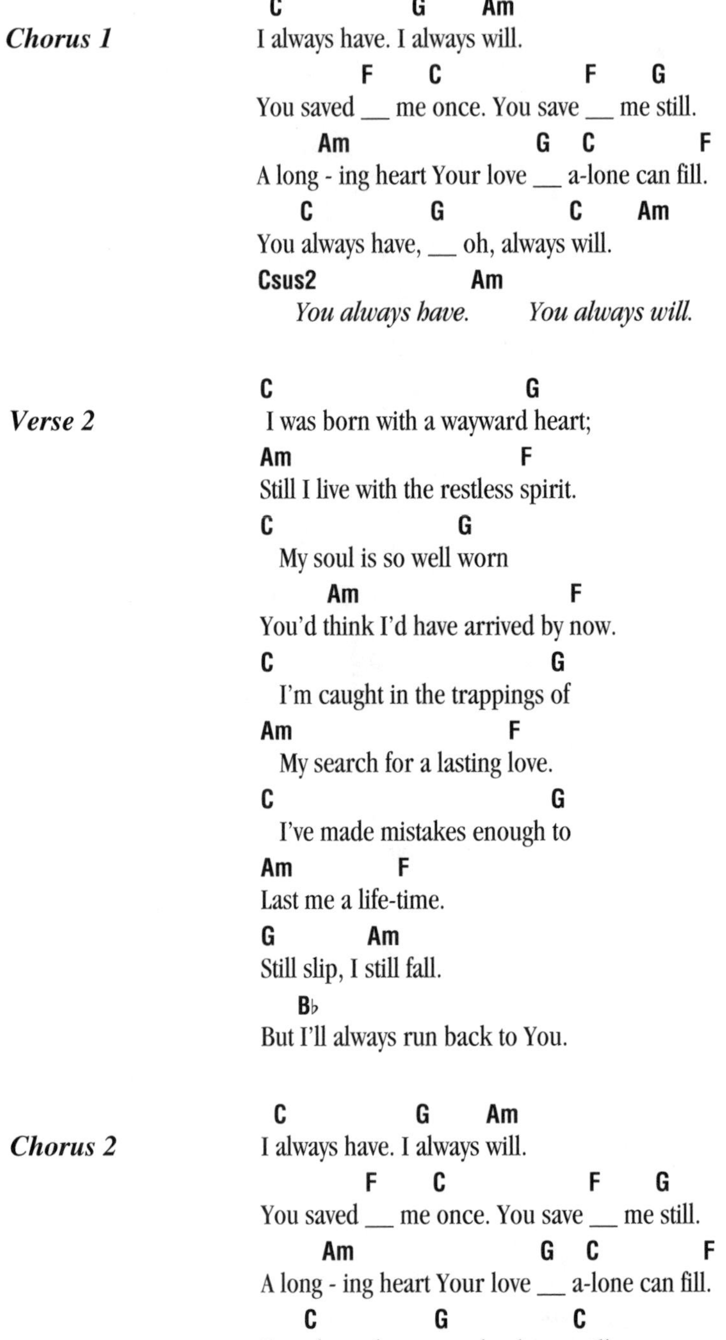

Chorus 1

```
 C            G      Am
I always have. I always will.
            F      C             F      G
You saved __ me once. You save __ me still.
      Am                     G   C          F
A long - ing heart Your love __ a-lone can fill.
    C             G              C      Am
You always have, __ oh, always will.
Csus2                  Am
    You always have.        You always will.
```

Verse 2

```
C                            G
 I was born with a wayward heart;
Am                           F
Still I live with the restless spirit.
C                   G
  My soul is so well worn
       Am                          F
You'd think I'd have arrived by now.
C                               G
  I'm caught in the trappings of
Am                          F
  My search for a lasting love.
C                               G
  I've made mistakes enough to
Am            F
Last me a life-time.
G           Am
Still slip, I still fall.
    B♭
But I'll always run back to You.
```

Chorus 2

```
 C            G      Am
I always have. I always will.
            F      C             F      G
You saved __ me once. You save __ me still.
      Am                     G   C          F
A long - ing heart Your love __ a-lone can fill.
    C             G              C
You always have, __ oh, always will.
```

Bridge

```
G
  I'm gonna keep trusting You.

  I see what You've seen me through.

  I'm goin' where You have gone.

  I'm letting You lead me,

  I'm letting You lead me home.

All my days,
F       C         G
Always, and forever.
                     (Never far.)
F     C              G
Never leave me, never.
                        (Here I'll stay.)
F       C        G                   F  C
Ever love__ me, ever.
                       (Here's my heart.)
   F      G   C    Am7
I'll always love You.
    C   G    Am
Love you, yeah, yeah.
```

Chorus 3

Repeat Chorus 1

Chorus 4

```
 C              G      Am
I always have. I always will.
           F      C                     F        G
You saved __ me once.  I know you'll save me still.
        Am7                      F   C          F
My long - ing heart Your love __ a-lone can fill.
     C            G         C
You always have, __ always will.
Am          C
  Oh, you al - ways will.
       Am              Csus2
You al  -  ways will.
```

Angels

Words and Music by Amy Grant, Gary Chapman,
Michael W. Smith and Brown Bannister

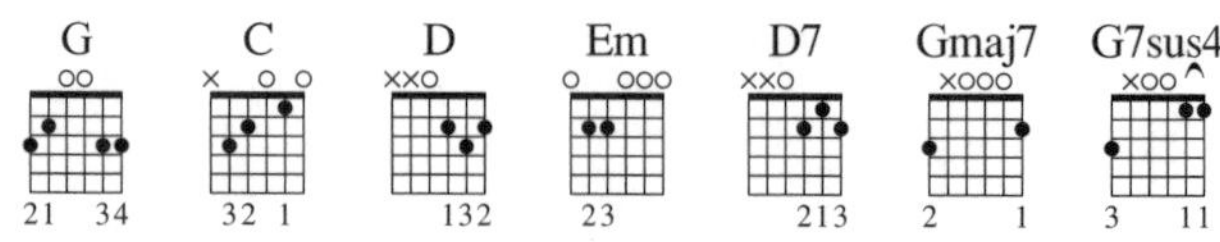

Intro ||: G | :|| *Play 4 times*

Verse 1

```
G
"Take this man to prison,"
           C              D  G
The man __ heard Her-od say,

And then four squads of soldiers came and
C           D   G
Carried him a - way.

Chained up between two watchmen,
C          D  G
Peter tried to sleep,

But beyond the walls an endless pray'r was
C         D  G
Lifting for his keep.
         C
Then a light cut through the darkness
```

```
    G
Of a lonely prison cell,
        C
And the chains that bound the man of God just
G
Opened up and fell,
    D
And running to his people
  C
Be-fore the break of day, there was
G
Only one thing on his mind,
C           D G
Only one thing to say:
```

Chorus 1

```
C             Em D7 G
Angels watching o - ver me,
C         D G
Ev'ry move I make.
C     Em       D7 G  C   D G
Angels watching o-ver me.
C             Em D7 G
Angels watching o - ver me,
C        D G
Ev'ry step I take,
C     Em       D7 G
Angels watching o-ver me.
|C    D  G |C    D  G|
```

Verse 2

```
   G
God only knows the times my life
   C            D G
Was threatened just to-day,

Reckless car ran out of gas
  C        D  G
Be-fore it ran my way.

Near misses all around me,
C       D G
Accidents un-known,

Though I never see with human eyes
   C            D  G
The hands that lead me home.
    C
But I know they're all around me,
  G
All day and through the night,
       C
When the enemy is closing in
 G
I know sometimes they fight
  D
To keep my feet from falling,
  C
I'll never turn away,
      G
If you're asking what's protecting me,
             C        D  G
Then you're gonna hear me say:
```

Chorus 2

```
C                 Em D7 G
Angels watching o  -  ver me,
C         D G
Ev'ry move I  make.
C     Em        D7 G  C    D  G
Angels watching o-ver me.
C                 Em D7 G
Angels watching o  -  ver me,
C        D G
Ev'ry step I  take,
C     Em        D7 G
Angels watching o-ver me.
|C    D   G |C     D |G      |Gmaj7    |G7sus4    |
```

Bridge

```
C  Em              D7  G      Gmaj7     G7sus4
An-gels watching o-ver me,
C  Em              D7 G   N.C.
An-gels watching o-ver me.
```

Got His...

Chorus 3

Repeat Chorus 1

Outro

```
C     Em       D   G
Angels watching o-ver me,
C     Em       D   G
Angels watching o-ver me,
C  Em          D7 G
An-gels watching o-ver me,
C              D   G
Angels watching o-ver me.
```

Though I never see with human eyes

```
            C          D  G
The hands __ that lead me home.
||: G        |          :|| Repeat and fade
```

Awesome God

Words and Music by
Rich Mullins

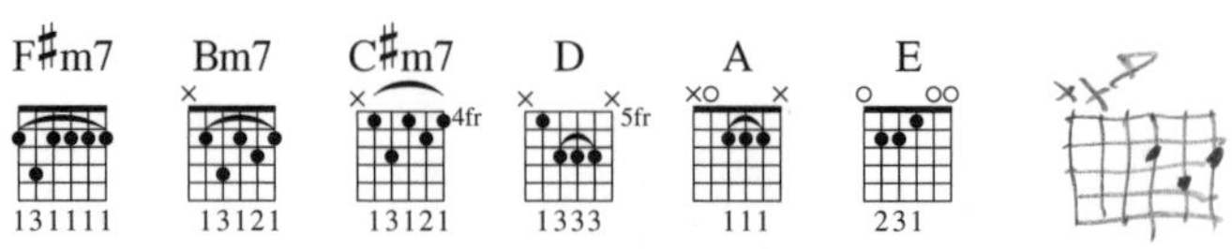

Intro | F♯m7 | Bm7 C♯m7 | F♯m7 | Bm7 C♯m7 |

Verse 1

```
              F♯m
When He rolls up His sleeve, He ain't just "puttin' on the Ritz."
    Bm7       C♯m7      F♯m
Our God is an awesome God!

There is thunder in His footsteps and lightnin' in His fist.
    Bm7       C♯m7      F♯m
Our God is an awesome God!
       Bm7
And the Lord wasn't jokin' when He kicked 'em out of Eden;
 C♯m7
It wasn't for no reason that He shed His blood.
      D                                 Bm7
His re-turn is very close and so you better be believin' that our
         C♯m7      F♯m
God is an awesome God!
```

Chorus 1

D A
Our God is an awesome God;
E F♯m
He reigns from heaven above.
D A
With wisdom, pow'r and love,
Bm7 C♯m7 F♯m
Our God is an awesome God!
D A
Our God is an awesome God;
E F♯m
He reigns from heaven above.
D A
With wisdom, pow'r and love,
Bm7 C♯m7 F♯m
Our God is an awesome God!
| Bm7 C♯m7 |

Verse 2

F♯m
And when the sky was starless in the void of the night,
Bm7 C♯m7 F♯m
Our God is an awesome God!

He spoke into the darkness and created the light.
Bm7 C♯m7 F♯m
Our God is an awesome God!
Bm7
The judgment and wrath He poured out on Sodom,
C♯m7
The mercy and grace He gave us at the cross.
D Bm7
I hope that we have not too quickly forgotten
C♯m7 F♯m
That our God is an awesome God!

Chorus 2 *Repeat Chorus 1*

Chorus 3

```
    D       A
Our God is an awesome God;
  E           F#m
He reigns from heaven above.
     D      A
With wisdom, pow'r and love,
    Bm7     C#m7    F#m
Our God is an awesome God!
    D       A
Our God is an awesome God;
  E           F#m
He reigns from heaven above.
     D      A
With wisdom, pow'r and love,
    Bm7     C#m7    F#m
Our God is an awesome God!
    Bm7     C#m7    F#m
Our God is an awesome God!
    Bm7     C#m7    F#m
Our God is an awesome God!
```

Don't Look at Me

Words and Music by Stacie Orrico
and Mark Heimermann

Melody:

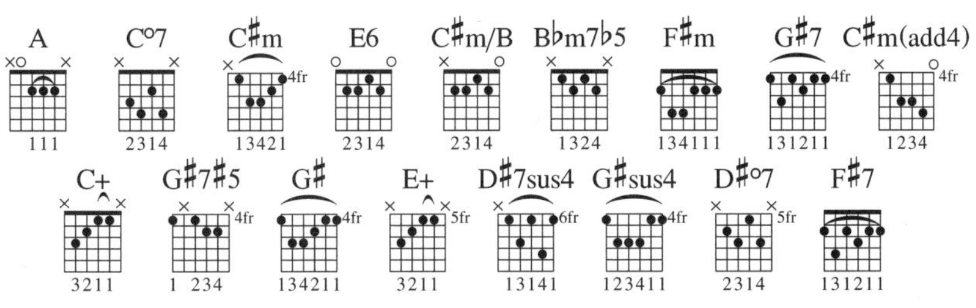

Chorus 1

A C°7 C♯m
Don't look at me if you're lookin' for per-fection.

E6 A C°7 C♯m/B
Don't look at me; I will only let you down.

B♭m7♭5 A C°7 C♯m
I'll do my best to point you in the right di-rection,

E6 F♯m
But don't look at me, no, no, no,

G♯7 C♯m
Don't look at me; look at Him.

Verse 1

C♯m(add4) C+
Sometimes I have a fear that you will see a mirror

G♯7♯5 F♯m A G♯ E+
And get the thought that it's the main at - trac - tion.

C♯m(add4) C+
But all that you detect is just what I reflect

G♯7♯5 F♯m A G♯ E+
Of the object of my own af - fec - tion.

F♯m D♯7sus4 G♯7
I'll lead you to the One I found;

F♯m G♯sus4 G♯
He'll give you ev'rything you need.

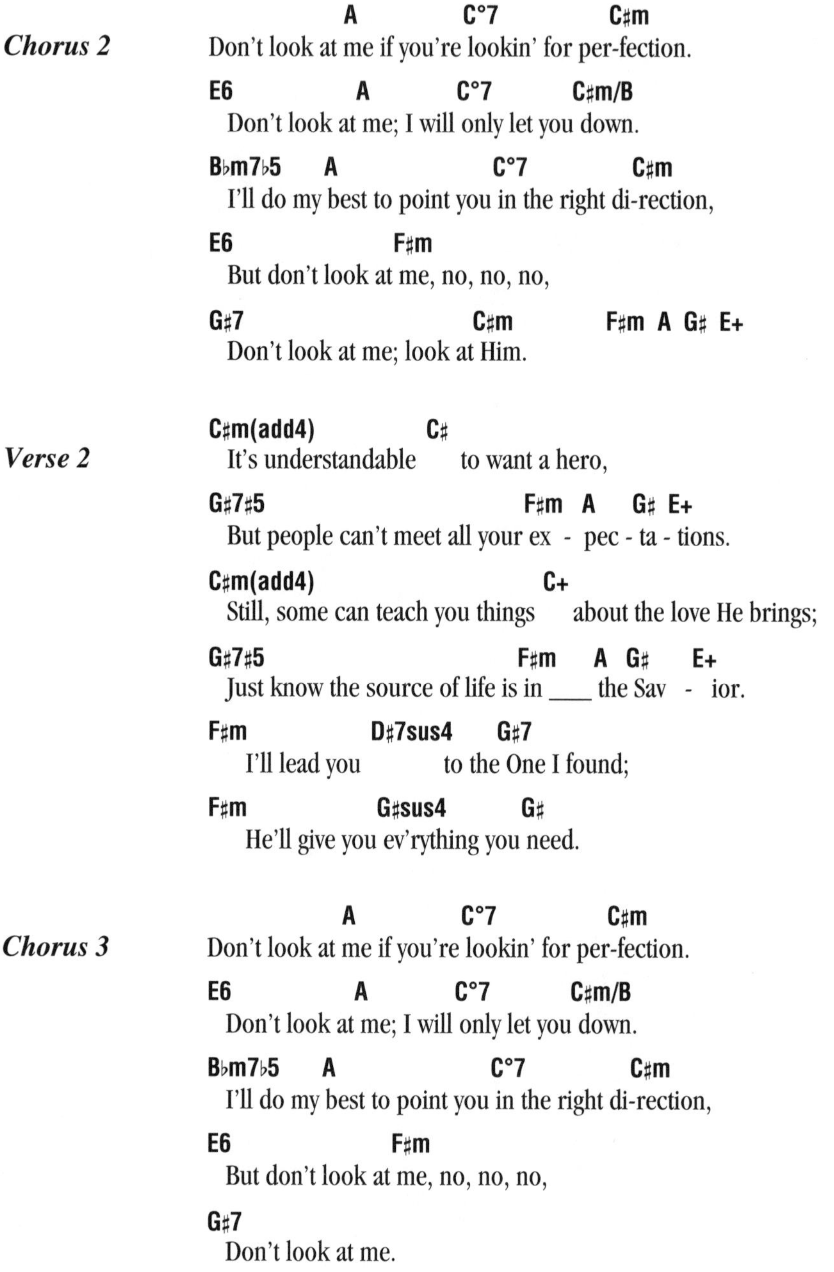

Chorus 2

A C°7 C♯m
Don't look at me if you're lookin' for per-fection.

E6 A C°7 C♯m/B
Don't look at me; I will only let you down.

B♭m7♭5 A C°7 C♯m
I'll do my best to point you in the right di-rection,

E6 F♯m
But don't look at me, no, no, no,

G♯7 C♯m F♯m A G♯ E+
Don't look at me; look at Him.

Verse 2

C♯m(add4) C♯
It's understandable to want a hero,

G♯7♯5 F♯m A G♯ E+
But people can't meet all your ex - pec - ta - tions.

C♯m(add4) C+
Still, some can teach you things about the love He brings;

G♯7♯5 F♯m A G♯ E+
Just know the source of life is in ___ the Sav - ior.

F♯m D♯7sus4 G♯7
I'll lead you to the One I found;

F♯m G♯sus4 G♯
He'll give you ev'rything you need.

Chorus 3

A C°7 C♯m
Don't look at me if you're lookin' for per-fection.

E6 A C°7 C♯m/B
Don't look at me; I will only let you down.

B♭m7♭5 A C°7 C♯m
I'll do my best to point you in the right di-rection,

E6 F♯m
But don't look at me, no, no, no,

G♯7
Don't look at me.

```
Bridge      C♯m                           D♯°7
              He's the One who lived a perfect life;

            E6                            F♯7
              He's the One who always gets it right.

            C♯m                        D♯°7
              He's the One and only guiding light;

            E6     F♯7
              Oh,       yeah.

            C♯m                  C°7
              He's ev'rything you want to be;

            C♯m/B                        B♭m7♭5
              He's the answer to your ev'ry need.

            A
              If you follow Him, then you will see He's

            G♯7
            Like no other, yeah.


Chorus 4    A             C°7                C♯m    E6
                                               Ooh,        ooh,

            A           C°7    C♯m/B
            Ooh.  Yeah.

            B♭m7♭5     A                  C°7              C♯m
              I'll do my best to point you in the right di-rection,

            E6                    F♯m
              But don't look at me, no, no, no,

            G♯7               A     C°7     C♯m
              Don't look at me.

            E6                A     C°7          C♯m/B      B♭m7♭5
              Don't look at me.        (I'll only let you go.)

                      A                  C°7              C♯m
            I'll do my best to point you in the right di-rection;

                                  F♯m
            But don't look at me, no, no, no,

            G♯7                          N.C.
              Don't look at me, look at Him.
```

Between You and Me

Words and Music by
Toby McKeehan and Mark Heimermann

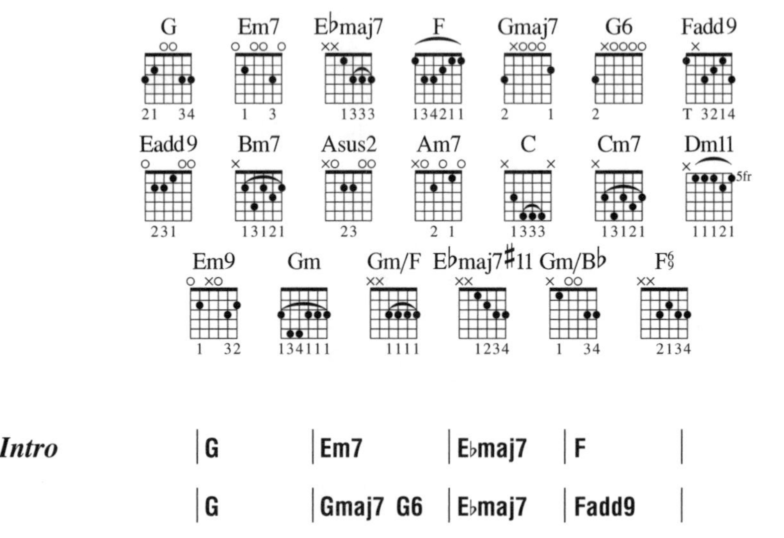

Intro

| G | Em7 | E♭maj7 | F |
| G | Gmaj7 G6 | E♭maj7 | Fadd9 | |

Verse 1

```
Eadd9                    Bm7
Sorrow is a lonely feel - ing,
   Asus2                     Am7
Un-settled is a painful place.
Eadd9                         Bm7
  I've lived with both for far __ too long now
Asus2                     Am7
Since we've parted ways.
         Eadd9                Bm7
I've been wrestling with my con - science
     Asus2          Am
And I found myself to blame.
C                       Cm7
  If there's to be any res - olution
C                         Cm7      Dm11
  I've got to peel my pride __ away.
```

Chorus 1

```
G
    Just between you and me
Em9                          E♭maj7
    I've got something to say,
                    Fadd9
Wanna get it straight

Before the sun goes down.
G
    Just between you and me
Em9                              E♭maj7
    Confession needs to be made,
                       Dm11
Recompense is my way
       C
To free - dom now.
G
    Just between you and me
C                             Fadd9
    I've got something to say.
```

Verse 2

```
       Eadd9                    Bm7
If con-fession is the road to heal  -  ing,
    Asus2                         Am7
For-giveness is the promised land,
Eadd9                   Bm7
    I'm reaching out in my __ conviction,
    Asus2                 Am7
I'm longing to make amends.
        Eadd9                          Bm7
So, I'm sorry for the words I've spo  -  ken,
    Asus2          Am
For I've betrayed a friend.
C                              Cm7
  We've got a love that's worth __ preserving
C                   Cm7         Dm11
    And a bond I will __ defend.
```

Chorus 2 *Repeat Chorus 1*

Interlude

| E♭maj7 | F | Gm | Gm/F |
| E♭maj7♯11 | F | Gm | F6/9 |

Bridge

E♭maj7
In my pursuit of God,

Fadd9
I thirst for holiness,

Gm
As I approach the Son,

Gm/B♭
I must consider this.

E♭maj7
Offenses unresolved,

Fadd9
They'll keep me from the throne.

Gm
Before I go to Him

Gm/B♭ **C**
My wrong must be a - toned.

Cm7
If there's to be any res - olution,

C **Cm7** **Dm11**
I've got to peel this pride __ away.

Solo

| G | Em9 | E♭maj7 | Fadd9 |
| G | Em9 | E♭maj7 | Dm11 C |

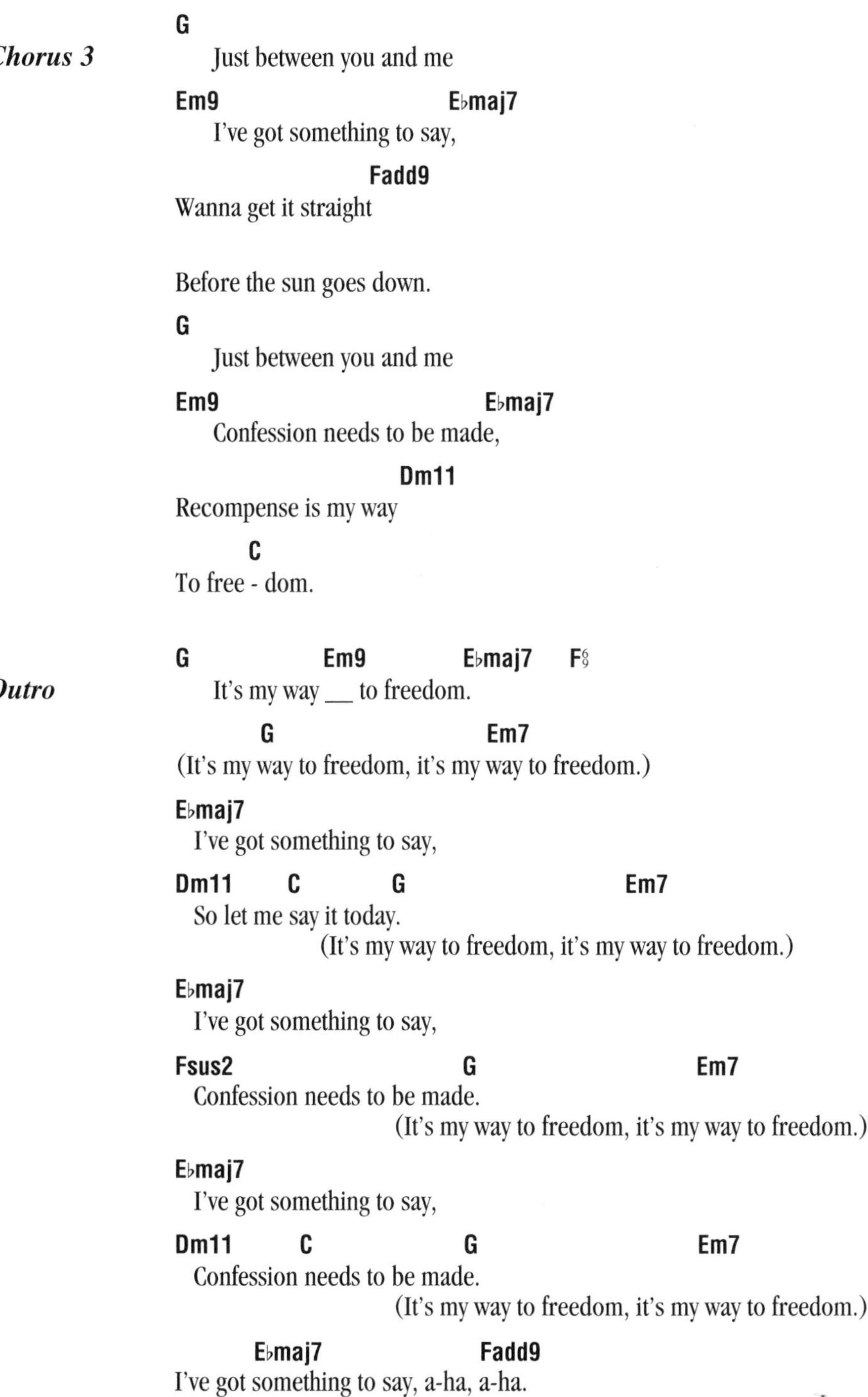

Chorus 3

G
Just between you and me
Em9 E♭maj7
I've got something to say,
Fadd9
Wanna get it straight

Before the sun goes down.
G
Just between you and me
Em9 E♭maj7
Confession needs to be made,
Dm11
Recompense is my way
C
To free - dom.

Outro

G Em9 E♭maj7 F6/9
It's my way __ to freedom.
G Em7
(It's my way to freedom, it's my way to freedom.)
E♭maj7
I've got something to say,
Dm11 C G Em7
So let me say it today.
(It's my way to freedom, it's my way to freedom.)
E♭maj7
I've got something to say,
Fsus2 G Em7
Confession needs to be made.
(It's my way to freedom, it's my way to freedom.)
E♭maj7
I've got something to say,
Dm11 C G Em7
Confession needs to be made.
(It's my way to freedom, it's my way to freedom.)
E♭maj7 Fadd9
I've got something to say, a-ha, a-ha.

Can't Live a Day

Words and Music by Ty Lacy,
Connie Harrington and Joe Beck

Melody:

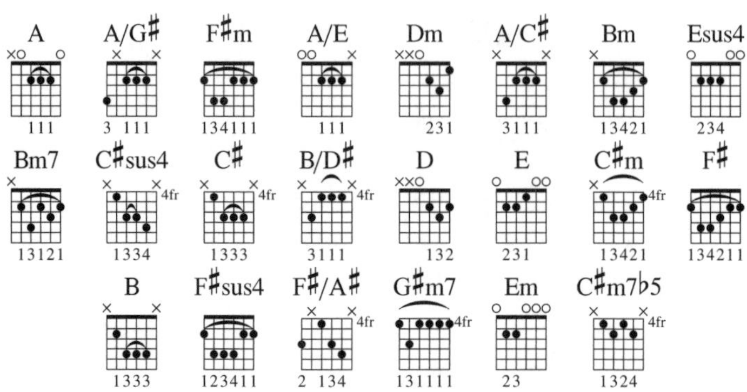

Intro | A A/G♯ | F♯m A/E | Dm A/C♯ | Bm Esus4 |

Verse 1

```
A        A/G♯            F♯m
I could live life alone
     A/E                  Dm                    A/C♯
And never fill the long - ings of my heart,
    Bm7                          Esus4
The healing warmth of some - one's arms.
      A         A/G♯                  F♯m
And I __ could live without dreams,
     A/E                    Dm                      A/C♯
And never know the thrill __ of what could be
     Bm7               C♯sus4       C♯              F♯m
With ev'ry star so far __ and out __ of reach.
        A/E                B/D♯
I could live without man - y things
       Esus4
And I __ could carry on.
```

Chorus 1

```
                    A               A/C#
But I couldn't face __ my life tomor - row

                  D
Without Your hope __ in my heart.

 A/C#        Bm             A/C#            E
I __ know I can't live a day __ without You.

                      A                       A/C#
Lord, there's no night __ and there's no morn - ing

                  D                 A/C#
Without Your lov - ing arms to hold __ me.

             Bm             A/C#   D
You're the heartbeat of all __ I do.

                   Esus4         A      A/G#        D      Esus4
I can't live a day __ without You.          No, no.
```

Verse 2

```
          A         A/G#             F#m
And oh, I __ could travel the world,

    A/E                  Dm           A/C#
See all the wonders beau - tiful and new.

       Bm7                 Esus4
They'd only make me think __ of You.

      A          A/G#          F#m
And I __ could have all life of-fered,

A/E                  Dm              A/C#
Riches that were far __ beyond compare,

   Bm7                 C#sus4     C#         F#m
To grant my ev'ry wish __ without __ a care.

    A/E             B/D#
Oh, I could do an - ything, oh, yes.

       Esus4
But if You weren't in it all...
```

Chorus 2

```
                   A                   A/C#
But I couldn't face __ my life tomor  -  row
                    D
Without Your hope __ in my heart.
  A/C#        Bm              A/C#              E
I __ know I can't live a day __ without You.
                      A                          A/C#
Lord, there's no night __ and there's no morn  -  ing
                D                   A/C#
Without Your lov - ing arms to hold __ me.
             Bm             A/C#   D
You're the heartbeat of all __ I do.
                Esus4          A
I can't live a day __ without You.
```

Bridge

```
        Bm
Oh, Je  -  sus,
       A/C#
I live __ because You live.
D                             E
    You're like the air I breathe.
         Bm
Oh, Je  -  sus,
             A/C#
Oh, I have __ because You gave.
D                           Esus4
    You're everything to me.
```

```
                N.C.
Chorus 3        Oh, I couldn't face my life tomorrow

                           E                B/D♯
                Without your hope __ in my heart I __ know

                 C♯m           B/D♯          F♯
                 I can't live a day __ without You.

                                B                         B/D♯
                Oh Lord, there's no night __ and there's no morn - ing

                         E                  B/D♯
                Without Your lov - ing arms to hold__ me.

                      C♯m             B/D♯        E
                You're the heartbeat of all __ that I do.

                         F♯sus4                 B                  B/D♯
                I can't live a day __ without You.
                                          I couldn't face __ my life tomor - row

                           E                B/D♯
                Without Your hope __ in my heart. I __ know,
                                                    I know.

                C♯m          B/D♯           F♯
                Can't live a day __ without You.

                              B                          B/D♯
                Lord, there's no night __ and there's no morn - ing

                         E                  B/D♯
                Without Your lov - ing arms to hold __ me.

                      C♯m             B/D♯    E
                You're the heartbeat of all __ I do.

                         F♯
                I can't live a day __ without You.

Outro           | A    F♯/A♯   | G♯m7   F♯       |

                | Em   B/D♯    | C♯m7♭5 B  A     | B
```

Come Quickly Lord

Words and Music by
Rebecca St. James and David Smallbone

Melody:

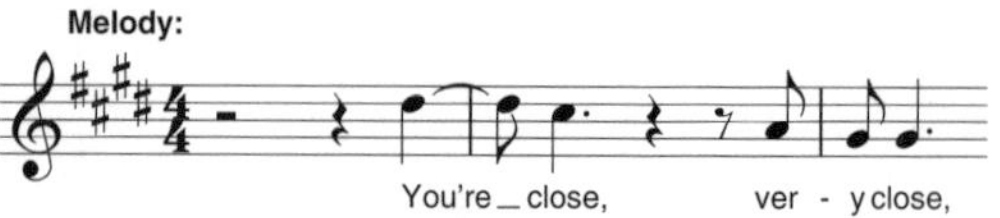

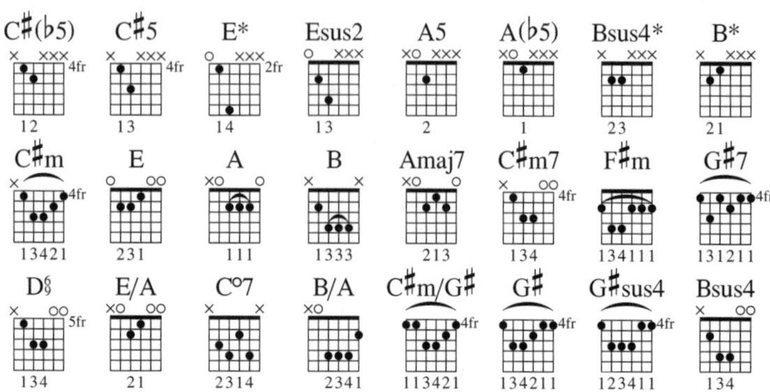

Intro ‖: C♯(♭5) C♯5 | E* Esus2 | A5 A(♭5) | Bsus4* B* :‖

Verse 1

```
          C♯m          E
You're __ close, ver-y close,
A                    B
   But Lord, I miss __ You.
              C♯m      E
Here's where ___ I,   I find hope:
A                  B
   You're coming __ soon.
      Amaj7                B
And I __ long so much to see You
       C♯m7      E
That I __ cry.
       Amaj7                B
Ev'ry  -  where are the signs
                     F♯m       G♯7
That the end is near.          I say
```

Chorus 1

```
                E          Bsus4
Come quick - ly, Lord,

                C♯m7                        D6/9
When the sun __ grows dark and the moon __ will shine no more.

        E/A         E
Quick  -  ly, Lord,

                 Bsus4                  C°7
When the stars __ fall out of the sky __ above.

              B/A              C♯m      B       Amaj7     B  N.C.
Won't You come, dear Lord?
```

Verse 2

```
    C♯m     E
Be ready is what I wanna be

A                   B
  When You come for me.

    C♯m      E
No sitting on my hands;

A                    Bsus4
  I won't be caught __ sleeping.

      Amaj7            B
And I __ long so much to see You

      C♯m7                   E
That I __ reach for the skies.

      Amaj7            B                          F♯m     G♯7
And I __ lift up my hands __ and I hold them high,     high.
```

Chorus 2

                E   Bsus4
Come quick - ly, Lord,

                C#m7   D6/9
When the sun __ grows dark and the moon __ will shine no more.

         E/A   E
Quick - ly, Lord,

                  Bsus4   C°7
When the stars __ fall out of the sky __ above.

               B/A
Won't You come, dear Lord?

Bridge

| F#m | |

C#m7   Amaj7
Come, dear Lord,

              C#m/G#   G#
Dear Lord.

         Amaj7   B
Come quickly, Lord Je - sus,

C°7   C#m7
   Please come for me.

         Amaj7   B
Come quickly, Lord Je - sus,

F#m   G#sus4
   Please come for me.

Amaj7 B   C°7   C#m
(Come, take us away __ to be with You.)

         Amaj7 B   F#m   G#sus4
(Come   take us away.)

```
Interlude   | E        | Bsus4    | C#m      | D6/9     |
            | E/A      | E        | Bsus4    | C°7      |


                      E          Bsus4
Chorus 3    Come quick - ly, Lord,

                      C#m7                              D6/9
            When the sun __ grows dark and the moon __ will shine no more.

                    E/A        E
            Quick  -  ly, Lord,

                        Bsus4                   C°7
            When the stars __ fall out of the sky __ above.

                    E          Bsus4
            Quick - ly, Lord,

                      C#m7                              D6/9
            When the sun __ grows dark and the moon __ will shine no more.

                    E/A        E
            Quick  -  ly, Lord,

                        Bsus4                   C°7
            When the stars __ fall out of the sky __ above.


                E     B        C#m   Dsus2
Outro       ||: Come take us a-way to be with You.

                  E/A E             Bsus4   C°7
            Come __  take us away.               :||     Repeat and fade
```

Dying to Reach You

Words and Music by
Michael Puryear and
Geoffrey Thurman

(Capo 1st fret)

D (132) Asus2 (23) G (21 34) C9 (21333) Bm (13421) Gm6 (2 34)

A (234) A/D (23) Em7 (1 3) D/F♯ (1 23) Em7add4 (1 24)

Intro

| D Asus2 | G Asus2 |
| D Asus2 | G Asus2 |

Verse 1

```
D                        Asus2    G
  He looked through tem-ples of time
                Asus2    D      Asus2  G  Asus2
To see you right where you stand.
D               Asus2      G
  He emptied all of Himself
                  Asus2      D    Asus2  G  Asus2
So He could reach out His hand
   C9
To give hope and meaning
      Bm             Gm6
To the wasted away.
D                 Asus2     G
  And you are one of the ones
                Asus2     D
That He was dy-ing to save.
A  G
   Oh, yeah.
```

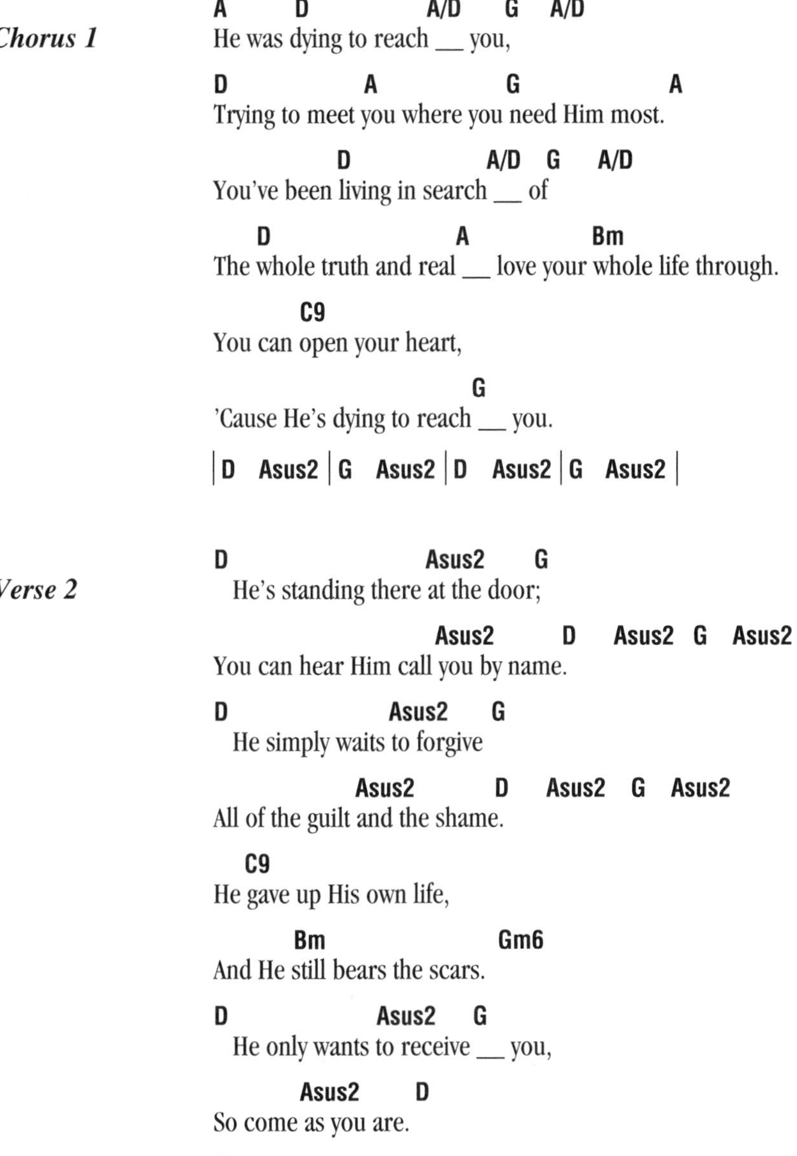

Chorus 1

A D A/D G A/D
He was dying to reach __ you,

D A G A
Trying to meet you where you need Him most.

D A/D G A/D
You've been living in search __ of

D A Bm
The whole truth and real __ love your whole life through.

C9
You can open your heart,

G
'Cause He's dying to reach __ you.

| D Asus2 | G Asus2 | D Asus2 | G Asus2 |

Verse 2

D Asus2 G
He's standing there at the door;

Asus2 D Asus2 G Asus2
You can hear Him call you by name.

D Asus2 G
He simply waits to forgive

Asus2 D Asus2 G Asus2
All of the guilt and the shame.

C9
He gave up His own life,

Bm Gm6
And He still bears the scars.

D Asus2 G
He only wants to receive __ you,

Asus2 D
So come as you are.

G A
Oh, yeah.

Chorus 2

```
A        D              A/D     G    A/D
He was dying to reach __ you,

D               A              G                A
Trying to meet you where you need Him most.

                D                  A/D  G    A/D
You've been living in search __ of

     D                   A              Bm
The whole truth and real __ love your whole life through.

          C9
You can open your heart,

                      G
'Cause He's dying to reach you.
```

Bridge

```
C9                                   Bm
    Oh, He has waited time and time before.

Em7                      D/F#               G          A
    You must be still __ and know that He is Lord.
```

Verse 3

```
D                             Asus2   G    Asus2
  He was dying to reach you,

D                        Asus2        G                        Asus2
    Trying to meet you where you need Him the most.

D                  Asus2       G          Asus2
Tell me, what are you look - ing for?

              D                     Asus2
Won't you     open your heart?

     G                Asus2
He's dying to reach__ you,
```

Chorus 3

```
D       A/D   G              A/D
     Dy-ing to reach you,

D                    A              G
     Trying to meet you where you need Him most.

A             D                A/D   G    A/D
You've been living in search __ of

    D                        A              Bm
The whole truth and real __ love your whole life through.

          C9
You can open your heart,

                        G
'Cause He's dying to reach you.

 D              Asus2     G      Asus2
(Dying to reach __ you.)

D              Asus2    G                  Asus2
Dying to reach __ you,     to reach you.

D              Asus2   G   Asus2
Dying to reach __ you.

| D     Asus2 G  |    Em7add4    |
```

El Shaddai

Words and Music by
Michael Card and John Thompson

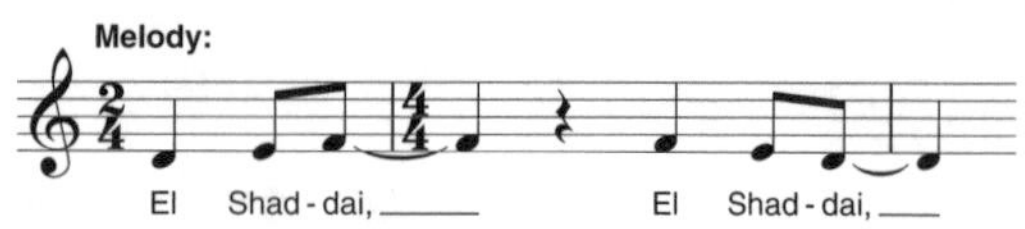

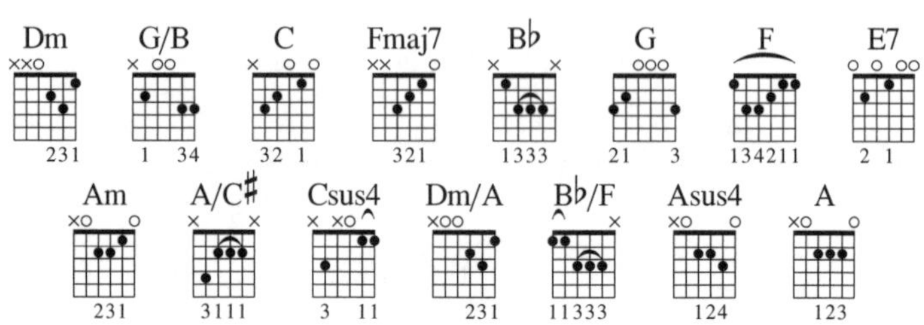

Intro

| Dm | G/B | C   G/B |
| Fmaj7 | B♭ | G |

Chorus 1

```
          Dm            G
El Shaddai, __ El Shaddai,
        C            F
El Elyon __ na Adonai,
          B♭                    E7
Age to age __ You're still the same,
          Am     G/B          A/C♯
By the pow - er of __ the name.
          Dm            G
El Shaddai, __ El Shaddai,
          C            F
Er kamka __ na Adonai,
        B♭                   G
We will praise and lift You high,
          C
El Shaddai.
```

```
                           Dm                      G
Verse 1        Through Your love __ and through the ram,
                         C               F
               You saved the son __ of Abraham.
                       B♭                  E7
               Through the pow - er of Your hand,
                           Am      G/B     A/C♯
               You turned the sea __ into __ dry land.
                       Dm                G
               To the out - cast on her knees,
                           C                F
               You were the God __ who really sees,
                    B♭                G                C     Csus4   C
               And by Your might You set your children free.

Chorus 2       Repeat Chorus 1

Interlude      | C     Csus4 | C        | B♭       | E7       |
               | C           | F        | Dm       | E7       |
               | Am    Dm/A  | Am       |

                           Dm                   G
Verse 2        Through the years __ You made it clear
                       C                 F
               That the time __ of Christ was near,
                       B♭                 E7
               Though the peo - ple couldn't see
                          Am        G/B      A/C♯
               What Messi  -  ah ought __ to be.
                             Dm                  G
               Through Your Word __ contained the plan,
                           C               F
               They just could __ not understand;
                          B♭                   G
               Your most awesome work was done
                     B♭/F       G
               In the frailty of Your Son.
```

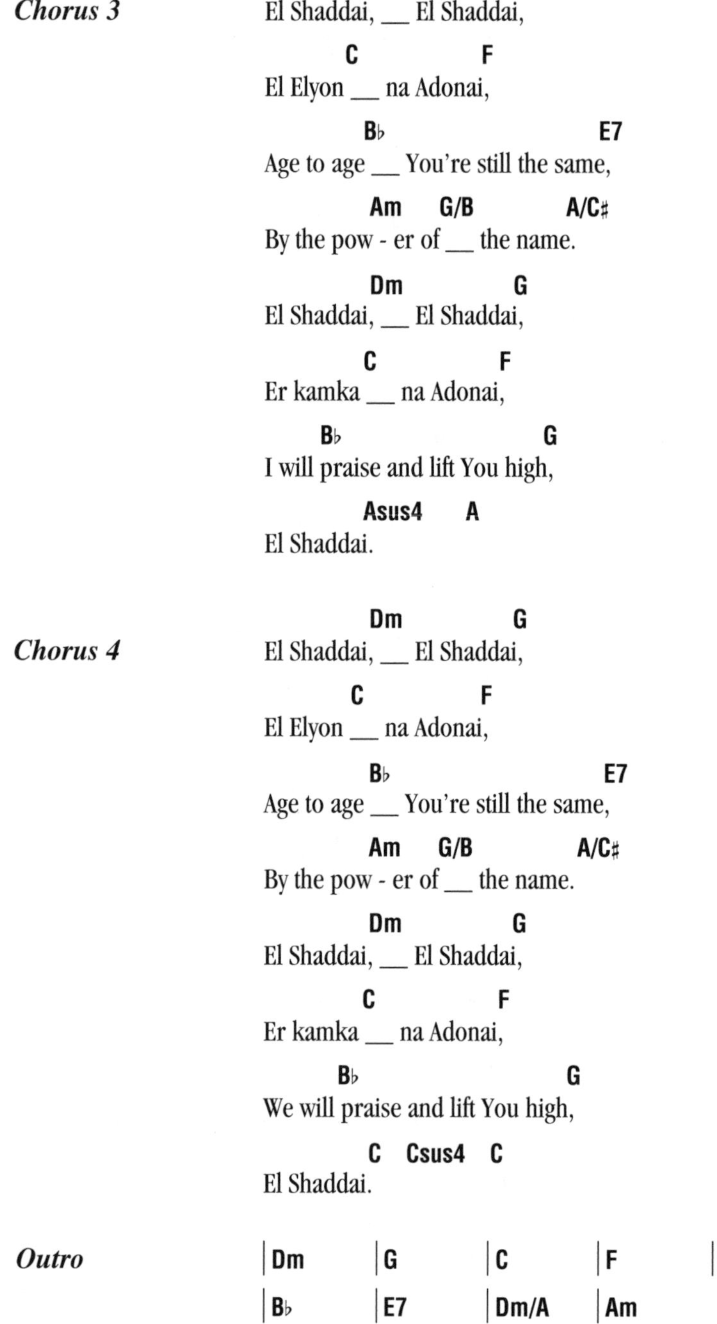

Chorus 3

```
                Dm              G
El Shaddai, __ El Shaddai,
            C               F
El Elyon __ na Adonai,
               B♭                         E7
Age to age __ You're still the same,
                Am     G/B           A/C♯
By the pow - er of __ the name.
                Dm             G
El Shaddai, __ El Shaddai,
               C              F
Er kamka __ na Adonai,
      B♭                         G
I will praise and lift You high,
               Asus4      A
El Shaddai.
```

Chorus 4

```
                Dm             G
El Shaddai, __ El Shaddai,
            C               F
El Elyon __ na Adonai,
                B♭                         E7
Age to age __ You're still the same,
                Am     G/B            A/C♯
By the pow - er of __ the name.
                Dm             G
El Shaddai, __ El Shaddai,
               C              F
Er kamka __ na Adonai,
          B♭                        G
We will praise and lift You high,
                C    Csus4    C
El Shaddai.
```

Outro

Dm	G	C	F
B♭	E7	Dm/A	Am

Find a Way

Words and Music by
Michael W. Smith and Amy Grant

Tune down 1 step:
(low to high) D–G–C–F–A–D

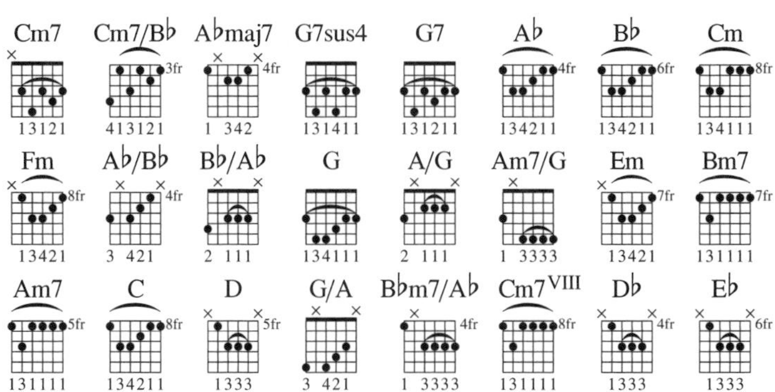

Intro

| Cm7 | Cm7/B♭ | A♭maj7 | Cm7 |
| | Cm7/B♭ | A♭maj7 | Cm7 |

Verse 1

```
      Cm7                       Cm7/B♭
You tell me your friends are dis - tant,
      A♭maj7               Cm7
You tell me your man's un-true.
                                    Cm7/B♭
You tell me that you've been walked __ on,
      A♭maj7         G7sus4   G7
And how you feel a-bused.
A♭                            B♭    Cm    B♭
So you stand here an angry young wom-an,
A♭                       B♭ Cm7  B♭
    Taking all the pain to  heart.
A♭                                B♭ Cm
  I hear you saying you want to see changes,
Fm                A♭/B♭        B♭/A♭
  But you don't know how to start.
```

```
              G                  A/G
Chorus 1      Love will find a way. (How do you know?)

              Am7/G            Em
              Love will find a way. (How can you see?)

                       Bm7     Am7                          Bm7
              I know it's hard to see the past and still believe

              C
              Love is gonna find a way.

                D           G                  A/G
              I know that love will find a way. (A way to go.)

              Am7/G              Em
              Love can make a way. (Only love can know.)

                     Bm7    Am7                         Bm7
              Leave behind the doubt, love's the on-ly out.

              C
              Love will surely find a way.


Interlude     | Cm7      | Cm7/B♭    | A♭maj7    | Cm7      |


              Cm7                            Cm7/B♭
Verse 2       I know this life is a strange __ thing,

                A♭maj7                 Cm7
              I can't answer all the why's.

                                      Cm7/B♭
              Tragedy always finds __ me

                  A♭maj7           G7sus4     G7
              Tak  -  en again by surprise.

              A♭                              B♭      Cm    B♭
              I could stand here an angry young wom-an,

              A♭                          B♭         Cm    B♭
                  Taking all the pain to __ heart.

              A♭                              B♭      Cm     B♭
                  But I know that love can bring chang-es,

              Fm                  A♭/B♭  B♭/A♭
                And so we've got to move on.
```

Chorus 2 *Repeat Chorus 1*

Bridge

```
B♭
If our God, His Son not sparing,

Came to rescue you,
C
Is there any circumstance
                          A♭/B♭  G/A
That He can't see you            through?
```

Chorus 3

```
A♭            B♭/A♭
Love will find a way. (How do you know?)
B♭m7/A♭          Fm
Love will find a way. (How can you see?)
        Cm7 VIII    B♭m7                Cm7 VIII
I know it's hard to see the past and still believe
D♭
Love is gonna find a way.
 E♭         A♭            B♭/A♭
I know that love will find a way. (A way to go.)
B♭m7/A♭             Fm
Love can make a way. (Only love can know.)
      Cm7 VIII  B♭m7                     Cm7 VIII
Leave behind   the doubt, love's the on-ly out.
D♭                                 E♭
Love will surely find a way.
```

Chorus 4 *Repeat Chorus 3 till fade*

Favorite Song of All

Words and Music by Dan Dean

Tune down 1/2 step:
(low to high) E♭–A♭–D♭–G♭–B♭–E♭

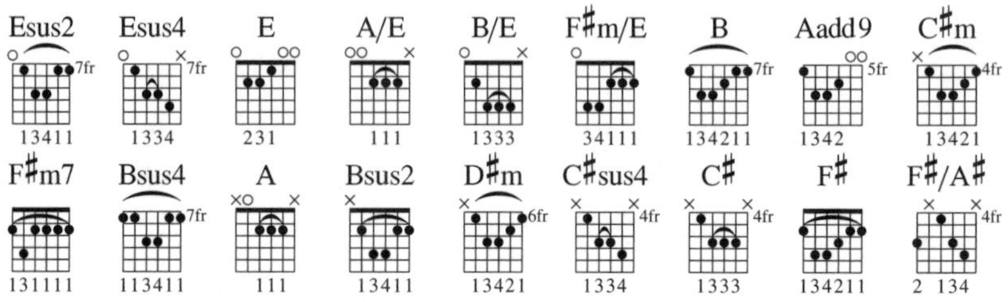

Intro | **Esus2** | **Esus4** | **Esus2** | **Esus4** |

Verse 1

```
  E                       A/E
He loves to hear the wind __ sing
     B/E                                E
As it whistles through the pines on mountain peaks
                              A/E
And He loves to hear the rain  -  drops
         F♯m/E                            B
As they splash to the ground in a magic melo - dy.
  Aadd9
He smiles in sweet approval
                                          Cm
As the waves crash to the rocks in harmony.
    F♯m7
Crea  -  tion joins in unity
                           Bsus4
To sing to Him majestic sym  -  phonies.
```

Chorus 1

```
B                       Aadd9
   But His fav'rite song of all
                        C♯m
Is the song of the redeemed
                              B
When lost sinners now made clean
                      E
Lift their voices loud and strong;
                                Aadd9
When those purchased by His blood
                      C♯m
Lift to Him a song of love.
                                   B
There's nothing more He'd rather hear,
           Bsus4          B
Nor so pleas  -  ing to His ear
                  E
As His fav'rite song __ of all.
```

Verse 2

```
A       E                 A/E
  And He loves to hear the an  -  gels
       B/E                   E
As they sing, "Holy, holy is the Lamb."
                       A/E
Heaven's choirs in harmo-ny
F♯m/E                     B
Lift up praises to the great "I __ Am."
       Aadd9
But He lifts His hands for silence
                                          C♯m
When the weakest saved by grace begins to sing
      F♯m7
And a million angels listen
                                  Bsus4
As a newborn soul sings, "I have been __ redeemed."
```

Chorus 2

```
B                                 Aadd9
     'Cause His fav'rite song of all
                               C#m
Is the song of the redeemed
                               B
When lost sinners now made clean
                           E
Lift their voices loud and strong;
                                 Aadd9
When those purchased by His blood
                          C#m
Lift to Him a song of love.
                                     B
There's nothing more He'd rather hear,
              Bsus4          B
Nor so pleas  -  ing to His ear
                     E
As His fav'rite song __ of all.
```

Bridge

```
              Aadd9
It's not just melodies and harmonies

That catches His attention.
              C#m7
It's not just clever lines and phrases

That causes Him to stop and listen
         F#m7
But when any heart set free,

Washed and bought by Calvary,
             Bsus4
Begins to sing.
```

Chorus 3

```
B                                Bsus2
    'Cause His fav'rite song of all
                              D♯m
Is the song of the redeemed
                                   C♯sus4      C
When lost sinners now made clean
                            F♯
Lift their voices loud and strong;
F♯/A♯                                    Bsus2
    When those purchased by His blood
                            D♯m
Lift to Him a song of love.
                                         C♯
There's nothing more He'd rather hear,
            C♯sus4          C♯
Nor so pleas  -  ing to His ear
                       F♯
As His fav'rite song __ of all.
```

Outro

```
F♯
    Holy, holy, holy is the Lamb.

Hallelujah, Hallelujah.

Holy, holy, holy is the Lamb.

Hallelujah, Hallelujah.
```

Find Us Faithful

Words and Music by Jon Mohr

(Capo 3rd fret)

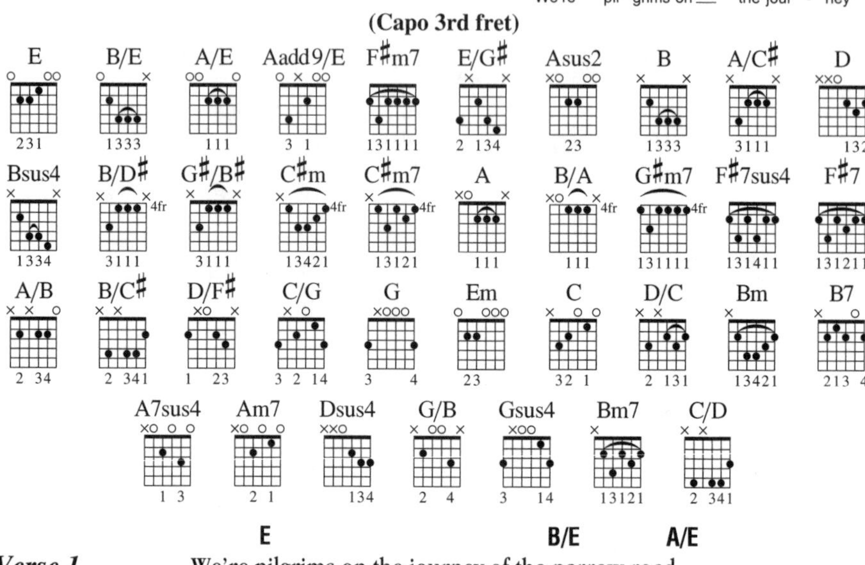

Verse 1

E **B/E** **A/E**
We're pilgrims on the journey of the narrow road,

E **Aadd9/E**
And those who've gone before us line the way.

F♯m7 **E/G♯** **Asus2** **B**
Cheering on the faith - ful, en-couraging the wea - ry,

A/C♯ **D** **F♯m7** **Bsus4**
Their lives a stirring testament to God's sustaining grace.

Verse 2

E **B/E** **A/E**
Sur-rounded by so great a cloud of witnesses,

E **Aadd9/E**
Let us run the race not only for the prize,

F♯m7 **E/G♯**
But as those who've gone before __ us,

Asus2 **B**
Let us leave to those behind __ us

A/C♯ **D** **F♯m7** **Bsus4** **B**
The heritage of faithfulness passed on through Godly lives.

```
                 B/D♯                                  A/E   E
Chorus 1   O may all who come behind us find us faith-ful.

                B                     G♯/B♯    C♯m   C♯m7
           May the fire of our devotion light their way.

                A                       B/A
           May the footprints that we leave

           G♯m7      G♯/B♯      C♯m
           Lead them __ to be-lieve,

                F♯7sus4          F♯7              Bsus4   B
           And the lives we live in-spire them to o-bey.

                A        G♯m7          F♯m7   A/B    A/E   E   C♯m
           O may all who come behind __ us find us faith-ful.
           | F♯m7    B/C♯  | F♯m7     E    | Aadd9/E       |

           E                                     B/E           A/E
Verse 3    After all our hopes and dreams have come and gone

                E                                        Aadd9/E
           And our children sift through all we've left be-hind,

                F♯m7                  E/G♯
           May the clues that they discov  -  er

                Asus2                  B
           And the mem'ries they uncov - er

              A/C♯                 D                  F♯m7              Bsus4   B
           Be-come the light that leads them to the road we each must find.
```

```
                   B/D#                                A/E   E
Chorus 2           O may all who come behind us find us faith-ful.

                   B                    G#/B#     C#m   C#m7
                   May the fire of our devotion light their way.

                   A                     B/A
                   May the footprints that we leave

                   G#m7      G#/B#    C#m
                   Lead them __ to be-lieve,

                   F#7sus4        F#7              Bsus4  B
                   And the lives we live in-spire them to o-bey.


                   D/F#                                C/G   G
Chorus 3           O may all who come behind us find us faith-ful.

                   D/F#        Em       D     B/D#       Em
                   May the fire of our __ devo - tion light their way.

                   C                     D/C
                   May the footprints that we leave

                   Bm        B7       Em
                   Lead them __ to be-lieve,

                   A7sus4         Am7              Dsus4  D
                   And the lives we live in-spire them to o-bey.

                   C        G/B          Am7   D      Gsus4 G
                   O may all who come behind __ us find us faith - ful.

                   Am7   G/B             C     C/D     N.C.
                   O may all who come behind __ us find us faith-ful.

                   | Am7   G/B   C   C/D   | G
```

The Great Divide

Words and Music by
Matt Huesmann and Grant Cunningham

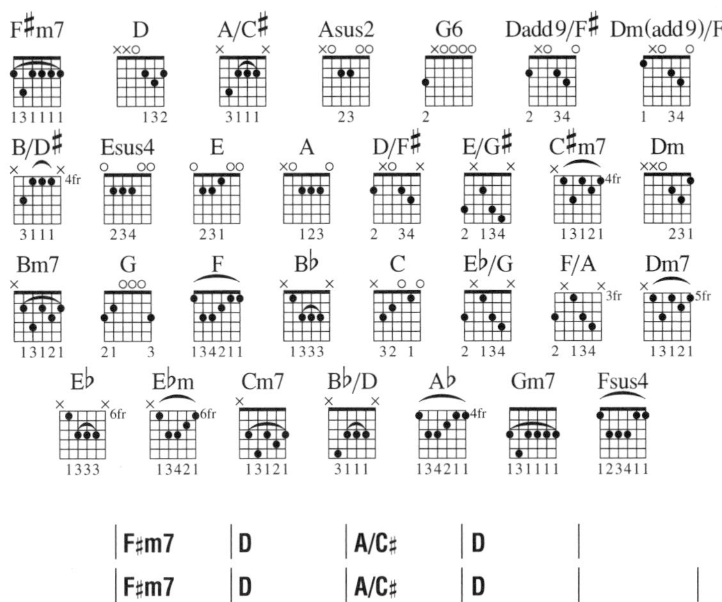

Intro

| F♯m7 | D | A/C♯ | D | |
| F♯m7 | D | A/C♯ | D | | |

Verse 1

```
Asus2              D              G6
Silence, trying to fathom the distance,

                         Dadd9/F♯            Dm(add9)/F
Looking out 'cross the canyon carved by my hands.

       Asus2
God is gracious.

          D         G6
Sin would still sepa-rate us

                        Dadd9/F♯               Dm(add9)/F
Were it not for the bridge His grace has made us.

    B/D♯           Esus4   E
His love will carry me.
```

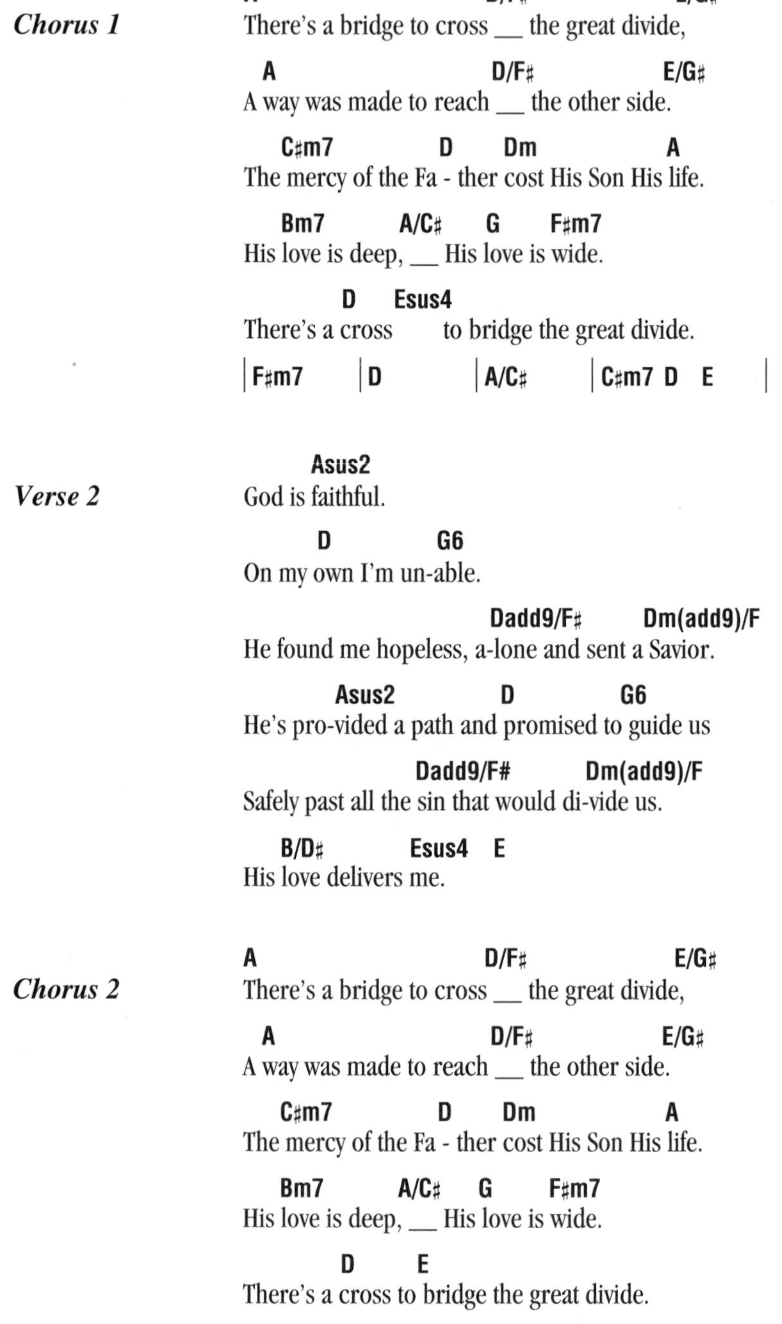

Chorus 1

```
A                          D/F♯                  E/G♯
There's a bridge to cross __ the great divide,

  A                          D/F♯                E/G♯
A way was made to reach __ the other side.

    C♯m7            D      Dm               A
The mercy of the Fa - ther cost His Son His life.

    Bm7          A/C♯     G       F♯m7
His love is deep, __ His love is wide.

           D      Esus4
There's a cross        to bridge the great divide.

| F♯m7      | D          | A/C♯        | C♯m7  D   E     |
```

Verse 2

```
        Asus2
God is faithful.

         D           G6
On my own I'm un-able.

                           Dadd9/F♯          Dm(add9)/F
He found me hopeless, a-lone and sent a Savior.

           Asus2              D           G6
He's pro-vided a path and promised to guide us

                   Dadd9/F#         Dm(add9)/F
Safely past all the sin that would di-vide us.

    B/D♯           Esus4   E
His love delivers me.
```

Chorus 2

```
A                          D/F♯                  E/G♯
There's a bridge to cross __ the great divide,

  A                          D/F♯                E/G♯
A way was made to reach __ the other side.

    C♯m7            D      Dm               A
The mercy of the Fa - ther cost His Son His life.

    Bm7          A/C♯     G       F♯m7
His love is deep, __ His love is wide.

           D       E
There's a cross to bridge the great divide.
```

Bridge

```
F♯m                E        D        A/C♯              Esus4   E     N.C.
    The cross that cost my Lord His life has given me mine.
```

Chorus 3

```
F                         B♭                  C
There's a bridge to cross __ the great divide.

F                         B♭                  C  E♭/G  F/A
There's a cross to bridge __ the great divide.    Whoa.

B♭                        E♭/G                F/A
There's a bridge to cross __ the great divide.

                B♭                      E♭/G              F/A
Whoa, whoa, a way was made to reach__ the other side.

     Dm7             E♭    E♭m               B♭
The mercy of the Fa - ther cost His son His __ life.

    Cm7          B♭/D     A♭      Gm7
His love is deep. __ His love is wide.

          Cm7    Fsus4
There's a cross       to bridge the great divide.

B♭/D            E♭                          B♭/D
There's a cross to bridge the great divide.

                  E♭                  B♭/D
A cross to bridge __ the great divide,

                  E♭
A cross to bridge __ the great...

B♭/D               E♭                  F       N.C.   B♭
There's a cross to bridge the great di-vide.
```

Fool for You

Words and Music by
Nichole Nordeman

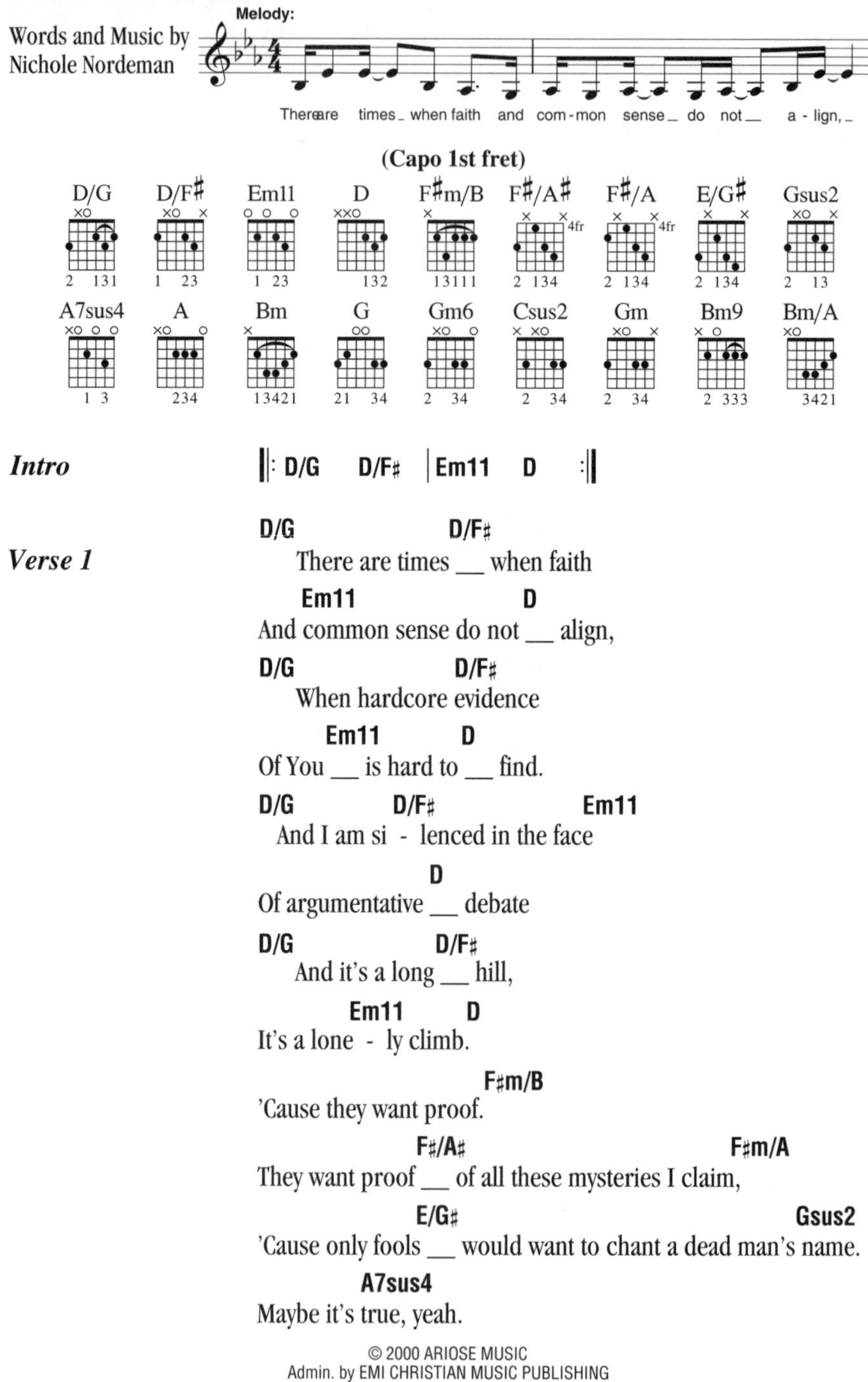

Intro

‖: D/G D/F♯ | Em11 D :‖

Verse 1

D/G **D/F♯**
There are times __ when faith
Em11 **D**
And common sense do not __ align,
D/G **D/F♯**
When hardcore evidence
Em11 **D**
Of You __ is hard to __ find.
D/G **D/F♯** **Em11**
And I am si - lenced in the face
D
Of argumentative __ debate
D/G **D/F♯**
And it's a long __ hill,
Em11 **D**
It's a lone - ly climb.

F♯m/B
'Cause they want proof.
F♯/A♯ **F♯m/A**
They want proof __ of all these mysteries I claim,
E/G♯ **Gsus2**
'Cause only fools __ would want to chant a dead man's name.
A7sus4
Maybe it's true, yeah.

```
                  D    A              Bm          G
Chorus 1             I __ would be a fool for You.
                  D      A              Bm          G
                     All __ because You asked me to.
                    Gm6
                  A simpleton who's seemingly naïve.
                    A7sus4  Gm6
                  I do be  -  lieve
                                Csus2                      D/G     D/F♯   Em11   D
                  You came and made Yourself a fool for __ me.
                  | D/G    D/F♯   | Em11    D      |

                  D/G        D/F♯            Em11
Verse 2              I admit __ that in my darkest hours
                              D
                  I've asked __ "What if ?"
                  D/G           D/F♯              Em11
                    What if we created some kind
                                D
                  Of manmade faith like this?
                  D/G            D/F♯
                    Out of good __ intention
                  Em11              D
                    Or emotional     invention
                  D/G            D/F♯
                     And after life is through
                       Em11          D            F♯m/B
                  There __ will be __ no You.
                                 F♯/A♯
                  'Cause they want proof
                                        F♯m/A
                  Of all these miracles I claim,
                                 E/G♯                              Gsus2
                  'Cause only fools __ believe that men can walk on waves.
                              A7sus4
                  Maybe it's true, yeah.
```

```
              D    A              Bm        G
Chorus 2        I __ would be a fool for You.

              D     A                Bm        G
                All __ because You asked me to.

                Gm6
              A simpleton who's seemingly naïve.

               A7sus4 Gm6
              I do be  -  lieve

                           Csus2                   D/G     D/F#   Em11  D
              You came and made Yourself a fool for __ me.


              Gm                      Bm9
Bridge          Unaware of popular - ity,

              Gm                            Bm   Bm/A
                Unconcerned with digni-ty,

                          E/G#
              You made me __ free.

              Gsus2
                That's proof enough for me.


Interlude     | D      A      | Bm     G      |
                                Ah.
              | D      A      | Bm     Gsus2  |
```

```
             D    A              Bm          G
Chorus 3        I __ would be a fool for You.

             D     A          Bm          G
                On - ly if You asked me to.

               Gm                              Gm6  A7sus4  D
             A simpleton who's only thinking of the cause of love.

              A             Bm          G
             I __ will speak Jesus' name.

             D                        A              Bm               G
               If that makes me cra - zy, they can call me crazed.

                Gm6
             I'm happy to be seemingly naïve.

              A7sus4
             I do believe

                          Csus2                          D/G    D/F#       Em11    D
             You came and made Yourself a fool for __ me.

             D/G    D/F#    Em11    D
                Ah, __

             D/G   D      Em11     D           D/G   D    Em11    D
                                A fool for You.

             D/G   D      Em11     D          D/G   D/F#     Em11
                             Do, do, do, do, do, do.
```

Friends

Words and Music by
Michael W. Smith and Deborah D. Smith

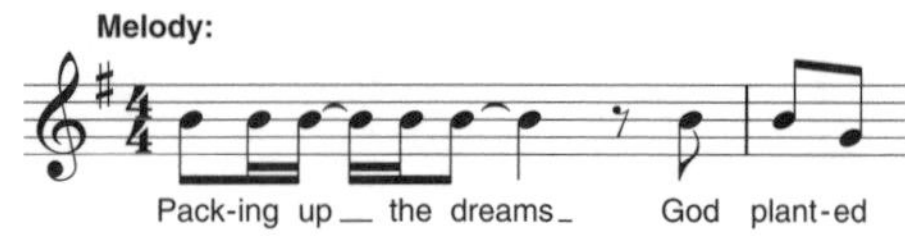

Melody:
Pack-ing up __ the dreams _ God plant-ed

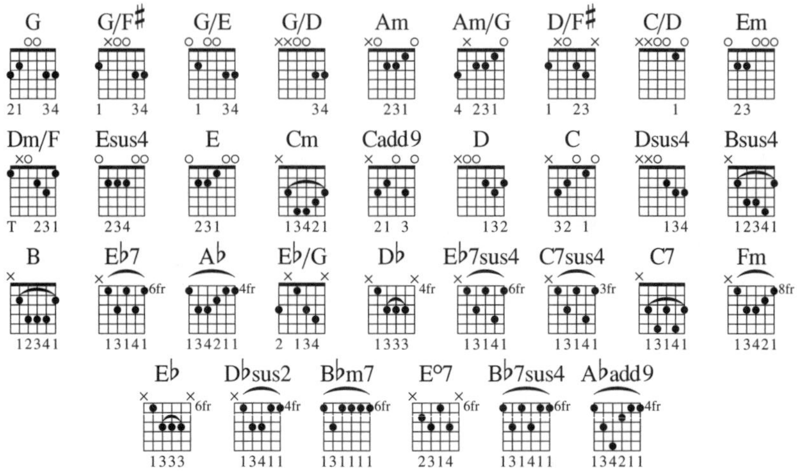
G G/F♯ G/E G/D Am Am/G D/F♯ C/D Em
Dm/F Esus4 E Cm Cadd9 D C Dsus4 Bsus4
B E♭7 A♭ E♭/G D♭ E♭7sus4 C7sus4 C7 Fm
E♭ D♭sus2 B♭m7 E°7 B♭7sus4 A♭add9

Intro

| G G/F♯ | G/E G/D | Am Am/G | D/F♯ C/D |

Verse 1

G   D/F♯   Em
Packing up the dreams __ God planted

Am   D/F♯
In the fertile soil of you;

G   D/F♯   Em
Can't believe the hopes __ he's granted

              Am   D/F♯
Means a chapter in your life is through.

                                          Dm/F   Esus4   E
But we'll keep you close __ as al-ways;

                Am   Cm
It won't e - ven seem you've gone,

                               G   D/F♯   Em
'Cause our hearts __ in big __ and small __ ways

          Am   D/F♯   Cadd9   D   G   C/D D
Will keep the love that keeps __ us strong.

Chorus 1

G D/F♯
And friends are friends forev - er

C Dsus4 D
If the Lord's the Lord of them.

G D/F♯
And a friend will not say "nev - er"

C Dsus4 D
'Cause the welcome will not end.

Bsus4 B
Though it's hard to let you go,

Em D Cadd9
In the Father's hands we know

Am D7sus4
That a lifetime's not too long

G G/F♯ C Dsus4 D
To live as friends.

Verse 2

G D/F♯ Em
With the faith and love __ God's given

Am D/F♯
Springing from the hope we know,

G D/F♯ Em
We will pray the joy __ you'll live in

Am D/F♯
Is the strength that now you show.

Dm/F Esus4 E
But we'll keep you close __ as al-ways;

Am Cm
It won't e - ven seem you've gone,

G D/F♯ Em
'Cause our hearts __ in big __ and small __ ways

Am D/F♯ Cadd9 D G C/D D
Will keep the love that keeps ___us strong.

Chorus 2

```
      G                        D/F#
And friends are friends forev  -  er
        C                      Dsus4  D
If the Lord's the Lord of them.
       G                       D/F#
And a friend will not say "nev  -  er"
             C                      Dsus4  D
'Cause the welcome will not end.
               Bsus4           B
Though it's hard to let you go,
       Em        D           Cadd9
In the Father's hands we know
        Am                    D7sus4
That a lifetime's not too long
                     G     Eb7
To live as friends.
```

```
                 A♭                        E♭/G
Chorus 3    And friends are friends forev  -  er
                  D♭                         E♭7sus4  E♭7
            If the Lord's the Lord of them.
                 A♭                          E♭/G
            And a friend will not say "nev  -  er"
                       D♭                         E♭7sus4  E♭7
            'Cause the welcome will not end.
                          C7sus4            C7
            Though it's hard to let you go,
                  Fm       E♭               D♭sus2
            In the Father's hands we know
                  B♭m7                    E♭7sus4  E♭7
            That a lifetime's not too long
                                 A♭    E♭/G   D♭
            To live as friends.
            E♭7sus4  E♭7             A♭   E♭/G   D♭
              To live __ as friends.
                                 C7sus4           C7
            Though it's hard __ to let you go,
                  Fm       E♭          D♭sus2
            In the Father's hands we know
                   B♭m7                    E♭7sus4
            That a lifetime's not too long
                   E°7    Fm
            To live __ as __ friends.
                  B♭7sus4                E♭7sus4
            No, a lifetime's not too long
                                 A♭   E♭/G   D♭   E♭7sus4  E♭7  A♭add9
            To live as friends.
```

Great Is the Lord

Words and Music by
Michael W. Smith and Deborah D. Smith

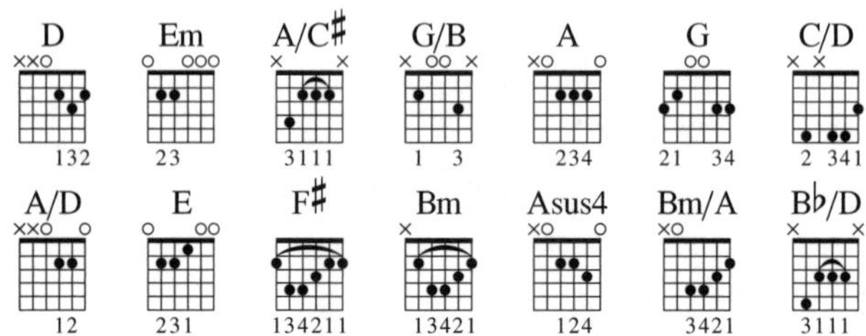

Intro ‖: D | :‖ *Play 4 times*

Verse 1

```
D                Em
Great is the Lord.
         A/C♯        D
He is holy and just,
         G/B          A                 G      D
By the power we trust in His love.
                 Em
Great is the Lord,
         A/C♯            D
He is faithful and true,
          G/B           A                 G      D
By His mercy He proves He is love.
```

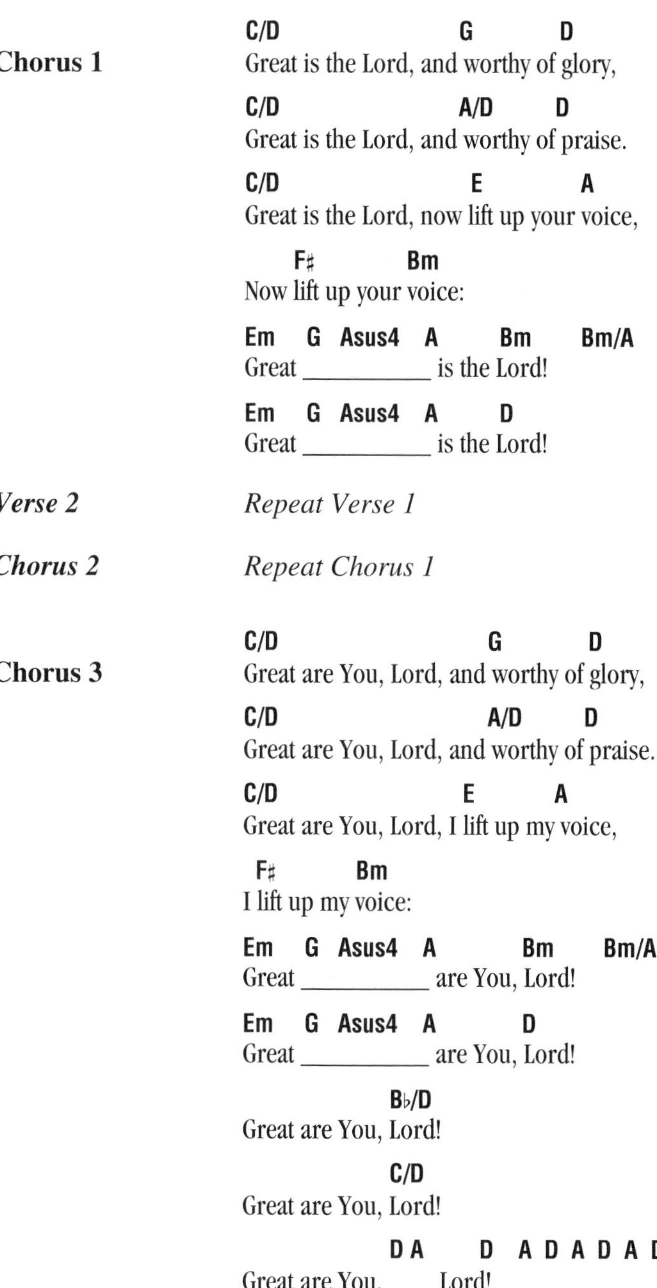

Chorus 1

```
C/D                G       D
Great is the Lord, and worthy of glory,
C/D                A/D     D
Great is the Lord, and worthy of praise.
C/D                  E        A
Great is the Lord, now lift up your voice,
     F♯         Bm
Now lift up your voice:
Em    G  Asus4   A       Bm      Bm/A
Great __________ is the Lord!
Em    G  Asus4   A       D
Great __________ is the Lord!
```

Verse 2 *Repeat Verse 1*

Chorus 2 *Repeat Chorus 1*

Chorus 3

```
C/D                      G       D
Great are You, Lord, and worthy of glory,
C/D                      A/D     D
Great are You, Lord, and worthy of praise.
C/D                     E       A
Great are You, Lord, I lift up my voice,
  F♯         Bm
I lift up my voice:
Em    G  Asus4   A          Bm      Bm/A
Great __________ are You, Lord!
Em    G  Asus4   A          D
Great __________ are You, Lord!
                 B♭/D
Great are You, Lord!
                 C/D
Great are You, Lord!
                 D A     D  A D A D A D
Great are You,        Lord!
```

He Walked a Mile

Words and Music by Dan Muckala

(Capo 2nd fret)

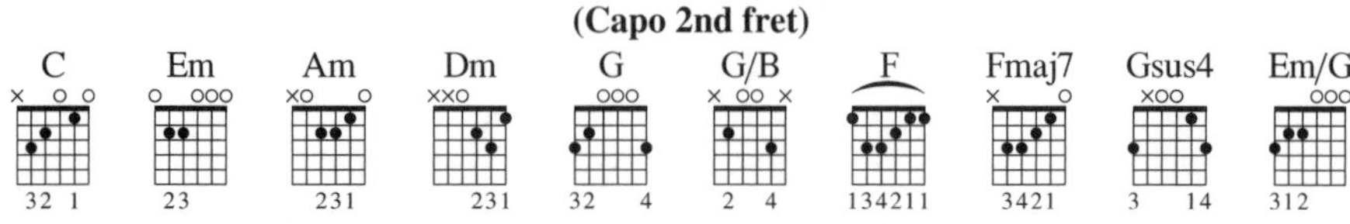

Intro

| C Em | Am | Em Am Dm | G |
| C Em | Am | Dm G | C | |

Verse 1

```
C                    Em     Am
Be-fore the threads of time be-gan,
     Em          Am   Dm        G
Was preordained __ a mighty plan
     C                 Em    Am
That I should walk with Him a-lone,
     Dm             G     C
The cords of trust un-broken.
                         Em       Am
But fate foresaw my wand'ring eye
      Em        Am        Dm    G
That none could __ yet re-strain;
   C        Em        Am
To violate the friendship, I
         Dm                G     C
Would cause Him so much pain.
```

Chorus 1

```
    G/B  Am   F        G
And ev'ry time I close my __ eyes,

 C          Fmaj7 Dm      G       Gsus4 G
I __ see the nails, I hear the __ cries.

            Am              Em/G
He did not keep Himself a-way,

            F         Dm G
He was no stranger to my pain;

He walked a mile in my shoes,
| C   Em | Am     | Em Am Dm | G

             C        Em
He walked a mile.
| Am     | Dm   G | C      |      |
```

Verse 2

```
C           Em          Am
Feet so dusty cracked with heat,

    Em      Am    Dm          G
But carried on __ by love's heartbeat.

  C             Am
A man of sorrows filled with grief;

    Dm             G     C
For-giveness was His anthem.

                     Em       Am
No feeble blow from tongue or pen

      Em  Am          Dm    G
Could ever __ sway my love for Him.

  C               Em     Am
A-cross the echoed hills He trod,

    Dm             G       C
And reached into my __ world.
```

Chorus 2

```
      G/B  Am    F         G
And ev'ry time I close my __ eyes,

 C          Fmaj7 Dm       G        Gsus4  G
I __ see the nails, I hear the __ cries.

              Am              Em/G
He did not keep Himself a-way,

              F          Dm G
He was no stranger to my pain;

He walked a mile in my shoes,
| C   Em  | Am       | Em  Am  Dm | G

                C         Em
He walked a mile.
| Am       | Dm    G | C
```

Chorus 3

Repeat Chorus 2

Outro

```
                C         Em
He walked a mile.
| Am      | Em  Am  Dm | G

                C      Em    Am
He walked a mile.

Dm         G     C
Woh, woh, woh, woh.

Dm         G     C     Dm    G   C
Woh, woh, woh, woh.
```

He Who Began a Good Work in You

Words and Music by
Jon Mohr

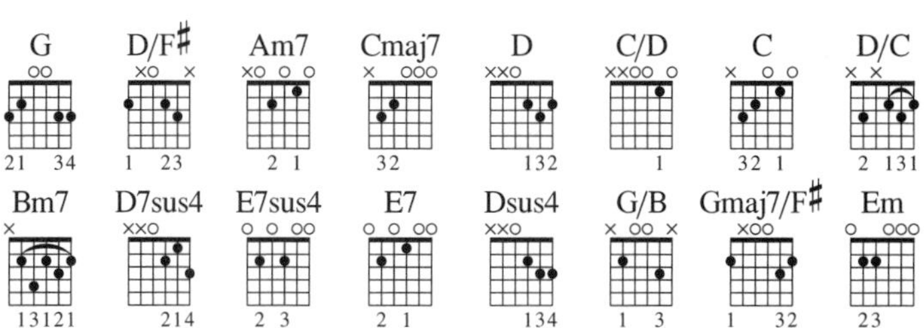

Intro | G D/F♯ | Am7 Cmaj7 D | G D/F♯ | C/D |

Chorus 1

```
G D/F♯     C           D     D/C  Bm7         D7sus4
He who be-gan a good work in     you,
G D/F♯     C           D     D/C E7sus4       E7
He who be-gan a good work in    you
             Am7                   D
Will be faith  -  ful to complete it.
              Am7                  Dsus4  D
He'll be faith  -  ful to complete it,
              Am7         G/B
He who start  -  ed the work
              C          C/D       G
Will be faith - ful to com-plete it in you.
```

Interlude

```
||: G        Gmaj7/F#  | C        Gmaj7/F#  :||
```

Verse 1

```
     G                 D/F#
If the struggle you're fac - ing

  C           G                C  G/B         Am7
Is slowly replac - ing your hope __      with de-spair,

C          D/F#        C
   Or the process is long

           D               D/C             G/B      C/D
And you're losing your song __ in the night,

G                D/F#           C              G
You can be sure __ that the Lord __ has His hand __ on you.

C                G/B          Am7        Em
Safe and secure,      He will never aban  -  don you.

D/F#             C
You are His treas-ure,

     D                      G     D/F#    C/D
And He finds His pleasure in you.
```

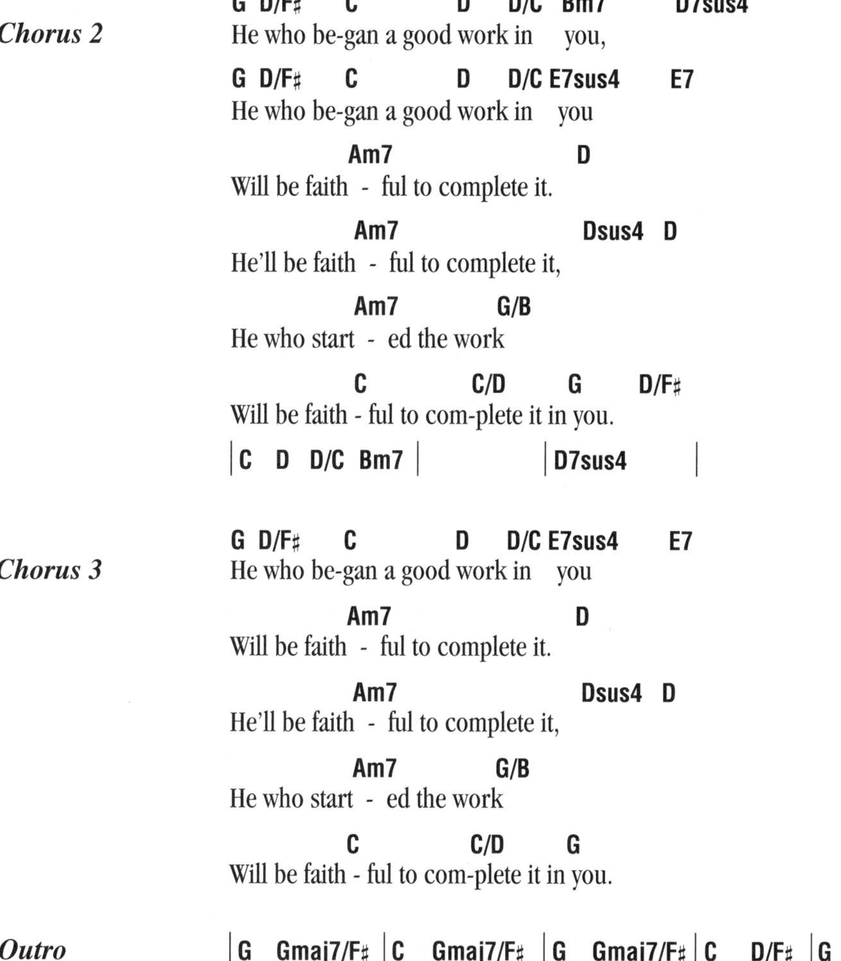

Chorus 2

G D/F♯ C D D/C Bm7 D7sus4
He who be-gan a good work in you,

G D/F♯ C D D/C E7sus4 E7
He who be-gan a good work in you

Am7 D
Will be faith - ful to complete it.

Am7 Dsus4 D
He'll be faith - ful to complete it,

Am7 G/B
He who start - ed the work

C C/D G D/F♯
Will be faith - ful to com-plete it in you.

| C D D/C Bm7 | | D7sus4 |

Chorus 3

G D/F♯ C D D/C E7sus4 E7
He who be-gan a good work in you

Am7 D
Will be faith - ful to complete it.

Am7 Dsus4 D
He'll be faith - ful to complete it,

Am7 G/B
He who start - ed the work

C C/D G
Will be faith - ful to com-plete it in you.

Outro

| G Gmaj7/F♯ | C Gmaj7/F♯ | G Gmaj7/F♯ | C D/F♯ | G

He Will Carry You

Words and Music by Scott Wesley Brown

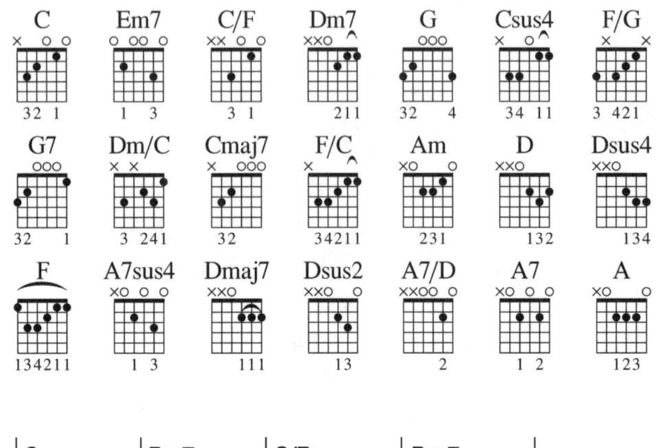

Intro

| C | Em7 | C/F | Dm7 |
| | G | Csus4 C | F/G G |

Verse 1

```
C                          Em7            Dm7     F/G
There is no problem too big He cannot solve it;
Dm7                        G7             Dm/C  C    F/G    G
There is no mountain too tall He cannot move  it.
C                       Em7               Dm7    F/G
There is no storm too dark God cannot calm it;
Dm7                       G7               Dm/C  C    F/G
There is no sorrow too deep He cannot soothe it.
```

Chorus 1

```
  G  C                                Cmaj7                Dm7     F/G
If He carried the weight of the world __ upon His shoul - ders,
Dm7                         F/G     G     C    F/C  C  F/G
I know, my brother, that He __ will carry you.
  G  C                                Cmaj7                Dm7     F/G
If He carried the weight of the world __ upon His shoul - ders,
Dm7                       F/G     G     C    F/C  C  F/G
I know, my sister, that He __ will carry you.
```

```
             G      Am         Em7 G            D          Dsus4
Bridge       He said, "Come unto Me   all who are weary,

             D    F     G          Csus4  C     F/G  G
             And I will give you rest."
```

Verse 2 *Repeat Verse 1*

```
             G C                                 Cmaj7              Dm7      F/G
Chorus 2     If He carried the weight of the world __ upon His shoul - ders,

             Dm7                      F/G      G      C    F/C  C  A7sus4
             I know, brother, that He __ will carry you.
```

```
                  D                              Dmaj7             Em7    Dsus2  A7/D
Outro        If He carried the weight of the world __ upon His shoul - ders,

             Em7                          A7sus4  A7    D        A7sus4
             I know, my brother, that He __ will carry you.

               A7 D                              Dmaj7             Em7    Dsus2  A7/D
             If He carried the weight of the world __ upon His shoul - ders,

             Em7                        A7sus4  A7    D
             I know, my sister, that He __ will carry you.

             A7sus4          G
                He will carry you.

             A               D
                He will carry you.
```

His Eyes

Words and Music by
Steven Curtis Chapman
and James Isaac Elliott

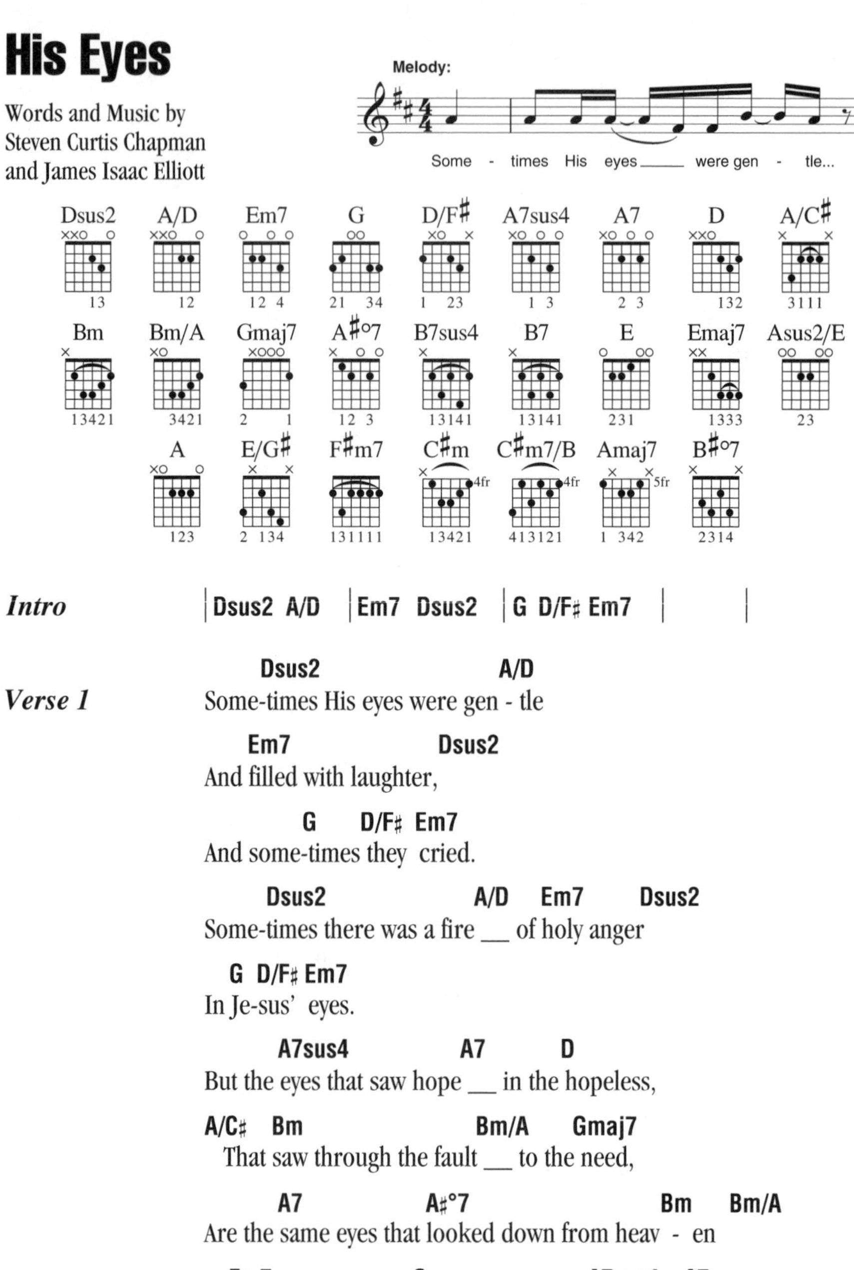

Intro | Dsus2 A/D | Em7 Dsus2 | G D/F♯ Em7 | |

Verse 1

Dsus2 A/D
Some-times His eyes were gen - tle

Em7 Dsus2
And filled with laughter,

G D/F♯ Em7
And some-times they cried.

Dsus2 A/D Em7 Dsus2
Some-times there was a fire __ of holy anger

G D/F♯ Em7
In Je-sus' eyes.

A7sus4 A7 D
But the eyes that saw hope __ in the hopeless,

A/C♯ Bm Bm/A Gmaj7
That saw through the fault __ to the need,

A7 A♯°7 Bm Bm/A
Are the same eyes that looked down from heav - en

Em7 G A7sus4 A7
In-to the deepest part __ of you and me.

```
               Gmaj7                   D
Chorus 1     And His eyes are always upon__ us.

                Gmaj7                  D
             His eyes never close in sleep,

             B7sus4 B7  Em7
             And        no  matter where you go,

                         A7         A♯°7   Bm    Bm/A   Gmaj7
             You will al - ways be in His eyes,

                          Dsus2   A/D    Em7    D     G   D/F♯  Em7
             In His eyes.


                  Dsus2                        A/D      Em7          Dsus2
Verse 2      Some-times His voice comes call  -  ing like rolling thunder,

                   G   D/F♯ Em7
             Or like driv-ing  rain.

                         Dsus2                  A/D          Em7         Dsus2
             And some-times His voice is qui  -  et and we start to wonder

                  G     D/F♯ Em7
             If He knows our  pain.

                A7sus4        A7           D      A/C♯
             But He who spoke peace to the water,

                  Bm                   Bm/A      Gmaj7
             Cares more for our hearts __ than the waves,

                      A7            A♯°7              Bm    Bm/A
             And the voice that once said, "You're for-given,"

                 Em7              G          A7sus4  A7    B7sus4  B7
             Still says, "You're for-given," to-day, _______ to  -  day.
```

```
                E                Emaj7      Asus2        E
Verse 3  Some-times I look above __ me when stars are shining,

              A   E/G♯ F♯m7
         And I feel so   small.

              E                   Emaj7    Asus2     E
         How could the God of heav - en and all creation

                   A    E/G♯ F♯m7
         Know I'm here at   all?

            B7sus4       B7       E
         But then in the si - lence    he whispers,

              C♯m        C♯m7/B      Amaj7
         "My child, I cre-ated you, too,

             B7             B♯°7          C♯m
         And you're my most precious cre-ation,

          F♯m7     A            A7sus4
         I even gave my Son for you."


           A7  A7sus4 Gmaj7                D
Chorus 2 And His     eyes are always upon __ you.

            Gmaj7            D
         His eyes never close in sleep,

         B7sus4 B7 Em7
         And      no matter where you go,

                     A7sus4   A♯°7  Bm  Bm/A  Gmaj7
         You will al - ways be in His eyes.

         D/F♯ Em7
           No matter where you go,

                     A7sus4   A7   Dsus2  A/D  Em7  D  G  D/F♯  Em7
         You will al - ways be in His eyes.

              Dsus2                A/D      Em7            D
         Some-times His eyes are gen - tle, and filled with laughter.
```

His Strength Is Perfect

Words and Music by
Steven Curtis Chapman and Jerry Salley

Melody:

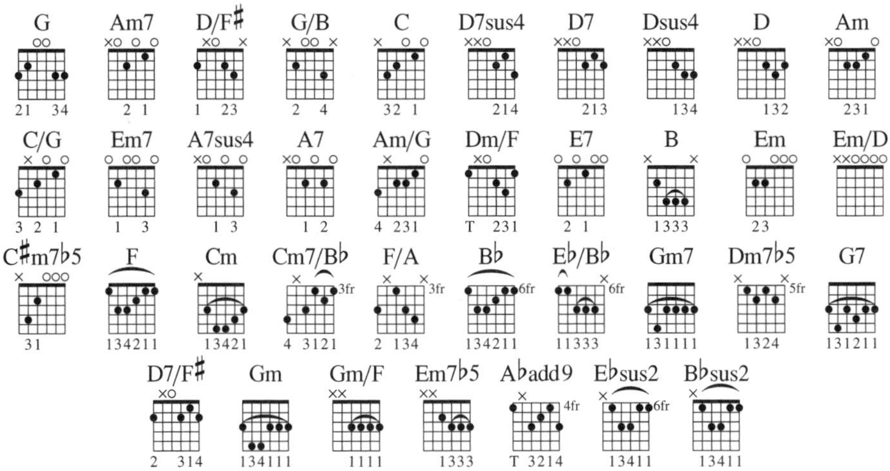

G Am7 D/F♯ G/B C D7sus4 D7 Dsus4 D Am
C/G Em7 A7sus4 A7 Am/G Dm/F E7 B Em Em/D
C♯m7♭5 F Cm Cm7/B♭ F/A B♭ E♭/B♭ Gm7 Dm7♭5 G7
D7/F♯ Gm Gm/F Em7♭5 A♭add9 E♭sus2 B♭sus2

Intro | G Am7 | D/F♯ | G/B C | D7sus4 | D7 |

Verse 1

```
G         Am7          Dsus4  D
I can do __ all things
          G/B               Am            G
Through Christ who gives __ me strength,
           C           G            Am       D              G  C/G  G  C/G
But some-times I won - der what He _ can do _ through me.
   G          Am           Dsus4  D
No great suc-cess to show,
   G/B      Am        Em7
No glory on __ my own
           C          G/B         A7sus4 A7     Am7
Yet in my weakness He is there __ to    let me know:
```

```
             D   G   Am        G Am     Am/G       D/F♯                    G    C/G
Chorus 1         His strength is per  -  fect when our strength is gone.

             G          Em7  Am Am/G      D/F♯         Dm/F
                 He'll carry us   when we can't carry on.

             E7                   Am    Am/G  D/F♯  B         Em    Em/D
                 Raised in His pow - er, the weak become strong.

             C♯m7♭5               Am   Am/G
                 His strength is per - fect,

             D/F♯                 C/G       G    Em7
                 His strength is perfect.

             | Am  Am/G | F        | D/F♯        |

             G           Am7        Dsus4   D
Verse 2      We can on  -  ly know

                 G/B        Am           G
             The power that __ He holds

                       C         G/B           Am              D             G  C/G  G  C/G
             When we truly see __ how deep __ our weak - ness goes.

                 G          Am      Dsus4   D
             His strength in us begins

                   G/B          Am        Em7
             Where ours comes to an end.

               C          G/B           A7sus4  A7       Am7
             He hears our humble cry __ and proves a-gain:
```

Chorus 2

```
D  G   Am     G Am    Am/G      D/F♯                  G   C/G
    His strength is per  -  fect when our strength is gone.

G        Em7  Am  Am/G    D/F♯        Dm/F
    He'll carry us   when we can't carry on.

E7                  Am    Am/G D/F♯  B        Em    Em/D
    Raised in His pow - er, the weak become strong.

C♯m7♭5               Am   Am/G
    His strength is per - fect,

F                     Cm   Cm7/B♭
   (His strength is per - fect.)

      F/A              B♭   E♭/B♭  B♭
When our strength is gone.

     Gm7  Cm  Cm7/B♭   F/A          Dm7♭5    G7
He'll carry us    when we can't carry on.

              Cm    Cm7/B♭  F/A  D7/F♯   Gm    Gm/F   Em7♭5
Raised in His pow - er, the    weak become strong.

               Cm   Cm7/B♭  F/A
His strength is per - fect,

               Dm7♭5
His strength is perfect.

G7                  Cm    Cm7/B♭  F/A  D7/F♯   Gm    Gm/F
    Raised in His power, __ the  weak become strong.

         Em7♭5
(Become strong.)

               Cm      Cm7/B♭      F/A
His strength is perfect.

               A♭add9  E♭sus2    B♭sus2
His strength is per   -   fect.
```

House That Mercy Built

Words and Music by
Matt Huesmann and Grant Cunningham

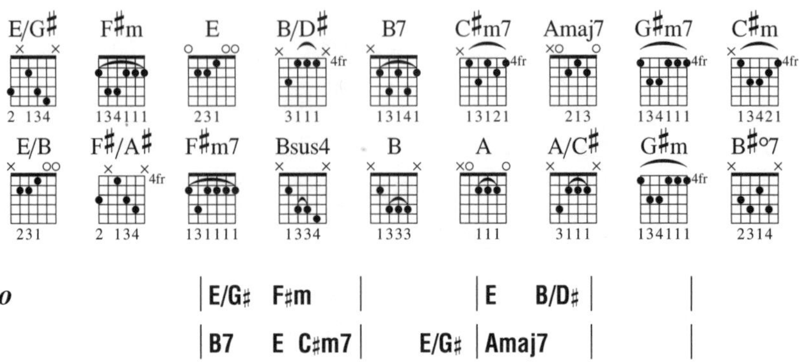

Intro

| **E/G♯ F♯m** | | **E B/D♯** | |
| **B7 E C♯m7** | **E/G♯** | **Amaj7** | |

Verse 1

E G♯m7 C♯m E/B
The light in the distance welcomes those
F♯/A♯ F♯m7 Bsus4 B
Way-faring souls come this far.
E B/D♯
A heart grows tired, faith grows cold
C♯m E/B
Wand'ring down the winding road.
F♯m7 E/G♯ A Bsus4
Just simply knock; the door will o - pen.

Chorus 1

B E B
There is a house that mercy built.
B7 E
There is a place where brokenness is healed.
Bsus4 B A/C♯ E/B A
There is a voice saying, "Peace, be still."
E/B B C♯m G♯m A
There is a house ____ that mercy built.
E/B B E
There is a house that mercy built.

Interlude | E B/D♯ | | B7 E C♯m7 | E/G♯ | Amaj7 | |

Verse 2

```
E              G♯m7                   C♯m    E/B
   Mercy will find you though you've given up
     F♯/A♯                  F♯m7   Bsus4  B
In the middle of what seems like no-where.
    E             B/D♯
He'll shelter you be-neath his wings.
   C♯m           E/B
His love will cover ev'ry need.
F♯m7          E/G♯            A      Bsus4
   Just simply seek and you will find.
```

Chorus 2

```
B        E                B
There is a house that mercy built.
         B7          E
There is a place where emptiness is filled.
         Bsus4  B          A/C♯   E/B A
There is a voice      saying, "Peace, be  still."
         E/B    B              C♯m  G♯m   A
There is a house ___ that mercy built.
         E/B    B       E     A/C♯
Rest in the house ___ that mercy built
    E/B     B
With blood and tears.
             E/G♯  A
We've nothing left to fear.
         E/B   B  B♯°7      C♯m  B  A       E/B
We live in grace ___ here in the safe em-brace of God.
```

| B | E/B B | Bsus4

Chorus 3

```
B           E                    B
There is a house that mercy built.

            B7            E
There is a place where grace has been revealed.

           Bsus4  B            A/C♯   E/B A
There is a voice          saying, "Peace, be  still."

           E/B     B               C♯m  G♯m   A
There is a house ____ that mercy built.

            E/G♯     A              E/G♯
Rest in the hope, ____ rest in the peace,

A                E/B        B      E
    For there is a house that mercy built.
```

Outro

```
| E    B/D♯ |           | B7      E |
|      E/G♯ | F♯m    B  |           | E
```

I'll Be Believing

Words and Music by
Geoffrey P. Thurman and Becky Thurman

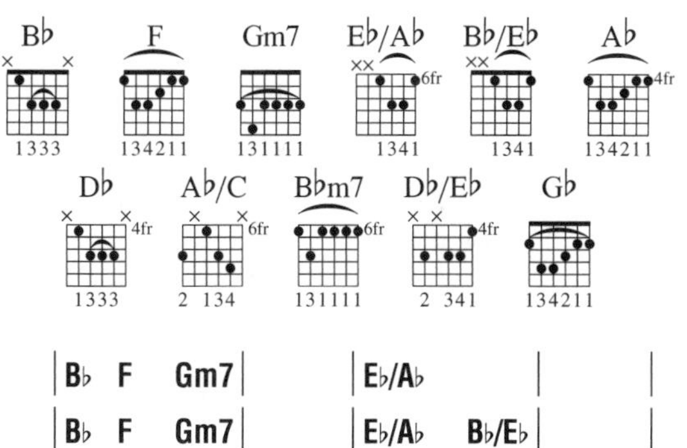

Intro

| B♭ F Gm7 | E♭/A♭ | |
| B♭ F Gm7 | E♭/A♭ B♭/E♭ | |

Verse 1

F Gm7
When I'm walking the straight and narrow,

F B♭/E♭
Sometimes life throws a little curve.

F Gm7
If I slip on the stones be-neath me,

A♭ B♭
Will I lose my nerve?

Verse 2

F Gm7
Looking up when I've hit the bottom,

F B♭/E♭
Giving thanks that the motion's stopped

F Gm7
I still have a rock to hold to

A♭ B♭/E♭
If the bottom drops.

D♭ A♭/C
Out here __ on my own I won't __ be alone.

B♭m7 A♭ D♭ D♭/E♭
I'll keep be-lieving you.

Chorus 1

```
Db          Ab
I'll be be-lieving.

                 Gb  Db
I will be be-liev-ing.

Bbm7  Ab/C    Db     Db/Eb
Oh, I'll be be - lieving you.

Db          Ab
I'll be be-lieving,

                 Gb  Db
I will be be-liev-ing.

Bbm7  Ab/C    Db     Db/Eb   Ab
Oh, I'll be be - lieving you.
```

Verse 3

```
   F                         Gm7
If I find all my hopes are hollow

     F                      Bb/Eb
Even if all my wells run dry?

      F                         Gm7
If I'm left here with next to nothing

     Ab                   Bb/Eb
And I don't know why.

          Db                          Ab/C
I'm here __ on my own, I won't __ be alone.

Bbm7 Ab/C    Db     Db/Eb
I'll    keep be-lieving you.
```

Chorus 2

```
D♭         A♭
I'll be be-lieving.
                G♭  D♭
I will be be-liev-ing.
B♭m7  A♭/C    D♭     D♭/E♭
Oh, I'll be be - lieving you.
D♭         A♭
I'll be be-lieving,
                G♭  D♭
I will be be-liev-ing.
B♭m7  A♭/C    D♭     D♭/E♭
Oh, I'll be be - lieving you.
```

Interlude

```
| F    Gm7 |        | F      B♭/E♭ |        |
| F    Gm7 |        | A♭    B♭/E♭  |        |
           D♭                          A♭/C
Out here __ on my own I won't __ be alone.
B♭m7  A♭         D♭      D♭/E♭
I'll     keep be-lieving you.
```

Chorus 3 *Repeat Chorus 2*

Outro

```
    D♭          A♭
||: I'll be be-lieving,
                G♭  D♭
I will be be-liev-ing.
B♭m7  A♭/C    D♭     D♭/E♭
Oh, I'll be be - lieving you.   :||
```

Repeat and fade

I Believe

Words and Music by
Fran King and Wes King

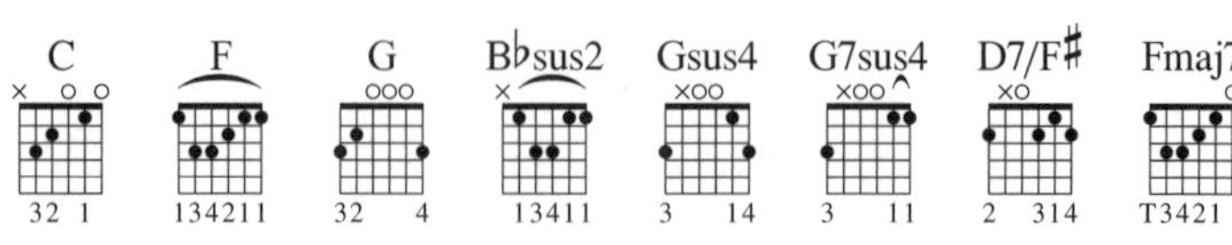

Verse 1

```
C           F G                 C  F
  I believe     in six days and a rest.
G                F  C              B♭sus2
  God is good,         I do confess.
C           F G             C      F
  I believe     in Adam and __ Eve,
G                     F
  In a tree in a garden,
C
  In a snake and a thief.
```

Chorus 1

```
C            F      Gsus4     G F
  I believe, __ I be-lieve,
G             F               C          G7sus4
  I believe in the Word of God, yeah, __ yeah.
C             F     Gsus4     G F
  I believe, __ I be-lieve,
G                  F        C       F
  'Cause He made __ me be-lieve.
| G    C F | G    F    | C        |
```

Verse 2

```
C                 F G                   C  F
  I believe Noah      built an ark of wood.
  G                           F C                    B♭sus2
A hundred and twenty years,       no one understood.
C           F   G          C   F
  I believe   El-ijah never died,
G                         F
  Called fire from heaven
C
  On a mountainside.
```

Chorus 2

```
C          F        Gsus4     G F
  I believe, __ I be-lieve,
G          F              C         G7sus4
  I believe in the Word of God, yeah, __ yeah.
C           F       Gsus4      G F
  I believe, __ I be-lieve,
G                  F         C         D7/F♯
  'Cause He made __ me be-lieve.
```

Bridge

```
          Fmaj7                      C
It's been passed down through ages of time,
        D7/F♯               Fmaj7
Written by hands of men, in-spired by the Lord.
   C                        Gsus4
His Word will remain to the end.
```

Verse 3

```
C                  F  G                        C  F
  I believe Isaiah        was a prophet of old;
G                          F  C
  The Lamb was slain        just as he foretold.
B♭sus2 C               F G                        C  F
Well,    I believe Jesus      was the Word made man
G                            F
  And He died for my sins
C N.C.
  And He rose again. Don't you know that...
```

Chorus 3

```
C          F        Gsus4     G F
  I believe, __ I be-lieve,
G          F              C         G7sus4
  I believe in the Word of God, yeah, __ yeah.
C           F       Gsus4      G F
  I believe, __ I be-lieve,
G                  F         C
  'Cause He made __ me be-lieve.
```

I Will Be Here

Words and Music by
Steven Curtis Chapman

(Capo 1st fret)

Dsus2 G6sus2 Asus4 D D/C♯ Bm7 F♯m/A Gsus2 D/F♯

Em7 A7sus4 A7 A/C♯ E9 A A/G Dadd9/F♯ G5

G5/F♯ F♯ B7 D/A E7sus4 E7 A♯°7

Intro | Dsus2 | Gsus2 | Dsus2 | Gsus2 |

Verse 1

Dsus2 **Asus4** **D**
Tomorrow morning, if you __ wake up

D/C♯ **Bm7** **F♯m/A** **Gsus2** **D/F♯**
And the sun does not appear,

Em7 **A7sus4** **A7** **Dsus2** **G6sus2**
I , ______ I will be here

Dsus2 **Asus4** **D**
If in the dark we lose sight__ of love,

D/C♯ **Bm7** **F♯m/A** **Gsus2** **D/F♯**
Hold my __ hand and have no fear

Em7 **A7sus4** **A7** **Dsus2** **D**
'Cause I, ______ I will be here.

Chorus 1

A/C♯ Bm7
I will be here

F♯m/A E9 A
When you feel like bein' qui - et.

A/G Dadd9/F♯ G5
When you need to speak your mind,

G5/F♯ Em7 F♯ B7
I ___ will lis - ten, and I will be here.

D/A Esus4 E7 Asus2
When the laughter turns to cry - ing,

A/G Dadd9/F♯ G5
Through the winning, losing and try - ing,

G5/F♯ Em7 Asus4
We'll be togeth - er,

Dsus2 G6sus2 Dsus2 G6sus2
'Cause I will be here.

Verse 2

Dsus2 Asus4 D
Tomorrow morning, if you__ wake up

D/C♯ Bm7 F♯m/A Gsus2 D/F♯
And the future is un - clear,

Em7 A7sus4 A7 Dsus2 G6sus2
I, _______ I will be here.

Dsus2 Asus4 D
As sure as seasons are made __ for change,

D/C♯ Bm7 F♯m/A Gsus2 D/F♯
Our lifetimes are made for __ years,

Em7 A7sus4 A7 Dsus2 D
So I, ______ I will be here.

Chorus 2

```
A/C♯           Bm7
I will be here,

 F♯m/A          E9                 A
  And you can cry on my shoul - der.

A/G             Dadd9/F♯                  G5
     When the mirror tells us we're old-er,

  G5/F♯    Em7
I will hold __ you.

      F♯             B7     D/A
And I will be here

    E7sus4    E              A     A/G
To watch you grow in beau - ty

               Dadd9/F♯                  G5
And tell you all the things you are to me.

D/F♯          Em7
I will be here.

A7          A♯°7
     Mm.
```

Bridge

```
Bm7           E7sus4    E7
I will be true

                  A      A/G       Dadd9/F♯
To the prom - ise I __ have made

   G             D/F♯        Em7
To you and to __ the One

                  A7sus4  A7     Em7    A7sus4  A7
Who gave you to           me.
```

Outro

```
|Dsus2    |Asus4   D   D/C♯|Bm7    F♯m/A   |Gsus2 D/F♯   |

Em7  A7sus4 A7          Dsus2
I, _______    I will be here.

G6sus2       Dsus2
  And just as sure

                    Asus4          D   D/C♯
As seasons are made __ for change,

    Bm7                  F♯m/A    G5          D/F♯
Our lifetimes are made __ for ___ years.

  Em7    A7sus4
So I, _______

A♯°7       Bm7
  I will be __ here.

D/A     Em7          Asus4    A
  We'll be together.

     Dsus2
I will be here.

|G6sus2    |Dadd9/F♯    |Em7    Asus4   |D
```

I'll Lead You Home

Words and Music by
Michael W. Smith and Wayne Kirkpatrick

Tune down 1/2 step:
(low to high) E♭–A♭–D♭–G♭–B♭–E♭

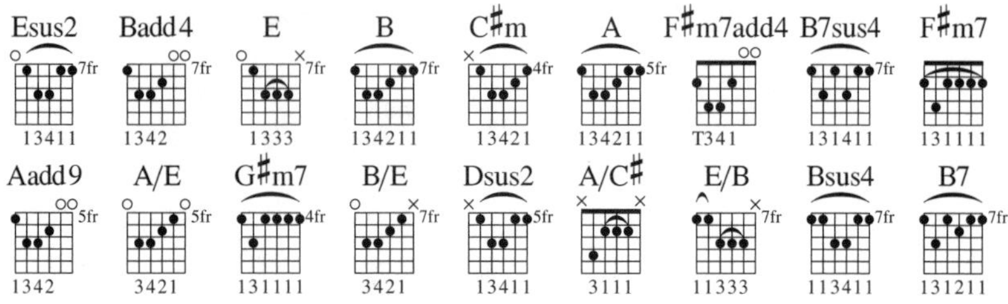

Intro

Esus2	Badd4	E	B	C♯m
A	F♯m7add4	B7sus4	E	

Verse 1

```
E                            B
    Wandering the road of desp'rate life,
C♯m                           A
    Aimlessly beneath a bar - ren sky.
F♯m7               B7sus4             E
    Leave it to Me,     I'll lead you home.
                              B
So afraid that you will __ not be found,
C♯m                                Aadd9
  It won't be long before your sun goes down.
F♯m7add4             B7sus4              E
  Just leave it to Me,     I'll lead you home.
```

```
                  A/E
Chorus 1     Hear Me calling,

                  E         G♯m7
             Hear Me calling.

             F♯m7
               Leave it to Me,

             B7sus4               E
                 I'll lead you home.

             |        |        A/E | E        |       A/E  B/E |


             E                        B
Verse 2        A troubled mind and doubter's heart,

             C♯m                              A
               You wonder how you ever got __ this far.

             F♯m7              B7sus4                E
                 Leave it to Me,      I'll lead you home.

                                             B
                 Vultures of darkness ate the crumbs you left,

             C♯m                          Aadd9
               And you've got no way to re-trace your steps.

             F♯m7add4           B7sus4                E
               Just leave it to Me,      I'll lead you home.
```

Chorus 2

```
          A/E
Hear Me calling,
          E
Hear Me calling.
G♯m7                    F♯m7
  You're lost and alone.
                 B7sus4
Leave it to Me,
                 E
I'll lead you home.
          A/E
Hear Me calling,
          E
Hear Me calling.
G♯m7                    F#m7
  You're lost and alone.
                 B7sus4
Leave it to Me,

I'll lead you home.
```

Dsus2		A/C♯	
F♯m7		E/B	Bsus4 B
A	F♯m7	E/B	B7
F♯m7	B7sus4 B7	E	

Verse 3

```
E                       B
  So let it go and turn it over to
C♯m                                  A
  The One who chose to give His life __ for you.
F♯m7
    Leave it to Me,
B7sus4              E
    I'll lead you home.
E                       B
  So let it go and turn it over to
C♯m                                  A
  The One who chose to give His life __ for you.
F♯m7
    Leave it to Me,
B7sus4              C♯m
    I'll lead you home.
F♯m7                B7sus4
    Leave it to Me,
                E
I'll lead you home.
```

Chorus 3

```
          A/E
Hear Me calling,
          E
Hear Me calling.
G♯m7
  You're lost and alone.
F♯m7
    Leave it to Me,
B7sus4              E
    I'll lead you home.
```

Chorus 4 *Repeat Chorus 3 till fade*

If This World

Words and Music by Michelle Tumes,
Tyler Hayes, Erik Sundin and Mark Heimermann

D · A · Bm · Gmaj7 · Asus4 · G

132 · 123 · 13421 · 2 1 · 124 · 21 34

Em7 · D/F♯ · A/C♯ · Gsus2 · Dmaj7/A · Dmaj7/E

12 4 · 1 23 · 3111 · 2 134 · 111 · 111

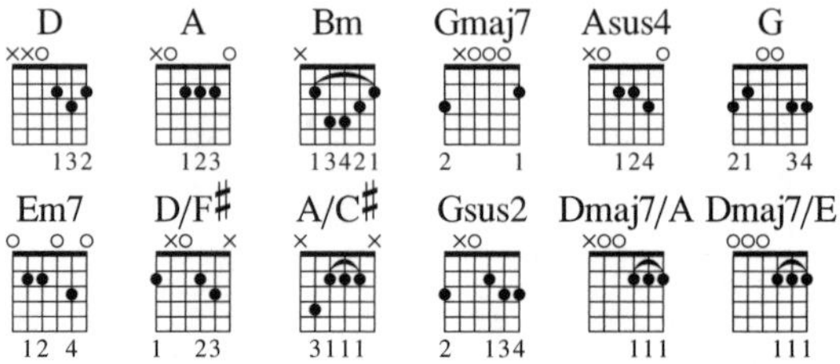

Intro

D **A**
‖: Na, na, na, na, na, na, na,

Bm
Na, na, na, na, na.

Gmaj7 A
Oh, yeah. :‖

Verse 1

D **Asus4**
Do you feel you've been disowned,

Bm **G** **A**
Left outside __ in the cold and without __ a home?

D **Asus4**
Do you think that no one cares

Bm **G** **A**
That you're lost __ and alone and without __ a prayer?

Em7 **D/F♯**
Don't give in __ to the lie

Asus4 **A** **Bm**
That there's no __ one you can turn to.

Em7 **D/F♯**
Don't lose heart, __ there is hope,

Asus4 **A**
There is some - one who will never desert __ you, oh.

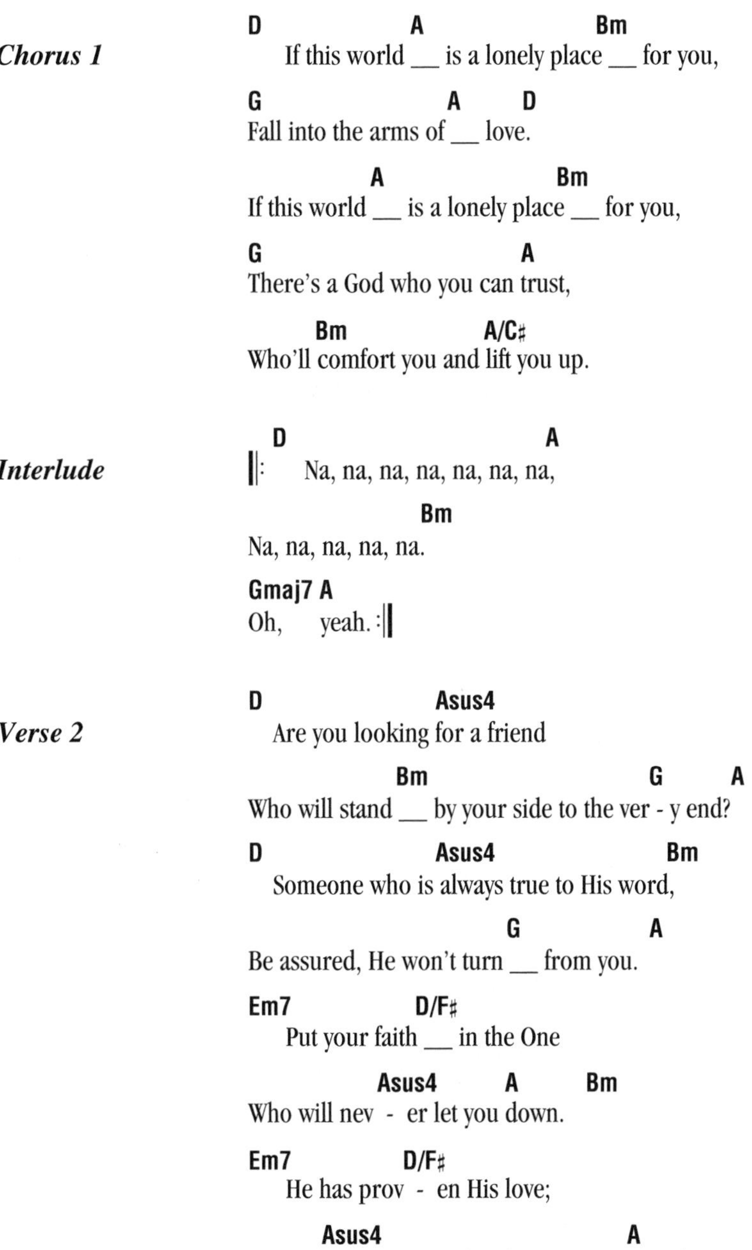

Chorus 1

D A Bm
If this world __ is a lonely place __ for you,

G A D
Fall into the arms of __ love.

A Bm
If this world __ is a lonely place __ for you,

G A
There's a God who you can trust,

Bm A/C♯
Who'll comfort you and lift you up.

Interlude

D A
‖: Na, na, na, na, na, na, na,

Bm
Na, na, na, na, na.

Gmaj7 A
Oh, yeah. :‖

Verse 2

D Asus4
Are you looking for a friend

Bm G A
Who will stand __ by your side to the ver - y end?

D Asus4 Bm
Someone who is always true to His word,

G A
Be assured, He won't turn __ from you.

Em7 D/F♯
Put your faith __ in the One

Asus4 A Bm
Who will nev - er let you down.

Em7 D/F♯
He has prov - en His love;

Asus4 A
Open up __ to all He has for you now, __ oh.

Chorus 2 *Repeat Chorus 1*

Bridge

```
Gsus2              Dmaj7/A             Dmaj7/E
   He hears your cry, He sees your tears,

                              Em7    D/F♯      Gsus2
He knows your pain and all __ your __ fears.

              Dmaj7/A             Dmaj7/E
He waits for you with open arms,

                         Em7     D/F♯     Gsus2
He longs to live inside __ your __ heart.

             Asus4          D
You'll never be alone again.
```

Chorus 3 *Repeat Chorus 1*

Outro

```
   D                             A
‖:   Na, na, na, na, na, na, na,

                  Bm
Na, na, na, na, na.

Gmaj7 A
Oh,    yeah. :‖  Play 3 times

| D          |
```

In Christ Alone

Words and Music by
Don Koch and Shawn Craig

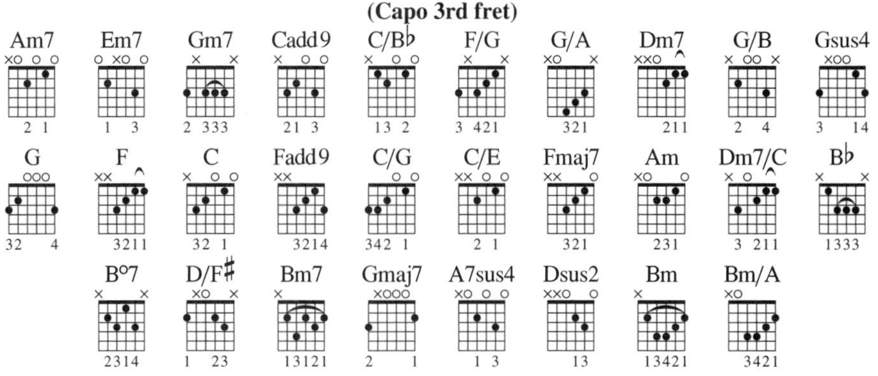

Intro | Am7 Em7 | Gm7 Cadd9 | C/B♭ F/G |

Verse 1

```
                    Cadd9
In Christ alone __ will I glory
           G/A            Dm7        Am7
Though I could pride my-self in battles won.
      G/B       Cadd9
For I've been blessed beyond measure,
      Dm7              Am7          Gsus4  G
And by His strength a-lone I over-come.
F                             G/B        C
Oh, I could stop and count __ suc-cesses
       Am7          G/B       Fadd9
Like diamonds in __ my hand,
             C/G
But those trophies are not equal
          Dm7             Gsus4  G
To the grace by which I stand.
```

Chorus 1

```
                Fadd9        C/E
In Christ a-lone I place my trust
                  Dm7         Gsus4       Cadd9
And find my glory in the power of the cross.
Am7        Fmaj7 Gsus4
  In ev'ry victo - ry,
            Cadd9  Am
Let it be said of me:
    Dm7                          Gsus4        G
My source of strength, my source of hope
                 Am7      Gm7  Cadd9     C/B♭ F/G
Is Christ a-lone.
```

Verse 2

```
                 Cadd9
In Christ alone __ I will glory,
    G/A          Dm7            Am7
For only by His grace I am re-deemed.
              Cadd9
And only His tender mercy
       Dm7                 Am7              Gsus4   G
Could reach beyond my weakness to my need.
F                       G/B   C
Now I seek no great  -  er honor
      Am7          G/B       Fadd9
Than just to know __ Him more
          C/G
And to count my gains but losses
        Dm7         E♭      Gsus4
To the glory of my Lord.
```

Chorus 2

Fadd9 C/E
In Christ a-lone I place my trust

Dm7 Gsus4 Cadd9
And find my glory in the power of the cross.

Am7 Fmaj7 Gsus4
In ev'ry victo - ry,

Cadd9 Am
Let it be said of me:

Dm7 Dm7/C B♭ B°7
My source of strength, _____ my source of hope...

Chorus 3

G D/F♯
In Christ a-lone I place my trust

Em7 G D/F♯
And find my glory in the power of the cross.

Bm7 Gmaj7 A7sus4
In ev'ry victo - ry,

Dsus2 Bm7
Let it be said of me:

Em7 A7sus4
My source of strength, my source of hope

Bm Bm/A
Is Christ a-lone.

Em7 A7sus4
My source of strength, my source of hope

D
Is Christ alone.

If We Answer

Words and Music by Douglas McKelvey,
Phil Naish and Scott Dente

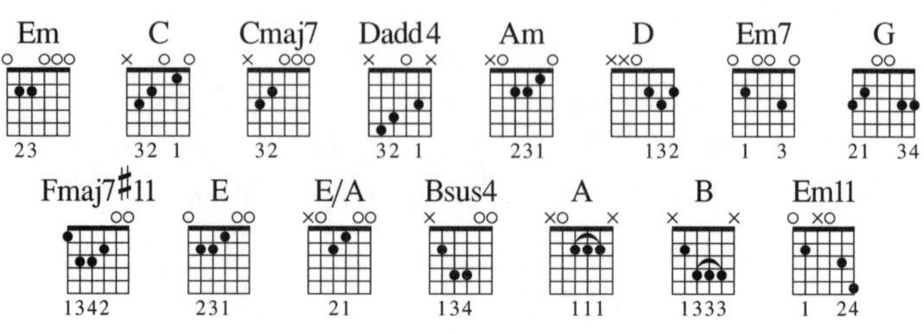

Intro

| Em | C | Em | C Cmaj7 |
| Em | C Dadd4 | Em | C Cmaj7 |

Verse 1

```
Em                 C
He is fierce and He __ is tender.
Em                     C
He's our judge and our __ defender,
Am                        C     Cmaj7
   And He calls us to sur-render,
        Em                 D
For He loves us to the core.
Em                   C
He is fright'ning and __ resplendent.
Em                C      Cmaj7
He is present and __ tran-scendent.
Am                        C
   He's enmeshed and inde-pendent
         Em                Dadd4
And He cannot love us more.
```

Chorus 1

```
        G                  D
So He calls our names
               C
And we fear __ Him for His goodness,
         Am                            Dadd4
For we know He won't be tamed.
        G                  D
So He calls our names
               C
And we won - der, if we answer,
          Am
Will we ever be the same?
          Fmaj7♯11
Will we ever be the same?
```

Verse 2

```
Em                     C
He's a comfort and __ a terror,
Em                 C
A destroyer and __ repairer.
Am                             C      Cmaj7
   He's more terrible and fairer
           Em                          D
Than our mortal tongues can say.
Em                  C
He is hidden and __ revealing.
Em                    C       Cmaj7
He's appalling and __ ap-pealing.
Am                                  C
   He's our wounding and our healing
         Em                 Dadd4
And He will not turn away.
```

Chorus 2 *Repeat Chorus 1*

Bridge

```
E            E/A        Bsus4
     (Holy Lamb of ___ God.)
          E/A                  E
And He cannot love us more.
                 A       B
(Holy Lamb __ of __ God.)
```

Verse 3

```
Em                C
He is wild, He __ is wonder.
Em                         C
He is whisp'ring and He is thunder.
Am                      C  Cmaj7
   He is over, He is un-der,
          Em                   Dadd4
And He suffered for our gain.
Em                      C
He's a comfort and __ a danger.
Em                   C
He's a father and __ a stranger.
Am                               C
   He's enthroned and in a manger,
          Em                         D
And He says we're worth His pain.
```

Chorus 3

```
         G                 D
So He calls our names
                C
And we fear __ Him for His goodness,
          Am                           D
For we know He won't be tamed.
         G                 D
So He calls our names
                C
And we won - der, if we answer,
          Am
Will we ever be the same?
          Fmaj7#11
Will we ever be the same?
            D                          Dadd4
No, we'll __ never be the same.
```

Interlude

```
|Em          |C           |Em          |C           |
```

Outro

```
          Em               Cmaj7    Em
And He calls our name.
Cmaj7                          Em11
   Oh, we'll never be the same.
Cmaj7                   Em11
   We will never be __ the same.
Cmaj7                         Em       C
     We will never be the same.
Em          C           Em              C         Em    Cmaj7
     (He com - forts and __ He loves __ us.)
```

If You Want Me To

Words and Music by
Ginny Owens and Kyle Matthews

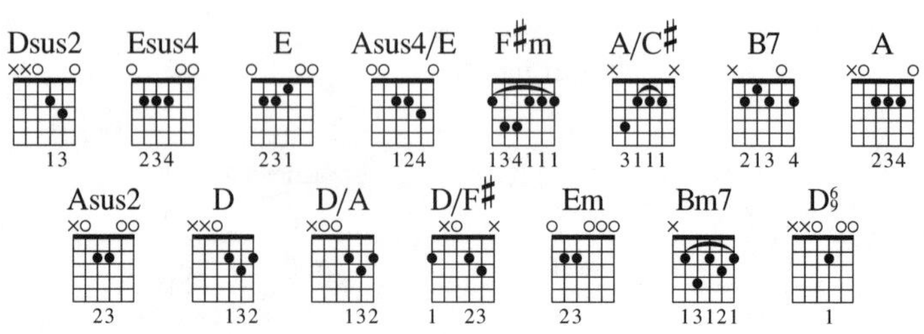

Intro | Dsus2 | Esus4 E |

Verse 1

```
       Asus4/E                          E            F♯m
The pathway is broken and the signs are un - clear.
    Dsus2             A/C♯          E                     F♯m
And __ I don't know the reason     why You brought me here.
      Dsus2         A/C♯            E          F♯m
But just because You love me the way that You do,
                A/C♯  B7                       Esus4         A
I'm gonna walk  through the valley if You __ want me to.
| Dsus2   E   | Asus2  A/C♯  |
```

Verse 2

```
              D          A/C♯          E              F♯m
No, I'm not who I was when I took my first step.
            D                A/C♯                          E                F♯m
And I'm __ clingin' to the __ promise You're not    through with me yet.
      D           A/C♯           E      F♯m
So if all of these trials bring me closer to You,
                D  A/C♯            B7      Esus4       A
Then I will go through the fi-re if You __ want me to.
```

```
             D/F♯        E                        Dsus2   E
Verse 3      It may not be the way I would have chosen,

                        F♯m      E          D            A/C♯    Esus4    E
             When You lead me through a world that's not my home.

             D          E                        Em     Dsus2
             But You nev - er said it would be easy,

                 Bm7                                 Esus4      E
             You only said I'll never go alone.

Interlude    | D6/9          |               | E       F♯m  | E      Asus2   |
             | Dsus2         |        Esus4  |         A    |                 |

                          D                   Asus2                 E         F♯m
Verse 4      So when the whole world turns against me and I'm all by my  -  self

                  D          A/C♯                          E       F♯m
             And I can't hear You answer my cries __ for __ help,

                  D             A/C♯                E                           F♯m
             I'll re-member the suff'ring that Your love put You through.

                      D    A/C♯                B7            E                  Asus2
             And I will walk through the dark  -  ness if You __ want me to.

                            D          A/C♯                         E           F♯m
Verse 5      'Cause when I cross over __ Jordan I'm gonna sing, gonna shout.

                         D          A/C♯                        E            F♯m
             I'm gonna look into Your eyes and see You never let me __ down.

                D           A/C♯              E                F♯m
             So take me on the pathway that leads me home __ to You,

                      D    A/C♯             B7         E          Asus2
             And I will walk through the val-ley if You want me to.

             | A      Dsus2 |               | E       F♯m  |                 |

                      D    A/C♯             B7       Esus4        A
             Yes, I will walk through the val-ley if You want me to.
```

In Heaven's Eyes

Words and Music by Phill McHugh

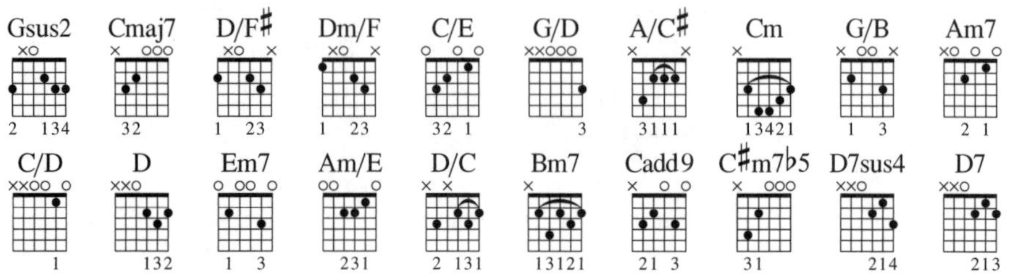

Intro

| Gsus2 | | Cmaj7 | |
| Gsus2 | | Cmaj7 | |

Verse 1

Gsus2 D/F♯
A fervent prayer rose up to heaven.

Dm/F C/E G/D
A fragile soul was losing ground.

A/C♯ Cm
Sorting through the earthly Babel,

G/B Am7 C/D
Heaven heard the sound.

Verse 2

D Gsus2 D/F♯ Dm/F
This was __ a life of no distinction,

Em7 Am/E G/D
No __ successes, only tries.

A/C♯ Cm
Yet gazing __ down on this un-lovely one,

Am7 C/D D/C
There was love in Heaven's eyes.

Chorus 1

```
                   G/B  Bm7             Cadd9     C/D
In Heaven's eyes          there are no losers.
   D/C             G/B   Bm7                Cadd9    C/D
In Heaven's eyes               no hopeless cause.
D/C    G/B         Cadd9  G/D            C♯m7♭5
   Only people like you with feelings like me,
  Am7                          D7sus4     D7
A-mazed by the grace we can find

In Heaven's eyes.
```

Interlude *Repeat Intro*

Verse 3

```
                 Gsus2                  D/F♯    Dm/F
The orphaned child, the wayward father,
                 C/E              G/D
The homeless traveler in the rain.
                  A/C♯            Cm
When life goes by and no one bothers,
         G/B                  Am7    C/D  D
Heaven feels the pain.
```

Verse 4

```
         Gsus2          D/F♯                    Dm/F
Looking __ down, God sees each heartache,
        Em7                 Am/E            G/D
Knows __ each sorrow,          hears each cry.
                A/C♯                   Cm
And looking __ up we'll see com-passion's fire,
  Am7                      C/D     D/C
A-blaze in Heaven's eyes.
```

```
                    G/B  Bm7           Cadd9    C/D
Chorus 2    In Heaven's eyes       there are no losers.

              D/C          G/B   Bm7              Cadd9   C/D
            In Heaven's eyes            no hopeless cause.

            D/C    G/B        Cadd9  G/D         C#m7b5
              Only people like you with feelings like me,

              Am7                    C/D   Bm7   C/D   D  D/C
            A-mazed by the grace we can find.


                    G/B  Bm7           Cadd9    C/D
Chorus 3    In Heaven's eyes       there are no losers.

              D/C             G/B   Bm7                   Cadd9   C/D
            In __ Heaven's eyes           there is no hopeless cause.

            D/C           G/B        Cadd9  G/D         C#m7b5
              There's only people like you with feelings like me,

                         Am7                       C/D       D
            And we're a-mazed by the grace we can find

            In Heaven's Eyes.

Outro       |Gsus2   |        |Cmaj7   |        |
            |Gsus2   |        |Cmaj7   |        |Gsus2
```

In the Name of the Lord

Words by Gloria Gaither,
Phill McHugh and Sandi Patty
Music by Sandi Patty

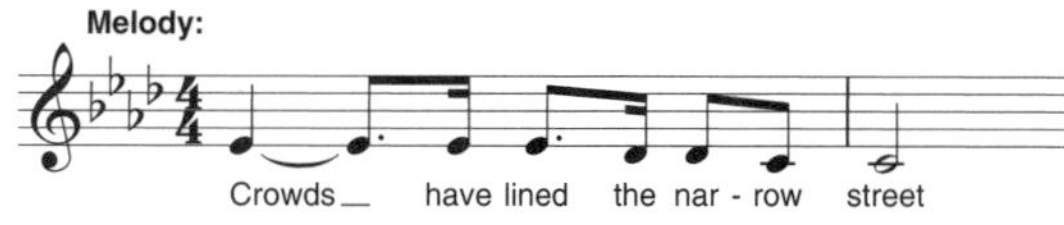

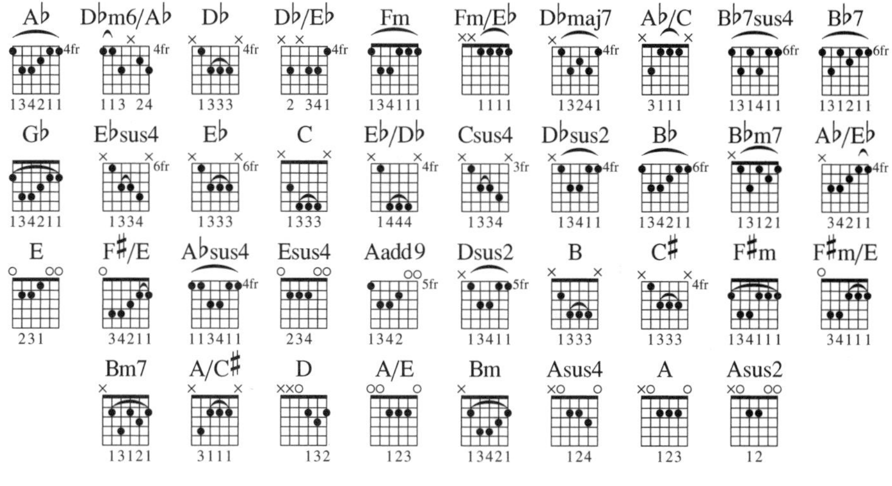

Intro

| A♭ | D♭m6/A♭ | A♭ | D♭m6/A♭ |

Verse 1

A♭ D♭m6/A♭ A♭
Crowds have lined the narrow street

D♭ D♭/E♭ A♭
To see this man from Gal - ilee;

Fm Fm/E♭
Just a carpenter some say,

D♭maj7 A♭/C
Leading fools a-stray,

B♭7sus4 B♭7 G♭ E♭sus4 E♭
Yet many kneel __ to give Him praise.

A♭ D♭m6/Ab A♭
And in His eyes they glimpse the pow'r

D♭ C Fm Fm/E♭
That sees the heart of all men,

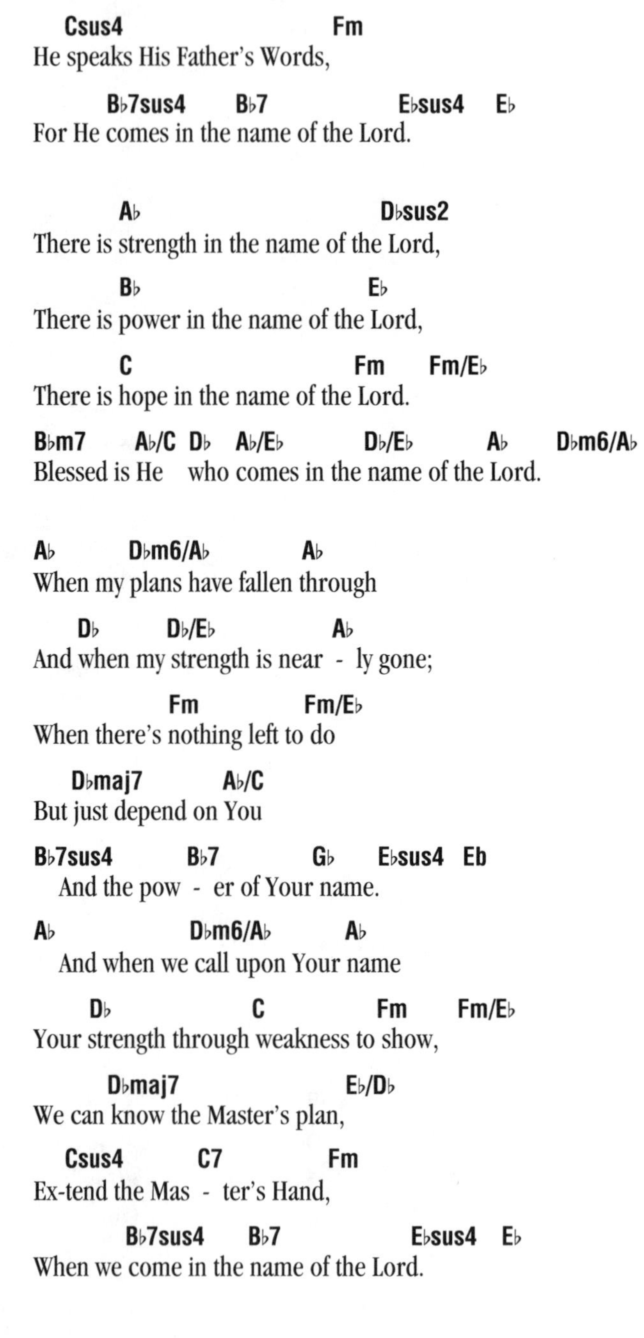

D♭maj7 E♭/D♭
And He knows His Father's mind,

Csus4 Fm
He speaks His Father's Words,

B♭7sus4 B♭7 E♭sus4 E♭
For He comes in the name of the Lord.

Chorus 1

A♭ D♭sus2
There is strength in the name of the Lord,

B♭ E♭
There is power in the name of the Lord,

C Fm Fm/E♭
There is hope in the name of the Lord.

B♭m7 A♭/C D♭ A♭/E♭ D♭/E♭ A♭ D♭m6/A♭
Blessed is He who comes in the name of the Lord.

Verse 2

A♭ D♭m6/A♭ A♭
When my plans have fallen through

D♭ D♭/E♭ A♭
And when my strength is near - ly gone;

Fm Fm/E♭
When there's nothing left to do

D♭maj7 A♭/C
But just depend on You

B♭7sus4 B♭7 G♭ E♭sus4 Eb
And the pow - er of Your name.

A♭ D♭m6/A♭ A♭
And when we call upon Your name

D♭ C Fm Fm/E♭
Your strength through weakness to show,

D♭maj7 E♭/D♭
We can know the Master's plan,

Csus4 C7 Fm
Ex-tend the Mas - ter's Hand,

B♭7sus4 B♭7 E♭sus4 E♭
When we come in the name of the Lord.

```
              A♭                              D♭sus2
Chorus 2      There is strength in the name of the Lord,

              B♭                            E♭
              There is power in the name of the Lord,

              C                          Fm       Fm/E♭
              There is hope in the name of the Lord.

              B♭m7      A♭/C  D♭   A♭/E♭        D♭/E♭       A♭
              Blessed is He    who comes in the name of the Lord.

                 E                 F♯/E             A♭sus4   A♭
Bridge        His name will be wor  -  shipped for-ever;

                 E          F♯/E          E♭sus4      Esus4
              Cre-ator, Re-deemer, and __ King.

              Aadd9                            Dsus2
Chorus 3      There is strength in the name of the Lord,

              B                        E
              There is power in the name of __ the Lord,

              C♯                         F♯m      F♯m/E
              There is hope in the name of the Lord.

              Bm7       A/C♯  D   A/E       F♯m   F♯m/E
              Blessed is He    who comes,

              Bm7       A/C♯  D   A/E       F♯m   F♯m/E
              Blessed is He    who comes,

              Bm7       A/C♯  D   A/E
              Blessed is He    who comes

              F♯m  Bm   Esus4 E   Asus4    A    D
              In the name of       the Lord.

                        A/C♯ Bm7  Asus4    A  Asus2  A
              The name of     the    Lord.
```

Jesus Freak

Words and Music by Toby McKeehan
and Mark Heimermann

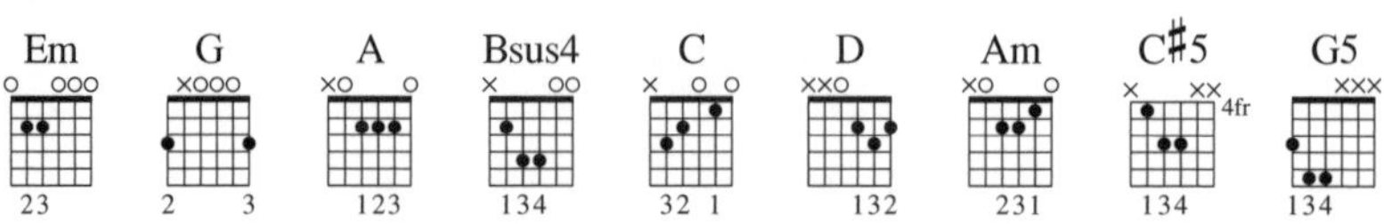

Intro

𝄆 Em G D | A Bsus4 𝄇 *Play 4 times*
Ha, ha.

Verse 1

```
Em       C     A
  Sepa-rated, I cut myself clean
          Em          C         A
From a past that comes back in my darkest dreams.
Em         C         A
  Been appre-hended by a spiritual force
          Em         C          A
And the grace that re-placed all the me I've divorced.
```

Pre-Chorus 1

```
        Em          C
I saw a man with a tat on his big fat belly.
A
It wiggled around like marmalade jelly.
  Em           C
It took me a while to catch what it said
 A
'Cause I had to match the rhythm of his belly with my head.
 Em         C           A
"Jesus saves" is what it raved in a typical tattoo green.
   Em         C
He stood on a box in the middle of the city
A
And he claimed he had a dream.
```

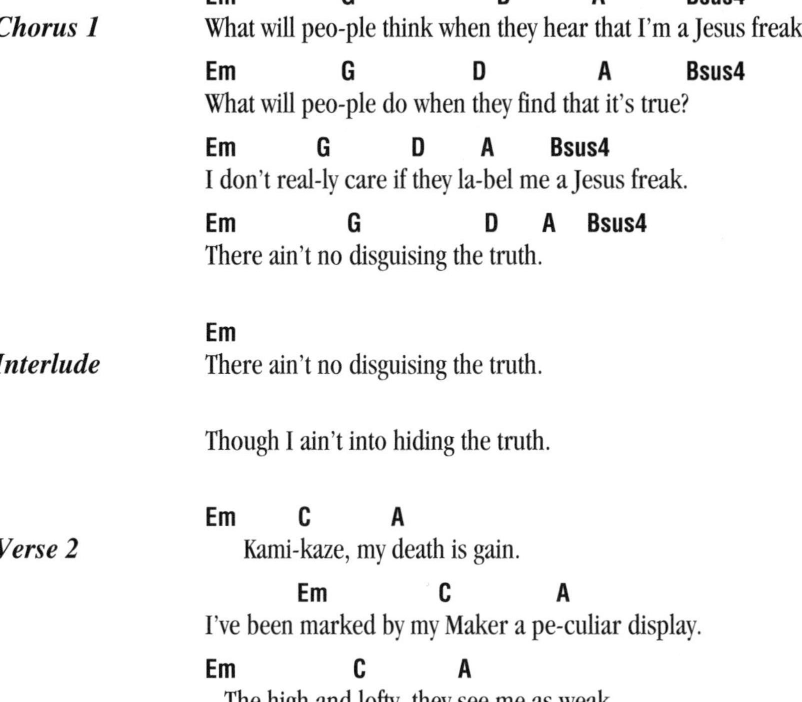

Chorus 1

```
Em            G                D          A          Bsus4
What will peo-ple think when they hear that I'm a Jesus freak?
Em            G              D            A          Bsus4
What will peo-ple do when they find that it's true?
Em         G          D      A       Bsus4
I don't real-ly care if they la-bel me a Jesus freak.
Em            G              D    A   Bsus4
There ain't no disguising the truth.
```

Interlude

```
Em
There ain't no disguising the truth.

Though I ain't into hiding the truth.
```

Verse 2

```
Em       C        A
    Kami-kaze, my death is gain.
           Em          C          A
I've been marked by my Maker a pe-culiar display.
Em          C         A
  The high and lofty, they see me as weak
          Em          C        A
'Cause I won't live and die for the power they seek, yeah.
```

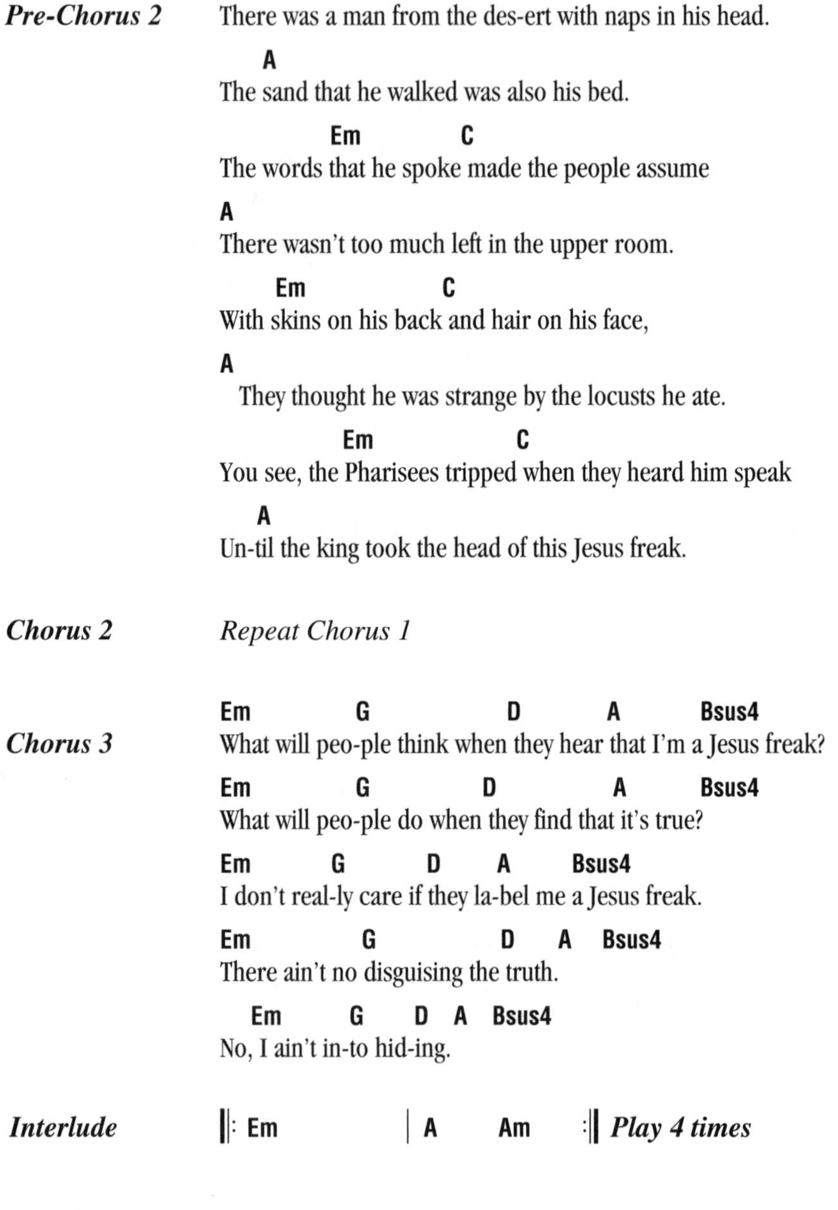

Pre-Chorus 2

Em C
There was a man from the des-ert with naps in his head.

A
The sand that he walked was also his bed.

Em C
The words that he spoke made the people assume

A
There wasn't too much left in the upper room.

Em C
With skins on his back and hair on his face,

A
They thought he was strange by the locusts he ate.

Em C
You see, the Pharisees tripped when they heard him speak

A
Un-til the king took the head of this Jesus freak.

Chorus 2 *Repeat Chorus 1*

Chorus 3

Em G D A Bsus4
What will peo-ple think when they hear that I'm a Jesus freak?

Em G D A Bsus4
What will peo-ple do when they find that it's true?

Em G D A Bsus4
I don't real-ly care if they la-bel me a Jesus freak.

Em G D A Bsus4
There ain't no disguising the truth.

Em G D A Bsus4
No, I ain't in-to hid-ing.

Interlude ‖: Em | A Am :‖ *Play 4 times*

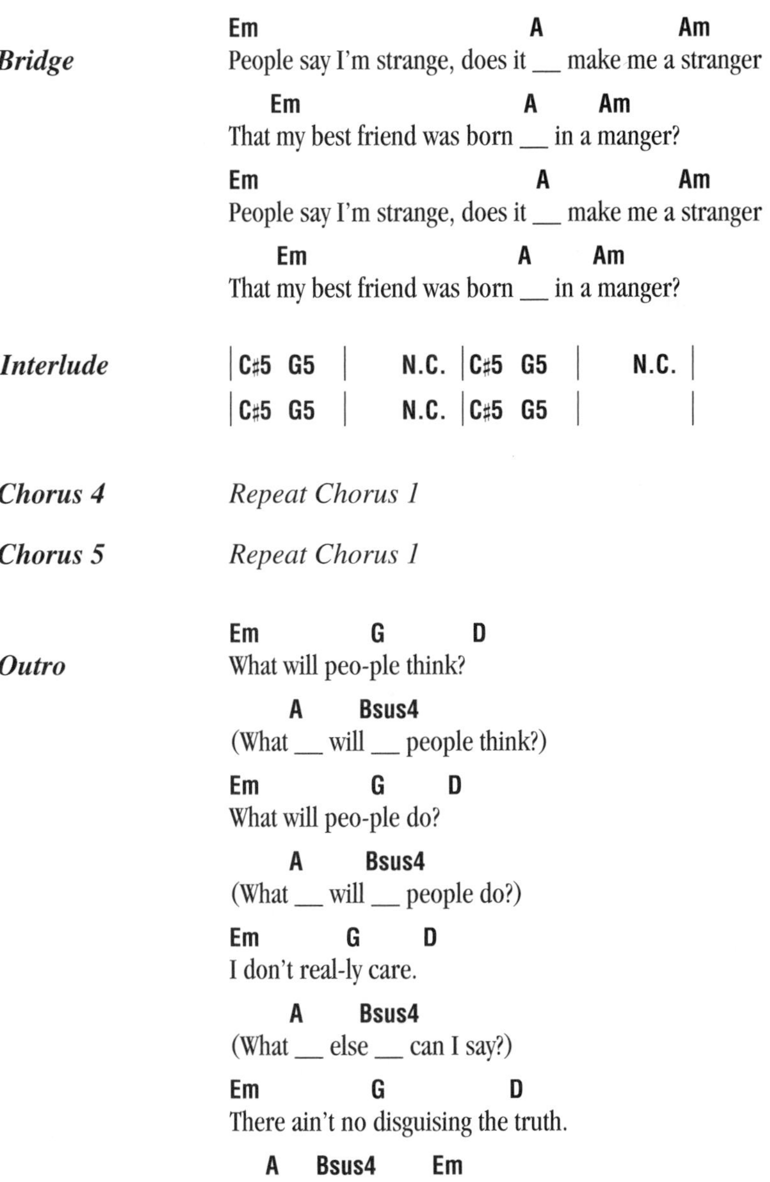

Bridge

Em A Am
People say I'm strange, does it __ make me a stranger
Em A Am
That my best friend was born __ in a manger?
Em A Am
People say I'm strange, does it __ make me a stranger
Em A Am
That my best friend was born __ in a manger?

Interlude

| C♯5 G5 | N.C. | C♯5 G5 | N.C. |
| C♯5 G5 | N.C. | C♯5 G5 | |

Chorus 4 *Repeat Chorus 1*

Chorus 5 *Repeat Chorus 1*

Outro

Em G D
What will peo-ple think?
A Bsus4
(What __ will __ people think?)
Em G D
What will peo-ple do?
A Bsus4
(What __ will __ people do?)
Em G D
I don't real-ly care.
A Bsus4
(What __ else __ can I say?)
Em G D
There ain't no disguising the truth.
A Bsus4 Em
(Je - sus is the way.)

Just One

Words and Music by
Connie Harrington and Jim Cooper

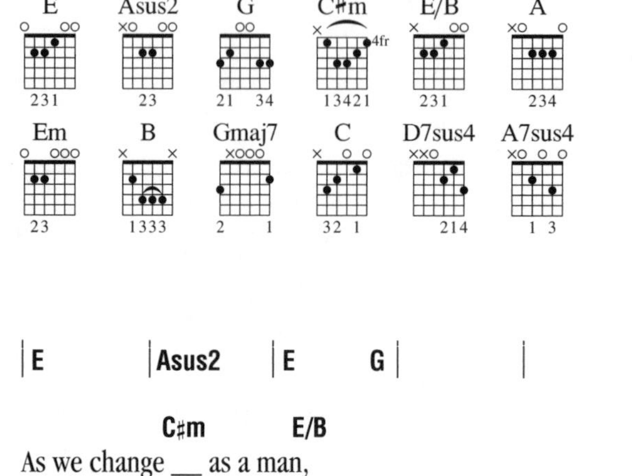

Intro | E | Asus2 | E G | | |

Verse 1

```
              C♯m          E/B
As we change __ as a man,
           A                      E
And the an - swers are a dime a doz - en,
              C♯m              E/B
Points of view __ are like sand
          G
Stretchin' out as far as the eye can see.
          Em                        C
There's a thousand diff'rent philos - ophies,
```

Chorus

```
                    E                              A
But there's just __ one book, and there's just __ one name
                 E                   G
With the pow - er to you and the grace to save.
                    E                        A
You can search __ the world for anoth - er way,
               Gmaj7                           A
But if you're lookin' for the road to beyond,
                     Asus2
There's just one.
```

Verse 2

```
                    C♯m                  E/B
There's just too __ much at stake
               A                   E
To be wast - ing time on imita - tions,
           C♯m             E/B
Promises __ and claims.
              G
There will never be a substitute
           Em                            B
For the blood, the Word, and the sim - ple truth,
                      E                              A
'Cause there's just __ one book, and there's just __ one name
                 E                   G
With the pow - er to you and the grace to save.
                    E                        A
You can search __ the world for anoth - er way,
               Gmaj7                           A
But if you're lookin' for the road to beyond,
```

```
                              C
Bridge        There's just one door __ to open,
                                                 D7sus4
              Where truth and hope will be wait  -  ing

              There on the other side.
                   C
              Just __ one story that's never ending
                       A7sus4           B
              With life ___ beginning in Jesus Christ.
              |E          |Asus2     |E     Gma7|          |
                                       Yeah.

                                   E                      A
Outro         ||: You can search __ the world for anoth - er way,
                          Gmaj7                          A
              But if you're lookin' for the road to beyond,
                                    E
              There's just one, just __ one book,
                                A                          E
              And there's just __ one name with the pow - er to heal
                        G
              And the grace to save.  :||  Repeat and fade
```

Let Us Pray

Words and Music by
Steven Curtis Chapman

(Capo 3rd fret)

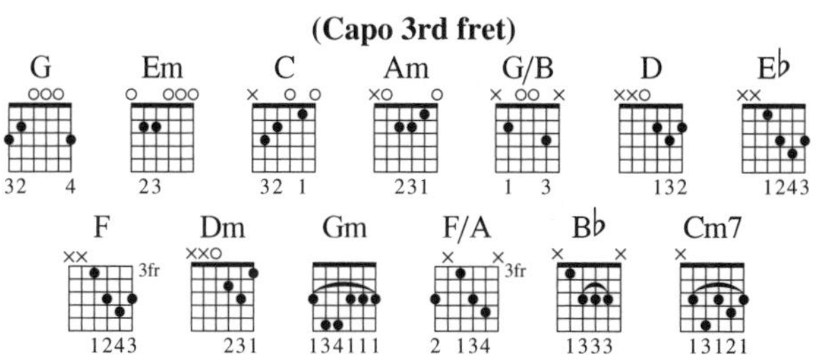

Intro ‖: G Gsus4 G | Gsus4 G :‖ *Play 4 times*

Verse 1

G Em
I hear you say your heart is ach - ing,

C
You've got trouble in the mak - ing,

Am
And you ask if I'll be praying for you, please.

G Em
And in keeping with conven - tion,

C
I'll say yes, with good inten - tions

Am
To pray later, making mention of your needs.

C G/B Em
But since we have __ this moment here at heaven's door,

C G/B
We should start knocking now.

D Em
What are we waiting for?

```
Chorus 1                 C
            Let us pray,
                     G/B            D             Am
            Let us pray, __ ev'rywhere __ in ev'ry way.
                 C                  G/B
            Ev'ry moment of the day,
                         D
            It is the right __ time.
                   C           G/B
            For the Father above,
                   D               Em
            He is lis - tening with love,
                          C              D
            And He wants __ to answer us,

            So let us pray.
            ||: G        Gsus4   G :|| Play 4 times

Verse 2     G                                 Em
              So when we feel the spirit mov - ing,
                                              C
            Prompting, prodding and behoov - ing,
                                      Am
            There is not time to be losing, let us pray.
            G                            Em
                Let the Father hear us say - ing
                                       C
            What we need to be convey - ing.
                                      Am
            Even while this song is playing, let us pray.
            C                   G/B          Em
              And just because __ we say the word "Amen,"
            C          G/B              D               Em
              It doesn't mean this conver-sation needs to end.
```

```
                C
Chorus 2   Let us pray,
                  G/B           D              Em
           Let us pray, __ ev'rywhere __ in ev'ry way.
               C              G/B
           Ev'ry moment of the day,
                   D
           It is the right __ time.
               C             G/B
           Let us pray without end,
                      D             Em
           And when we fin - ish, start again.
                          C                  D
           Like breathing out __ and breathing in,

           Oh, let us pray.

           E♭               F/A                        Dm
Bridge        Let us approach __ the throne of grace with con - fidence,
                     Gm       F     B♭
           As our prayers __ draw us near
                     E♭              Cm7
           To the One __ who knows our needs
                     D              N.C.
           Before we even call His name.
```

Chorus 3

```
                C
Let us pray,
                G/B                 D                  Am
Let us pray, __ ev'rywhere __ in ev'ry way.
        C                     G/B
Ev'ry moment of the day,
                 D
It is the right __ time.
          C               G/B
For the Father above,
          D                   Em
He is lis - tening with love,
                  C                    D
And He wants __ to answer us,
                  C                 G/B
Oh, let us pray, __ let us pray,
      D                   Em
Ev'ry-where in ev'ry way.
        C                     G/B                 D
Ev'ry moment of the day, __ it is the right __ time.
                  C                   G/B              D
And let us pray __ without end, __ and when we finish,
               Em                        C                  D
Start again, __ like breathing out __ and breathing in.
```

Outro

G
‖: Whoa, let us pray.

Oh, let us pray, yeah. :‖

Our Father, which art in heaven,

Hallowed be Thy name.

Thy kingdom come, Thy will be done

On earth as it is in heaven.

‖: Let us pray.

Let us pray, let us pray,

Oh, let us pray, yeah. :‖ ***Play 4 times***

A Little More

Words and Music by Jennifer Knapp

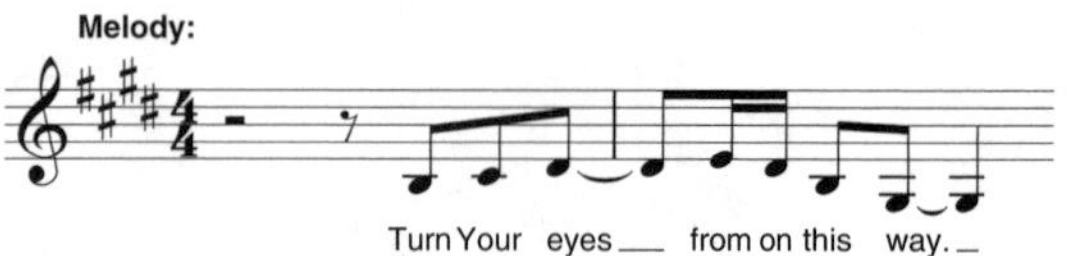

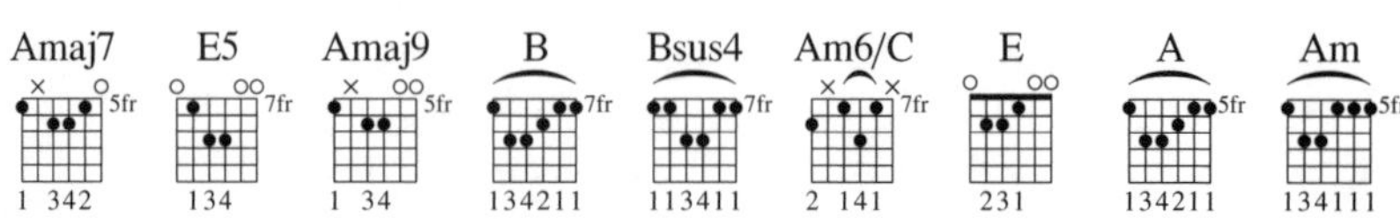

Intro | Amaj7 | E5 | Amaj7 | E5 |

Verse 1

```
Amaj7             E5
    Turn Your eyes __ from on this way.
Amaj7            E5
    I have proved __ to live a dastardly day.
  Amaj7                E5
I ___      hid my face __ from the saints
              Amaj7                        E5
And the an  -  gels who sing of Your glo - ry.
Amaj9             E5
    What you had in __ mind,
           Amaj9                E5
Said-a,           ooh, my weak-ness shines.

Shine, show me grace.
```

Chorus 1

```
Amaj9
  A little more than I can give,
E                              B
    Little more than I deserve,
                  Amaj9
Unearth this ho-liness I can't earn.

It's a little more than I can give,
E                              B     Amaj9
    Little more than I deserve,               oh.
```

Verse 2

```
Amaj7        E5
    For all the sin that lives in me,
Amaj7       E5
    It took a nail to set me free.
     Amaj7           E5                   Amaj7
Still, ___     what I do __ I don't wanna do
                  E5
And so goes the sto - ry.
Amaj9            E5
    What You had in __ mind,
        Amaj9            E5
Said-a,        when we seek we'll find.

Shine, show me grace.
```

Chorus 2

```
Amaj9
  A little more than I can give,
E                              B
    Little more than I deserve,
                 Amaj9
Unearth this ho-liness I can't earn.

It's a little more than I can give,
E                              B     Bsus4
    Little more than I deserve,
       Amaj7
Yeah, __ah, dah.
```

Bridge

```
Amaj7
    With all this motivation,
Am6/C                         E
I ___ still find a hesitation    deep in my soul.
E          Amaj7
Oh, and        despite all my demanding,
Am6/C
I ___ still find You understanding.
E                                      B          Amaj7  E   Amaj7
  Show me grace, show me grace __ I know is,
B
Oh.
```

Chorus 3

```
     N.C.
It's a     little more than I can give,
E                        B
    Little more than I deserve,
                Amaj9
Unearth this ho-liness I can't earn.

It's a little more than I can give,
E                        B
    Little more than I deserve,
Amaj7
Yeah, yeah.
```

Outro

```
| Amaj7  | Am6/C  | E      |        |
| Amaj7  | Am     | E
```

A Maze of Grace

Words and Music by
Grant Cunningham and Charlie Peacock

Melody:

(Capo 3rd fret)

Em7 (12 4) Cmaj7 (32) Em (23) D (132) G (32 4) C (32 1)

Intro ‖: **Em7** | **Cmaj7** :‖ *Play 4 times*

Verse 1

```
Em        Cmaj7
  I run.      I fall.
Em          Cmaj7
  I walk.       I sometimes crawl.
Em         Cmaj7
  I give.     I take.
Em                  Cmaj7
  I bend, and yet __ somehow I break.
Em                   Cmaj7                 Em
  I get dizzy from all __ this spinning 'round.
                           Cmaj7                 Em
I'm determined but won  -  der where I'm bound.
                                 Cmaj7         Em
I've learned to follow the sweet __ familiar sound
             Cmaj7
Of Your voice.
```

Chorus 1

```
                Em7                   Cmaj7
The straight __ and narrow twists __ and turns.
            Em7             Cmaj7
I make __ my way, and every day
         Em7          D G   Em7
I live __ I learn to fol-low You.
         D    G  Em7      D       G
You walk me through a maze of grace.
```

Interlude

| Em7 | Cmaj7 | Em7 | Cmaj7 |

Verse 2

```
Em         Cmaj7
   I stand.    I sway.
Em                  Cmaj7
   I reach for You.    I push away.
Em             Cmaj7
   I'm spent.     I'm saved.
Em           Cmaj7
   I disobey, __ yet I behave.
Em                      Cmaj7                 Em
   In my personal strug - gle to break free,
                                 Cmaj7          Em
The only piece for the puz - zle that I need
                                Cmaj7          Em
Is just to follow the sweet __ familiar lead
             Cmaj7
Of Your love.
```

Chorus 2 *Repeat Chorus 1*

Interlude

```
||: Em    |        |        |        :||
||: Em7   |        |        |        :||
|         |        |        | C   D   |
```

Chorus 3

```
              Em7                   Cmaj7
The straight __ and narrow twists __ and turns.
          Em7              Cmaj7
I make __ my way, and every day
       Em7           D  G   Em7
I live __ I learn to fol-low You.
      D    G  Em7       D       G
You walk me through a maze of grace.
          Em7                Cmaj7
I'm lost __ in You and there __ I'm found.
              Em7          Cmaj7              Em7
You're gent - ly guiding every time I turn __ around.
     D G            D  G  Em7   D      G
It's no surprise to see my life's a maze of grace.
```

Chorus 4

Repeat Chorus 3

Outro

```
Gm7
      Ah.
```

Live Out Loud

Words and Music by
Steven Curtis Chapman and Geoff Moore

Tune down 1/2 step:
(low to high) E♭–A♭–D♭–G♭–B♭–E♭

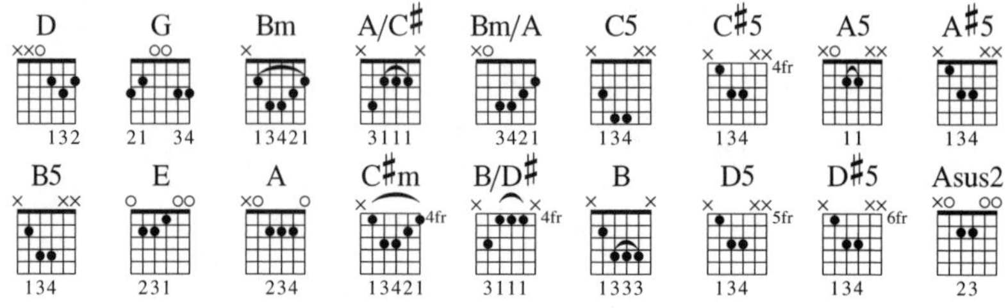

Intro ‖: D G | D G :‖ *Play 4 times*

Verse 1

```
          D
Imagine this:
                 G
I get a phone call from Regis.
D                    G
    He says, "Do you want to be a millionaire?"
D                     G                       Bm N.C.
  They put me on the show and I win with two lifelines to spare.
     A/C#    D
Now picture this:
          G
I act like nothing ever happened
D               G
  And bury all the money in a coffee can.
Bm               A/C#             D        G
  Well, I've been given more than Regis ever gave away.
Bm       A/C#               D                  G
  I was a dead man who was called to come out of my grave.
Bm               A/C#     G                 N.C.
  And I think it's time for makin' some noise.
```

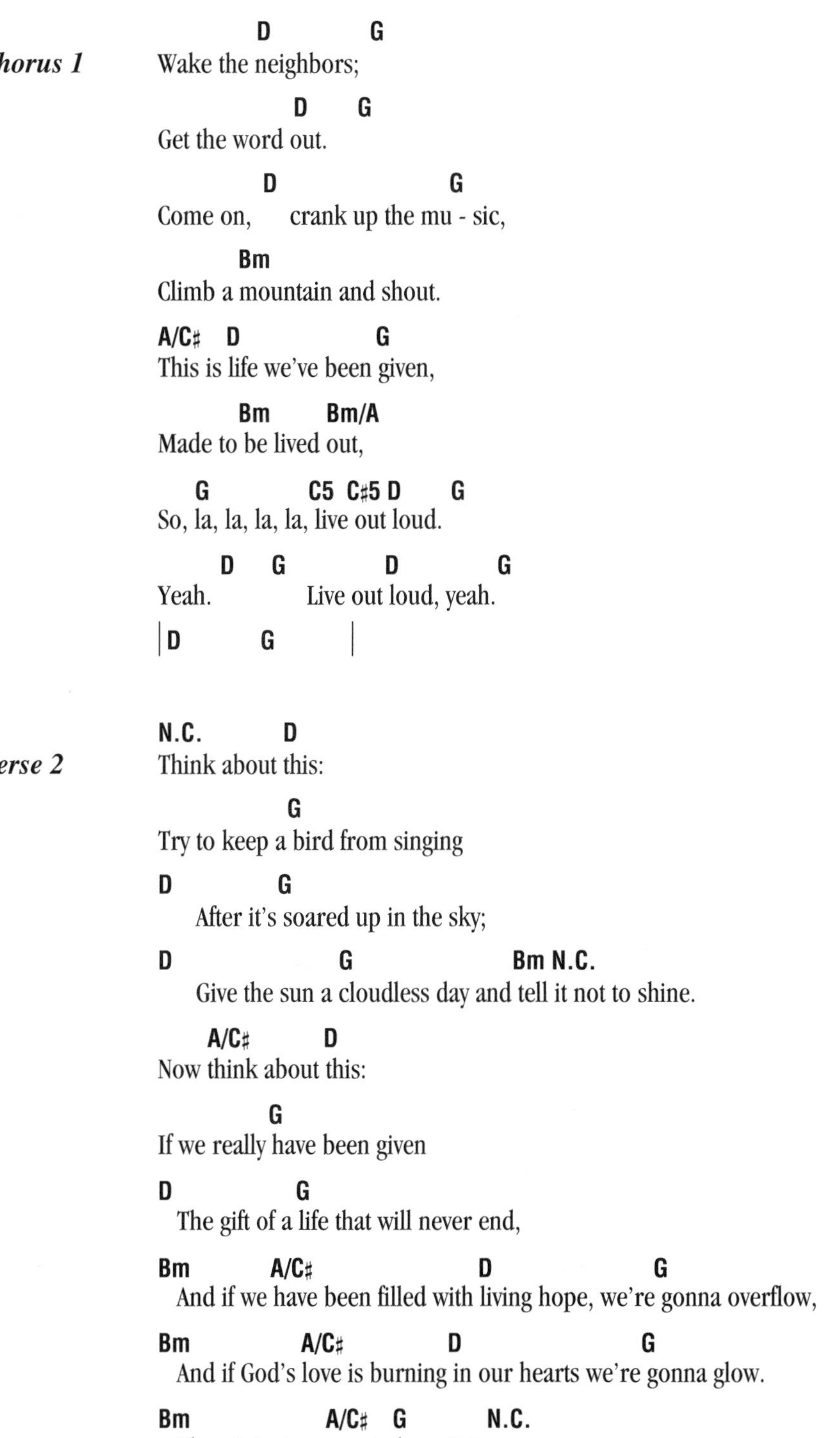

Chorus 1

D G
Wake the neighbors;

D G
Get the word out.

D G
Come on, crank up the mu - sic,

Bm
Climb a mountain and shout.

A/C♯ D G
This is life we've been given,

Bm Bm/A
Made to be lived out,

G C5 C♯5 D G
So, la, la, la, la, live out loud.

D G D G
Yeah. Live out loud, yeah.

| D G |

Verse 2

N.C. D
Think about this:

G
Try to keep a bird from singing

D G
After it's soared up in the sky;

D G Bm N.C.
Give the sun a cloudless day and tell it not to shine.

A/C♯ D
Now think about this:

G
If we really have been given

D G
The gift of a life that will never end,

Bm A/C♯ D G
And if we have been filled with living hope, we're gonna overflow,

Bm A/C♯ D G
And if God's love is burning in our hearts we're gonna glow.

Bm A/C♯ G N.C.
There's just no way to keep it in.

```
                 D          G
Chorus 2         Wake the neighbors;

                      D     G
                 Get the word out.

                  D                 G
                 Come on,   crank up the mu - sic,

                     Bm
                 Climb a mountain and shout.

                 A/C#  D              G
                 This is life we've been given,

                     Bm      Bm/A
                 Made to be lived out,

                   G          A5 A#5 Bm
                 So, la, la, la, la, live out loud.

Bridge           | Bm     G     | Bm     G      |
                                          Live out
                 | Bm     G     | C5  C#5  D    |
                  loud.

                       Bm   G
                 Ev'rybod - y,    come on,
                 | Bm     G     | Bm     G      |

                 C5  C#5      D
                      I want to hear ev'rybody sing.

                 Bm   G    Bm   G
                   La, la, la,   la, la, la, la,

                 Bm   G    C5  C#5 D
                   La, la, la, live out loud, loud, loud.

                 Ev'ry corner of creation is a living declaration.

                                  A5 B5  C5   A/C# D  N.C.
                 Come join the song we were made to   sing.
```

```
                          E            A
Chorus 3        Wake the neighbors;

                              E      A
                Get the word out.

                          E                     A
                Come on,      crank up the mu - sic,

                        C#m
                Climb a mountain and shout.

                B/D#   E                 A
                This is life we've been given,

                        C#m      B
                Made to be lived out,

                    A           D5  D#5  E
                So, la, la, la, la, live out  loud.  :||

Chorus 4        Repeat Chorus 3 (w/ voc. ad lib)

Outro           ||: E      Asus2   | E       Asus2   :||  Repeat and fade
```

Love in Any Language

Words and Music by John Mays and Jon Mohr

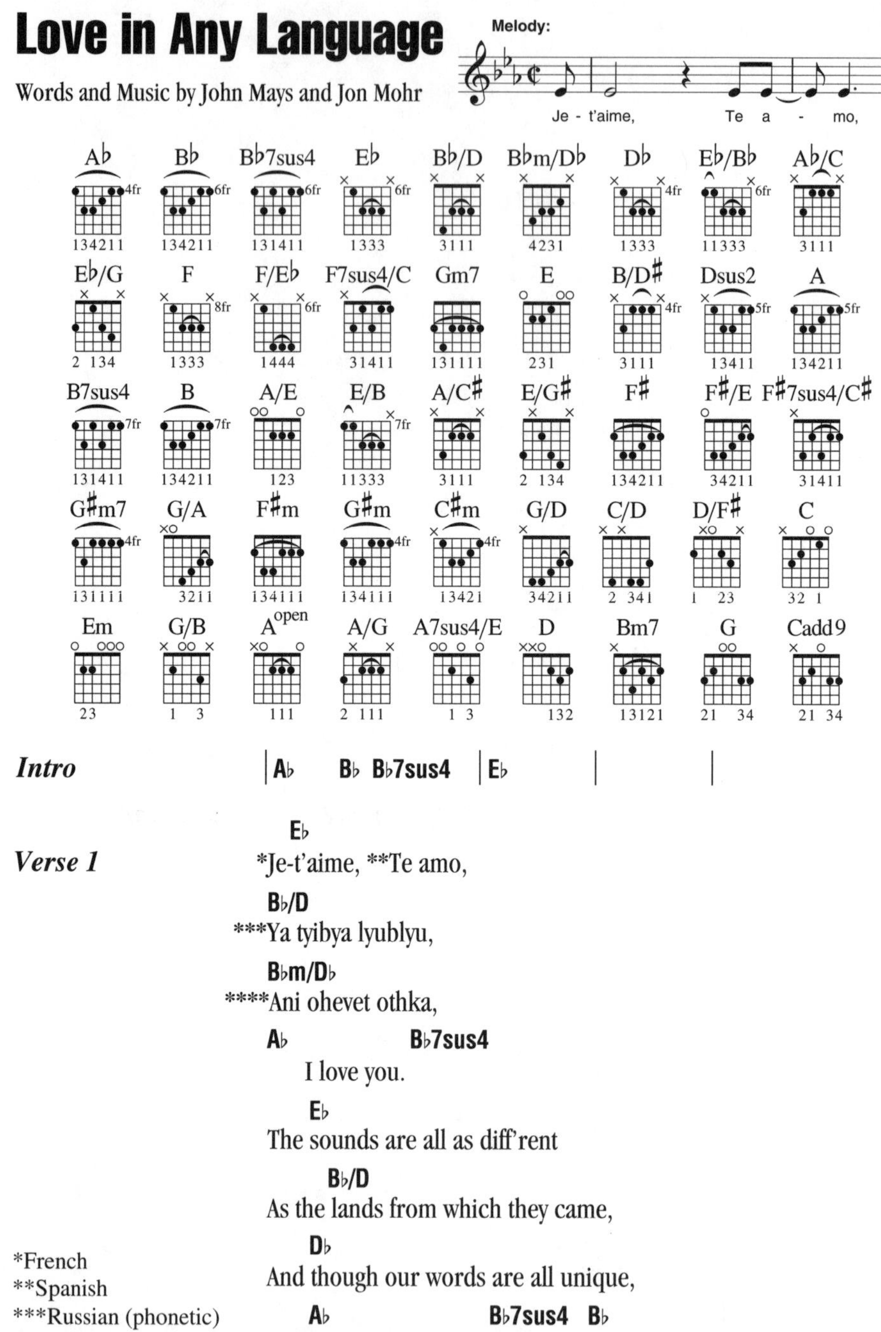

Intro | **A♭ B♭ B♭7sus4** | **E♭** | | |

Verse 1

E♭
*Je-t'aime, **Te amo,

B♭/D
***Ya tyibya lyublyu,

B♭m/D♭
****Ani ohevet othka,

A♭ B♭7sus4
I love you.

E♭
The sounds are all as diff'rent

B♭/D
As the lands from which they came,

D♭
And though our words are all unique,

A♭ B♭7sus4 B♭
Our hearts are still the same.

*French
**Spanish
***Russian (phonetic)
****Hebrew

Chorus 1

E♭
Love in any language,
A♭
Straight from the heart,
B♭
Pulls us all together,
A♭ E♭/B♭ B♭7sus4 B♭
Nev-er apart.
E♭ B♭/D A♭/C
And once we learn __ to speak __ it,
A♭ E♭/G F F/E♭
All the world __ will hear
B♭ F7sus4/C B♭ Gm7
Love in an - y lan - guage
A♭ B♭ B♭7sus4 E♭
Fluently spo - ken here.

Verse 2

E♭
We teach the young our diff'rences,
B♭
Yet look how we're the same;
B♭m/Db
We love to laugh, we dream our dreams,
A♭ B♭7sus4
We know the sting of pain.
E♭
From Leningrad to Lexington
B♭/D
The farmer loves his land,
D♭
And daddies all get misty-eyed
A♭ B♭7sus4 B♭
To give their daughter's hand.
E
Oh, maybe when we realize
B/D♯
How much there is to share,
Dsus2
We'll find too much in common
A B7sus4 B
To pre-tend it isn't there.

```
               E
*Chorus 2*     Love in any language,
               A/E
               Straight from the heart,
               B
               Pulls us all together,
               A   E/B         B7sus4  B
               Nev-er   apart.
                    E                  B/D♯            A/C♯     E/B
               And once we learn __ to speak __ it,
               A               E/G♯            F♯  F♯/E
               All the world __ will hear
               B/D♯        F♯7sus4/C♯     B          G♯m7
               Love in an - y          lan  -  guage
               A          B   B7sus4  E
               Fluently spo  -  ken     here.

                              G/A
*Bridge*       Though the rhetoric of governments
                    A
               May keep us worlds apart,
               B7sus4                   B
               There's no misinter - preting
                    F♯m   G♯m   A  C♯m  B
               The lan  -  guage of  the   heart.

               G/D
*Chorus 3*     Love in any language,
               C/D
               Straight from the heart,
               D/F♯
               Pulls us all together,
               C   G/D       C/D
               Nev-er   apart.
                    G                  D/F♯            Em    G/D
               And once we learn __ to speak __ it,
               C               G/B             A   A/G
               All the world __ will hear
               D/F♯      A7sus4/E        D          Bm7
               Love in an - y          lan  -  guage
               C               D             G     C/D
               Fluently spo - ken here.
```

Chorus 4 *Repeat Chorus 3*

Chorus 5

```
G/D
Love in any language,
C/D
Straight from the heart,
D/F♯
Pulls us all together,
C   G/D      C/D
Nev-er   apart.
     G              D/F♯          Em     G/D
And once we learn __ to speak __ it,
C            G/B          A^open  A/G
All the world __ will hear
D/F♯      A7sus4/E      D          Bm7
Love in an - y            lan  -  guage
C            D          G     G/B
Fluently spo - ken here.
D/F♯      A7sus4/E  D         Bm7
Love in an  -  y     lan - guage
C            D          G
Fluently spo - ken here.
D/F♯      A7sus4/E      D          Bm7
Love in an  -  y          lan  -  guage
C            D          G
Fluently spo - ken here.
D/F♯      A7sus4/E      D          Bm7
Love in an  -  y          lan  -  guage
C       D       Cadd9      D   G
Fluently spoken here!
```

Love Will Be Our Home

Words and Music by Steven Curtis Chapman

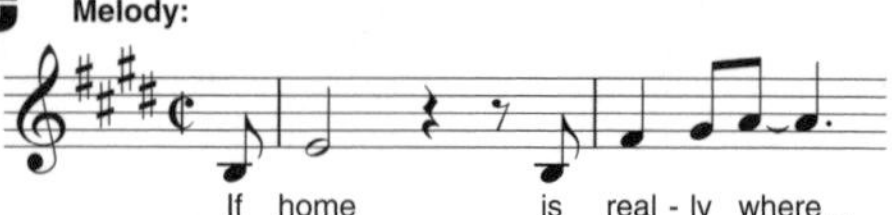

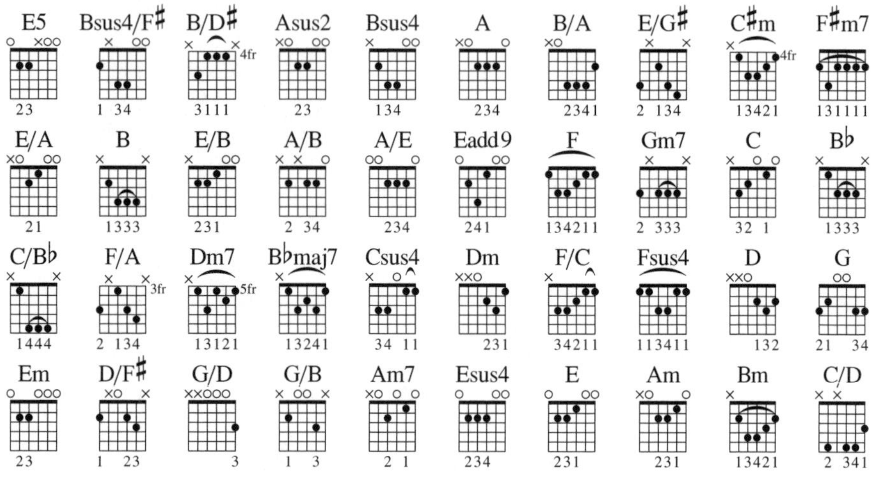

Intro | E5 | | | |

Verse 1

```
E5      Bsus4/F♯          B/D♯  E5
If home is really where the heart  is,

     Asus2               Bsus4       E5
Then home must be a place __ we all can __ share.

     A                B/A
For even with our dif-f'rences,

     E/G♯                     C♯m
Our hearts are much the same.

     F♯m7          E/G♯    E/A    Bsus4   B
For where love is, we come to-gether there.
```

Verse 2

```
         E                     B/D♯
Wher-ever there is laugh  -  ter ringing,

C♯m                      E/B
   Someone smiling,        someone dreaming,

A                      E/G♯
We can live togeth  -  er there.

F♯m7        A/B      E
Love will be __ our home.

                                B/D♯
Wherever there are chil  -  dren singing,

C♯m                     E/B
   Where a tender      heart is beating,

A                     E/G♯
We can live togeth  -  er there

        F♯m7       A/B        E        A/E   E   Eadd9
'Cause love will be __ our home.
```

Bridge

```
      F          Gm7                        C  F
With love, our hearts can be a fam  -  'ly,

     B♭                          C/B♭          F/A         F
And hope can bring this fam  -  'ly face to __ face.

     B♭                        C/B♭
And though we may be far apart,

     F/A                  Dm7
Our hearts can be as one

        Gm7                 F/A    B♭maj7  Csus4    C
When love brings us to-gether in one ___ place.
```

Verse 3

```
     F                C
Wher-ever there is laugh - ter ringing,

Dm                  F/C
   Someone smiling,      someone dreaming,

B♭                F/A
We can live togeth  -  er there.

Gm7        C      F
Love will be __ our home.

                                    C
Where there are words of kind - ness spoken,

Dm                     F/C
   Where a vow is nev  -  er broken,

B♭                F/A
We can live togeth  -  er there

         Gm7       C        Fsus4    F
'Cause love will be __ our home.
```

Chorus 1

```
C         B♭                    F
Love will, love will be our home.

C         B♭             F
Love will, love will be our home.

C         B♭                    F
Love will, love will be our home.

C         B♭             Dm     B♭maj7
Love will, love will be our home.
```

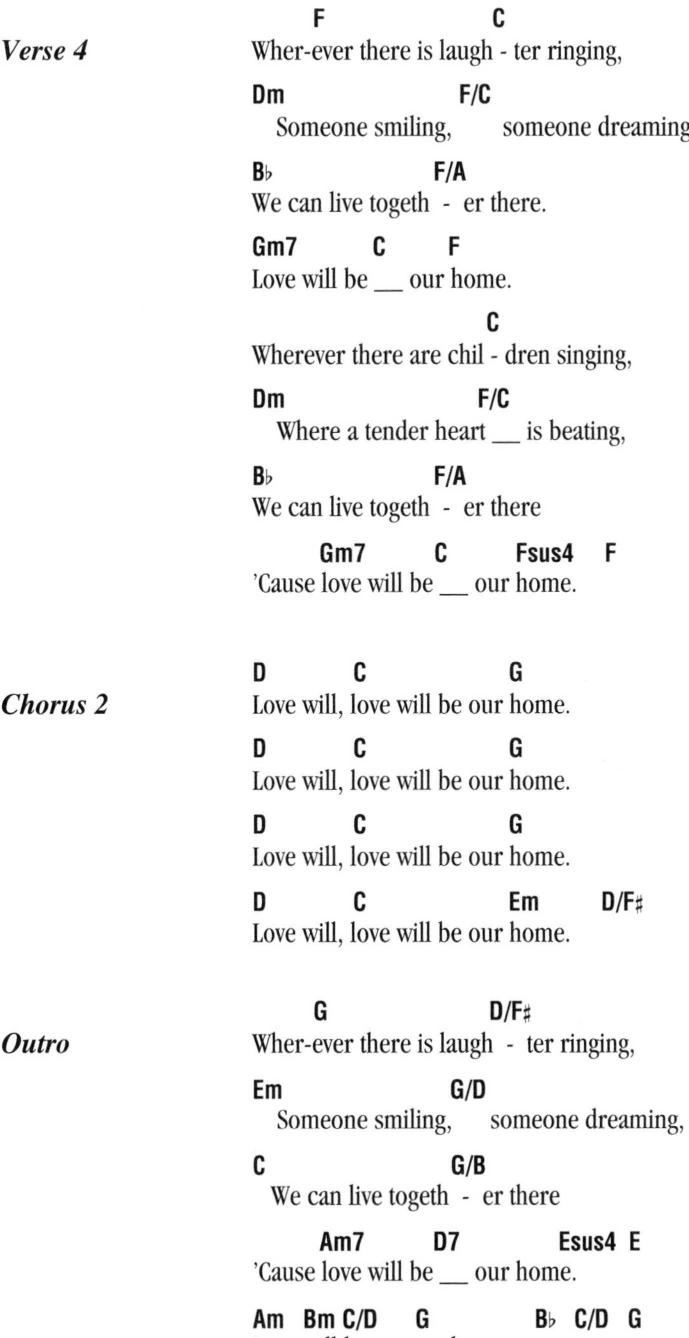

Verse 4

F C
Wher-ever there is laugh - ter ringing,

Dm F/C
Someone smiling, someone dreaming,

B♭ F/A
We can live togeth - er there.

Gm7 C F
Love will be __ our home.

C
Wherever there are chil - dren singing,

Dm F/C
Where a tender heart __ is beating,

B♭ F/A
We can live togeth - er there

Gm7 C Fsus4 F
'Cause love will be __ our home.

Chorus 2

D C G
Love will, love will be our home.

D C G
Love will, love will be our home.

D C G
Love will, love will be our home.

D C Em D/F♯
Love will, love will be our home.

Outro

G D/F♯
Wher-ever there is laugh - ter ringing,

Em G/D
Someone smiling, someone dreaming,

C G/B
We can live togeth - er there

Am7 D7 Esus4 E
'Cause love will be __ our home.

Am Bm C/D G B♭ C/D G
Love will be our __ home.

Magnificent Obsession

Words and Music by Steven Curtis Chapman

Tune down 1/2 step:
(low to high) E♭–A♭–D♭–G♭–B♭–E♭

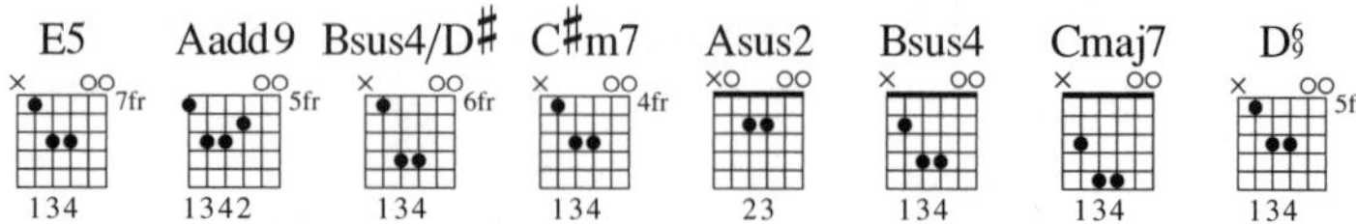

Intro

||: E5 | Aadd9 :|| *Play 3 times*

| E5 Aadd9 | |

Verse 1

```
E5                               Bsus4/D♯
  Lord, You know how much          I want to know so much
C♯m7                    Asus2       Bsus4
  In the way of answers and explana-tions.
E5                          Bsus4/D♯
  I have cried and prayed,      and still I seem to stay
C♯m7                     Asus2        Bsus4
  In the middle of life's      complica-tions.
Cmaj7
  All this pursuing leaves me
D6/9
Feeling like I'm chasing down the wind,
Cmaj7
  But now it's brought me back to You
Bsus4
  And I can see again.
```

Chorus 1

E Bsus4
This is ev'rything I want.

C♯m7 Asus2
This is ev'rything I need.

E Bsus4 C♯m7 Bsus4 Asus2
I want this to be my one consum-ing pas - sion.

E Bsus4
Ev-'rything my heart desires,

C♯m7 Asus2
Lord, I want it all to be

C♯m7
For You, Jesus.

Cmaj7 D$^{6}_{9}$ E5
Be my mag-nificent obses - sion.

Aadd9
Yeah.

| E5 | Aadd9 |

Verse 2

E5
So capture my heart again.

Bsus4/D♯
Take me to depths I've never been,

C♯m7 Asus2 Bsus4
Into the riches of Your grace and Your mer-cy.

E
Return me to the cross

Bsus4/D♯
And let me be completely lost

C♯m7 Asus2 Bsus4
In the wonder of the love that You've shown me.

Cmaj7
Cut through these chains that tie me down

D$^{6}_{9}$
To so many lesser things.

Cmaj7
Let all my dreams fall to the ground

Bsus4
Until this one remains.

Chorus 2

```
E         Bsus4
   This is ev'rything I want.
C#m7   Asus2
         This is ev'rything I need.
E                Bsus4                         C#m7  Bsus4 Asus2
   I want this to be my one consum-ing      pas  -  sion.
E       Bsus4
   Ev-'rything my heart desires,
C#m7  Asus2
        Lord, I want it all to be
C#m7
   For You, Jesus.
Cmaj7          D6/9              E5
   Be my mag-nificent obses  -  sion.
D6/9                          Cmaj7
   My magnificent obses  -  sion.
D6/9                            E5
   Yeah, yeah, yeah, yeah.
```

Bridge

```
| E5            |               |

You are ev'rything I want,

And You are ev'rything I need.

Lord, You are all my heart desires.
          Cmaj7        D6/9
You are ev'rything to me.
```

Chorus 3

```
E      Bsus4
  You are ev'rything I want.

C#m7  Asus2
        You are ev'rything I need.

E                Bsus4                       C#m7 Bsus4 Asus2
  I want You to be my one consum-ing     pas  -  sion.

E      Bsus4
  Ev-'rything my heart desires,

C#m7 Asus2                        C#m7
       Lord, I want it all to be      for You,

            Cmaj7              D6/9
I want it all to be for You.

E                    Bsus4                      C#m7
  'Cause You are ___ ev'rything I want.

Asus2
You are ev'rything I need.

E                Bsus4                       C#m7 Bsus4 Asus2
  I want You to be my one consum-ing     pas  -  sion.

E     Bsus4                            C#m7
  Ev-'rything my heart desires,

Asus2                         C#m7
Lord, I want it all to be        for You, Jesus.

Cmaj7          D6/9               Cmaj7      D6/9
  Be my mag-nificent obses  -  sion.
```

Outro

```
||: E     Bsus4    | C#m7    Asus2    |
|  E     Bsus4    |  C#m7    Bsus4    Asus2     |
|  E     Bsus4    | C#m7    Asus2    |
|  C#m7           | Cmaj7  D6/9      :||
```

Mercy Came Running

Words and Music by
Dan Dean, Dave Clark and Don Koch

Tune down 1/2 step:
(low to high) E♭–A♭–D♭–G♭–B♭–E♭

Intro

| C | | | |

Verse 1

```
F/A                     C/G
    Once there was a holy place,
F                 C/F       F
    Evidence of God's em-brace.
Dm7                              C
    And I can almost see mer - cy's face
F                           C/F   F
Pressed against the veil.
F/A                         C/G
    Looking down with longing eyes,
F                       C/F  F
    Mercy must have real-ized
Dm7                            C
    That once His blood was sacrificed
F                            C/F    F
Freedom would prevail.
                 Dm7
And as the sky grew dark
              C/E
And the earth began to shake,
        C/G       G         F            C/E  Dm7
With justice no longer in __ the way,
```

Chorus 1

                         C   Am7   Gsus4
Mercy came a runnin' __ like a pris'ner set free,

G   C/E   F   G
Past all my fail - ures to the point of my need;

           Gsus4   C   Am7 Gsus4 G
When the sin that I car - ried was all I could see

             F   C/E
And when I could not reach mercy,

Dm7   Gsus4   C   Csus4
Mercy came a runnin' __ to me.

Verse 2

F/A   C/G
    Once there was a broken heart,

F   C/F   F
    Way too human from the start,

Dm7   C
    And all the years left it torn __ apart,

F   C/F   F
Hopeless and afraid.

F/A   C/G
    Walls I never meant to build

F   C/F   F
    Left this pris'ner unful-filled.

Dm7   C
    Freedom called but even still

   F   C/F   F
It seemed so far away.

      Dm7
I was bound by the chains

          C/E
From the wages of my sin,

C/G   G   F   C/E Dm7
Just when I felt like giv - in' in,

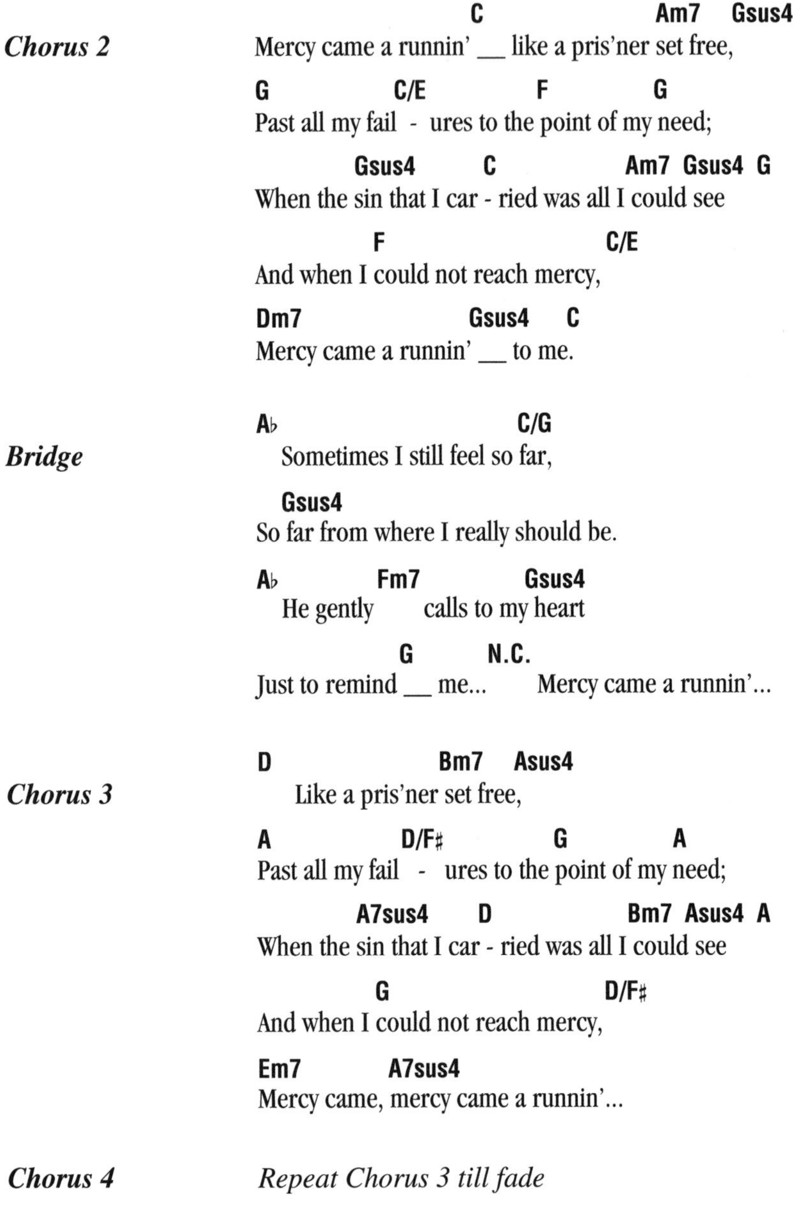

Chorus 2

C Am7 Gsus4
Mercy came a runnin' __ like a pris'ner set free,
G C/E F G
Past all my fail - ures to the point of my need;
Gsus4 C Am7 Gsus4 G
When the sin that I car - ried was all I could see
F C/E
And when I could not reach mercy,
Dm7 Gsus4 C
Mercy came a runnin' __ to me.

Bridge

A♭ C/G
Sometimes I still feel so far,
Gsus4
So far from where I really should be.
A♭ Fm7 Gsus4
He gently calls to my heart
G N.C.
Just to remind __ me... Mercy came a runnin'...

Chorus 3

D Bm7 Asus4
Like a pris'ner set free,
A D/F♯ G A
Past all my fail - ures to the point of my need;
A7sus4 D Bm7 Asus4 A
When the sin that I car - ried was all I could see
G D/F♯
And when I could not reach mercy,
Em7 A7sus4
Mercy came, mercy came a runnin'...

Chorus 4

Repeat Chorus 3 till fade

My Utmost for His Highest

Words and Music by Twila Paris

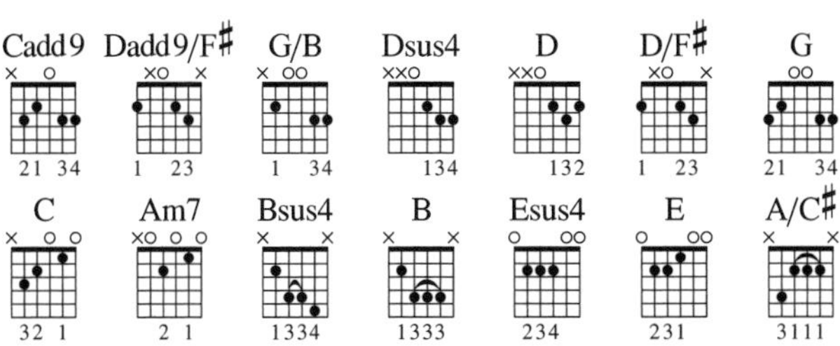

Intro

| Cadd9 Dadd9/F♯ | Cadd9 Dadd9/F♯ |
| G/B Cadd9 | Dsus4 D |

Verse 1

```
G/B                 Cadd9          Dsus4
    When the Sav - ior came to earth,
        G/B                 Cadd9      Dsus4
Answer to the endless fall,
G/B              Cadd9        Dsus4
    He became __ a man by birth
         G/B                  Cadd9
Then He died to save us all.
D/F♯                  Cadd9
May we never come __ to Him
         Dsus4          D
With half __ a heart.
D/F♯                 G                  C
All that He deserves __ is nothing less
          D          G
Than all I am and all you are.
```

```
C      D        C      D
For His highest, I give my utmost.

G/B   C      D     G/B  C
To the King of Kings, to the Lord of Hosts,

       D    G/B   C
For His glory, for His goodness,

G/B  C     G/B    C     D   G
I will give my utmost for His high-est.

| Cadd9    Dadd9/F#  | Cadd9              |
```

Verse 2

```
G/B          Cadd9     Dsus4
   Standing in __ this holy place,

     G/B              Cadd9    Dsus4
Let us all remember here,

G/B          Cadd9     Dsus4
   Covered on  -  ly by His grace,

      G/B                   Cadd9
We are bought with blood so dear.

D/F#              Cadd9          Dsus4     D
May we never bring __ with lesser of  -  fering,

D/F#         G            C
He alone is wor - thy to receive

         D/F#
The life we live,

         G
The song we sing.
```

```
                C        D            C         D
*Chorus 2*      For His highest, I give my utmost.

                G/B    C         D       G/B    C
                To the King of Kings, to the Lord of Hosts,

                         D       G/B     C
                For His glory, for His goodness,

                G/B  C         G/B       C        D     G
                I will give my utmost for His high-est.


                C                      G/B
*Bridge*        Any dream that tries

                                    D/F♯             G/B
                To turn my heart __ will be de-nied.

                C                G                       D
                Anything at all __ that weighs me down

                       C       Am7   Bsus4      B
                I will gladly cast a-side.


                D        Esus4   E    D        Esus4    E
*Chorus 3*      For His highest,      I give my utmost.

                A/C♯   D         E      A/C♯   D
                To the King of Kings, to the Lord of Hosts,

                         Esus4   E A/C♯    D
                For His glory,         for His goodness,

                D/C♯ D         A/C♯    D       E     A
                I will give my utmost for His high-est.

                D        Esus4   E          D
                For His glory,        for His goodness,

                D/C♯ D         A/C♯    D       Esus4   E    Cadd9    Dadd9/F♯
                I will give my utmost for His high       -      est.

                | Cadd9    Dadd9/F♯ | G/B    Cadd9    | Dsus4   D    | E
```

My Will

Words and Music by
Toby McKeehan, Michael Tait,
Joey Elwood and Daniel Pitts

Melody:

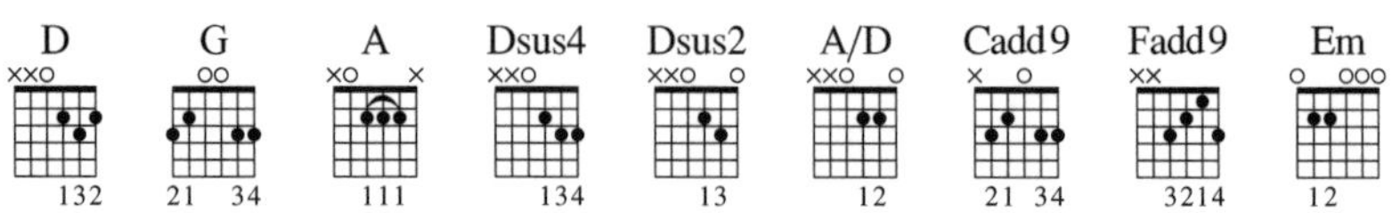

Intro

‖: D | :‖ *Play 3 times*
| D |

Verse 1

D G
I'm setting the stage __ for the things I love,
D A
And I'm now the man __ I once couldn't __ be.
D G
And nothing on earth __ could now ever move me,
D A D
I now have the will and the strength a man needs.

Chorus 1

D G
It's my will, __ and I'm not mov - in',
A
'Cause if it's Your __ will
D G
Then nothing can shake __ me.
D G
And it's my will __ to bow and praise __ You,
A Dsus4 D Dsus2 D
I now have the will to praise my God.

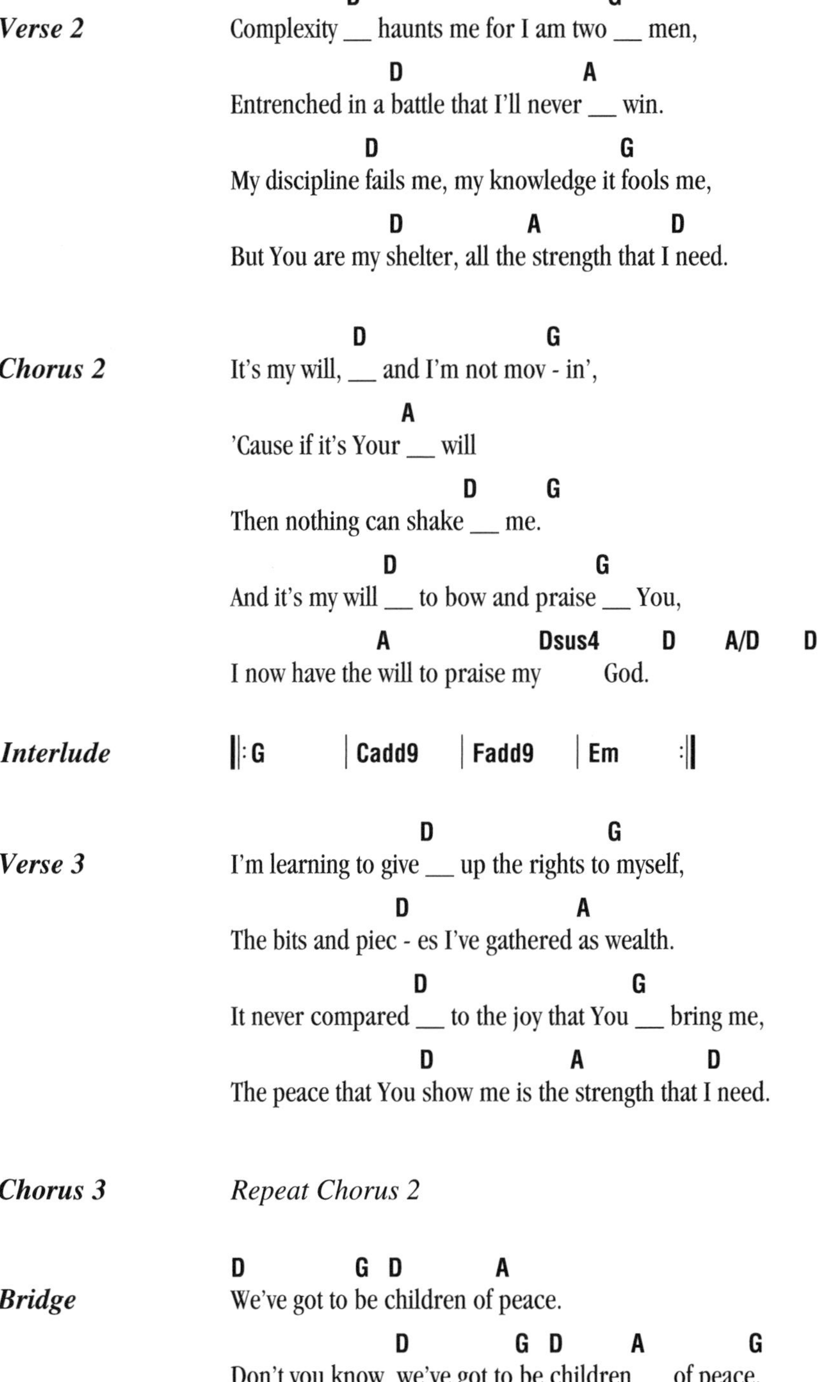

Verse 2

D G
Complexity __ haunts me for I am two __ men,
D A
Entrenched in a battle that I'll never __ win.
D G
My discipline fails me, my knowledge it fools me,
D A D
But You are my shelter, all the strength that I need.

Chorus 2

D G
It's my will, __ and I'm not mov - in',
A
'Cause if it's Your __ will
D G
Then nothing can shake __ me.
D G
And it's my will __ to bow and praise __ You,
A Dsus4 D A/D D
I now have the will to praise my God.

Interlude

‖: G | Cadd9 | Fadd9 | Em :‖

Verse 3

D G
I'm learning to give __ up the rights to myself,
D A
The bits and piec - es I've gathered as wealth.
D G
It never compared __ to the joy that You __ bring me,
D A D
The peace that You show me is the strength that I need.

Chorus 3

Repeat Chorus 2

Bridge

D G D A
We've got to be children of peace.
D G D A G
Don't you know we've got to be children __ of peace.

Chorus 4

```
                  D
And it's my will,

                   G
And I'm not mov - in',

                   D
'Cause if it's Your will

                             A
Then nothing can shake __ me.

                  D
And it's my will

                    G
To bow and praise __ You.

                    D    A
I now have the will __       to praise my
```

Interlude

```
G                           Cadd9
  It's Your will, it's Your will ___ not mine.
  God.

Fadd9                       Em
  It's Your will, it's Your will.

G                        Cadd9
It's Your will, it's Your will ___ not mine.

Fadd9                       Em
  It's Your will, it's Your will.
```

Outro

```
                  D
And it's my will, __ I'm not movin',

                   N.C.
'Cause if it's your will then nothing can save me.

And it's my will to bow and praise you.

I now have the will to praise my God.

(Don't you know we've got to be children of peace.

Don't you know, we've got to be children of peace.)
```

No You

Words and Music by Shauna Bolton,
Errol Johnson, Chrissy Conway
and Joe Priolo

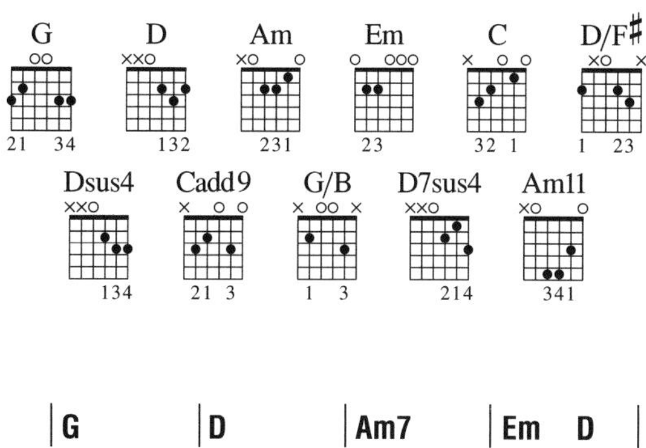

Intro

| G | D | Am7 | Em D |
| G | D | C | Em D |

Verse 1

G D/F♯
Been feeling so cra - zy lately,

Am Dsus4 D
When it seems that You're not around.

G D/F♯
The sun and the moon __ shine bright,

Am Dsus4
But my eyes are all Yours now.

Cadd9 Dsus4
Don't know how I'd live __ without You.

Cadd9 D Em D
I don't remember how __ it used to feel.

Cadd9 G/B
Lord, I can't imag - ine if

Am D7sus4
I had __ no You to hold ___ me.

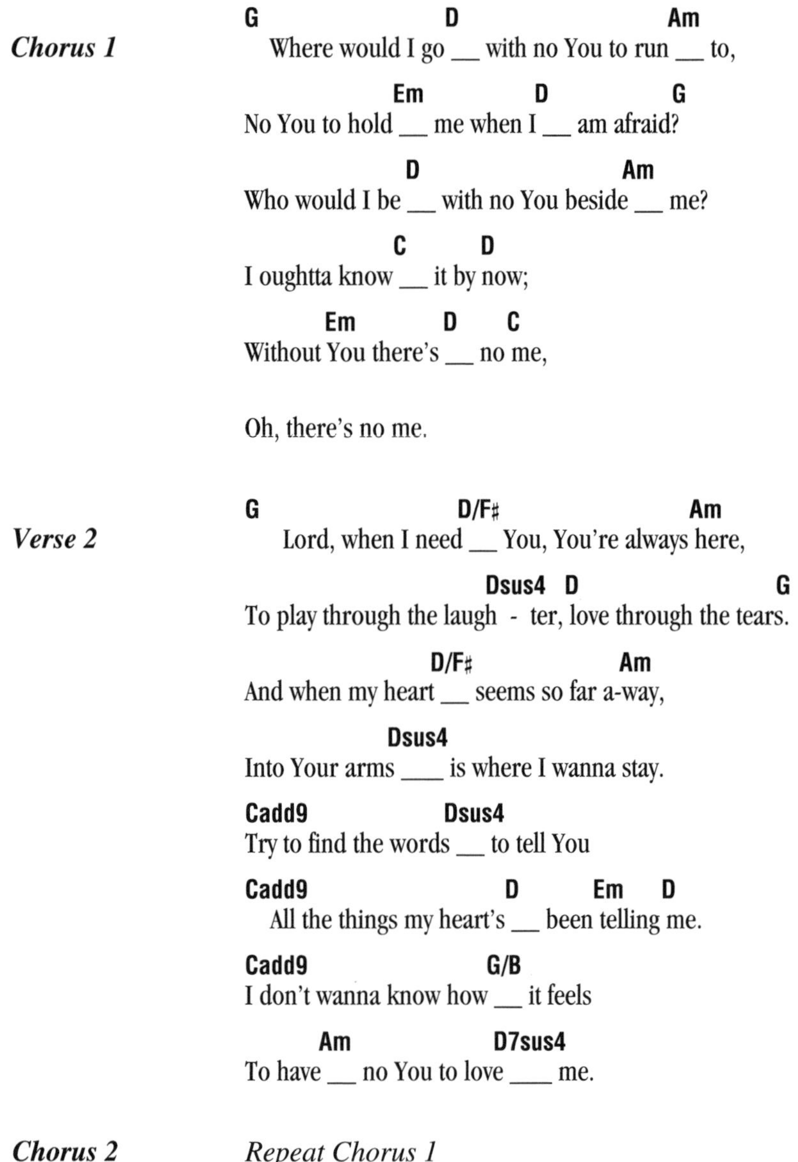

Chorus 1

G D Am
Where would I go __ with no You to run __ to,

Em D G
No You to hold __ me when I __ am afraid?

D Am
Who would I be __ with no You beside __ me?

C D
I oughtta know __ it by now;

Em D C
Without You there's __ no me,

Oh, there's no me.

Verse 2

G D/F# Am
Lord, when I need __ You, You're always here,

Dsus4 D G
To play through the laugh - ter, love through the tears.

D/F# Am
And when my heart __ seems so far a-way,

Dsus4
Into Your arms ___ is where I wanna stay.

Cadd9 Dsus4
Try to find the words __ to tell You

Cadd9 D Em D
All the things my heart's __ been telling me.

Cadd9 G/B
I don't wanna know how __ it feels

Am D7sus4
To have __ no You to love ___ me.

Chorus 2

Repeat Chorus 1

Chorus 3

```
G                     D                      Am
  Where would I go __ with no You to run __ to,
              Em            D            G
No You to hold __ me when I __ am afraid?
                D                   Am
Who would I be __ with no You beside __ me?
              C      D
I oughtta know __ it by now:  Without You,
```

Chorus 4 *Repeat Chorus 1*

Interlude

```
| G         | D         | Am        | Em   D  |
| G         | D         | Am11      | C    D  |
         Em        D       Cadd9
Without You there's __ no me,

Oh, there's no me.
```

Chorus 5 *Repeat Chorus 1*

Outro

```
||: G | D | Am   | Em  D | G             |
|   G | D | Am11 | C   D | Em  D  Cadd9 :||
```
Repeat and fade

Oh Lord, You're Beautiful

Words and Music by Keith Green

Melody:

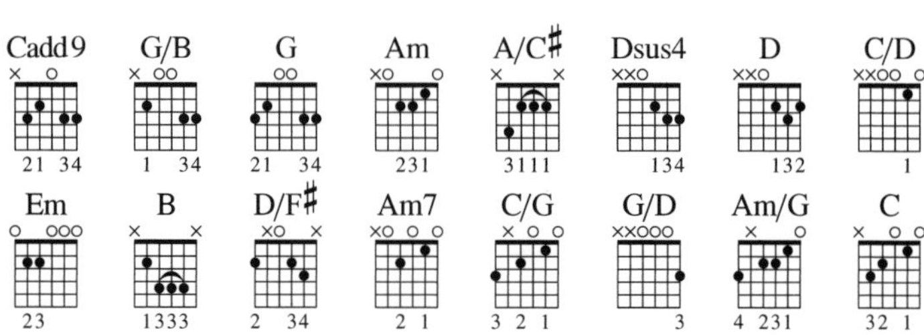

Intro | Cadd9 | G/B G | Am A/C♯ | Dsus4 D C/D |

Verse 1

G G/B Cadd9 G/B D C/D
Oh, Lord, You're beau - ti - ful.
G G/B Cadd9 G D
Your face is all I seek,
Em B Em D/F♯ G
For when Your eyes are on this child,
G/B Cadd9 G D Cadd9 G Cadd9
Your grace a - bounds to me.

Verse 2

D G G/B Cadd9 G/B D C/D
Oh, Lord, please light the fire
G G/B Cadd9 G/B D
That once burned bright and clear.
Em B Em D/F♯ G G/B
Re-place the lamp of my first love
Cadd9 G/B D Cadd9
That burns with holy fear.

Bridge 1

```
G   Am7 G/B Cadd9 G/B   Am    C/G  D/F#
  I want  to   take    Your Word and shine it all around,

G           Am7      G/B Cadd9 A/C#   G/D
  But first,      help me  just to live it, Lord.

D G   Am7  G/B Cadd9 G/B
  And when I'm do   -   ing well,

Am           Am/G  D/F#
    Help me __ to never seek a crown,

B                     Em    D      C    D      G     G/B
    For my reward      is giving glo  -  ry to You.

|Cadd9   G/B   |D            |C/D         |
```

Verse 3

Repeat Verse 1

Bridge 2

```
G   Am7 G/B Cadd9 G/B   Am    C/G  D/F#
  I want  to   take    Your Word and shine it all around,

G           Am7      G/B  Cadd9 A/C#  G/D
  But first,      help me  just to live it, Lord.

D G   Am7  G/B Cadd9 G/B
  And when I'm do   -   ing well,

Am           Am/G  D/F#
    Help me __ to never seek a crown,

B                     Em    D      C    D       Cadd9
    For my reward      is giving glo  -  ry to You.

|G/B    G     |Am      A/C#|G/D    D
```

Verse 4

```
C/D G    G/B          Cadd9  G/B  D    C/D
Oh,  Lord,     You're beau  -  ti  -  ful.
      G    G/B     Cadd9 G/B D
Your face        is all      I    seek,
    Em          B        Em  D/F#      G    G/B
For when Your eyes are on  this child,
       Cadd9 G   D           Cadd9     G
Your grace   a - bounds to me.
C/D    G    G/B           Cadd9   G/B   D    C/D
   Oh, Lord,      You're beau  -  ti  -  ful.
      G    G/B     Cadd9 G/B D
Your face        is all      I    seek,
    Em          B        Em  D/F#      G    G/B
For when Your eyes are on  this child,
       Cadd9  G  D           Cadd9
Your grace   a - bounds to me.
| G/B    G     | Am       A/C# | G/D   D   G
```

People Need the Lord

Words and Music by
Phill McHugh and Greg Nelson

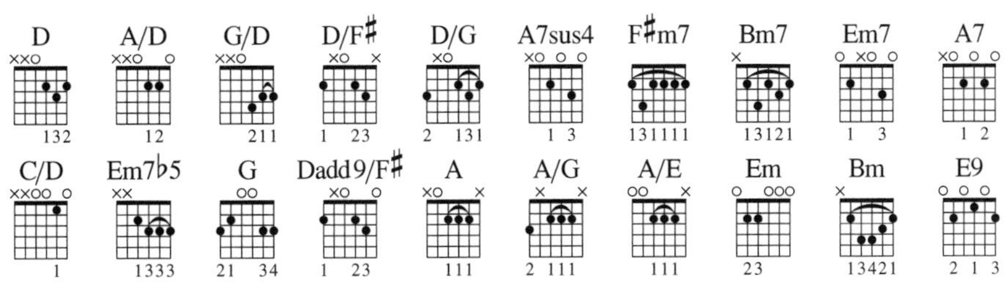

Intro | D | A/D G/D | D/F♯ | D/G A7sus4 |

Verse 1

```
D                A/D     G/D
   Ev'ry day they pass me by.
D             A/D        G/D
   I can see it in their eye;
F♯m7              Bm7
   Empty people filled with care,
Em7                      A7sus4   A7
   Headed who knows where.
D                        A/D         G/D
   On they go through __ private pain,
C/D          D/F♯   Gsus4  G
   Living fear to fear.
Em7♭5                    D/F♯
   Laughter hides the silent cries
G          Em7          A7sus4  A7  A7sus4  A7
   Only Jesus hears.
```

Chorus 1

```
D                         Em7
    People need the Lord.
Dadd9/F♯                  G
    People need the Lord.
A          A/G    D/F♯           G
    At the end of broken dreams __
Em7                      A7sus4  A7  A7sus4  A7
    He's the open door.
D                        Em7
    People need the Lord.
Dadd9/F♯                 G
    People need the Lord.
A             A/G     D/F♯  G
    When will __ we realize?
Em7         A7sus4  D
    People need the Lord.
| A/D   G/D   | D/F♯      | D/G    A7sus4    |
```

Verse 2

```
D                        A/D       G/D
    We are called to take His light
D                          A/D                G/D
    To a world where wrong seems right;
F♯m7                       Bm7
    What could be too great a cost for
Em7                      A7sus4    A7
    Sharing life with one who's lost?
D                             A/D             G/D
    Through His life our __ hearts can feel
C/D        D/F♯       Gsus4   G
    All the grief they bear.
Em7♭5                        D/F♯
    They must hear the words of life
G          Em7             A7sus4  A7  A7sus4  A7
    Only we can share.
```

Chorus 2

```
D                           Em7
    People need the Lord.

Dadd9/F♯                    G
    People need the Lord.

A          A/G    D/F♯          G
    At the end of broken dreams __

Em7                        A7sus4  A7  A7sus4  A7
    He's the open door.

D                           Em7
    People need the Lord.

Dadd9/F♯                    G
    People need the Lord.

A              A/G    D/F♯   G
    When will __ we realize?

A/E          A/G       D/F♯        G
    That we __ must give our lives __

    Em     A7       Bm    E9
For People need the Lord.

Em7        A7       D
    People need the Lord.

| A/D   G/D   | D/F♯      | D/G    A7    | D
```

Pleasures of the King

Words and Music by Fred MacKrell and Rob Mathes

C Csus4 C6 Dm/C Am Em F G Gsus4 E/G♯
D Dsus4 C/G F/A Dm7 G7sus4 C/B Am/G Fmaj7 A♭/C
D♭ E♭m/D♭ D♭/C B♭m Fm7 G♭ A♭7 A♭7sus4 E♭ E♭sus4
D♭/A♭ G♭/B♭ E♭m7 G♭maj7 E♭/G A♭ G♭sus4 Amaj7 B/A E/G♯
Asus2 F♯m11 Amaj7/E D♭sus4 D♭6 D♭maj7 G♭/D♭ D♭sus2

Intro

```
||: C   Csus4 | C   C6 :||  Play 3 times
|   C   Csus4 | C        |
```

Verse 1

```
 C              Csus4     C
To raise majes - tic moun - tains,
 Dm/C                    C
To cause the sea to roar,
 Am                      Em
To brush a crimson set-ting sun,
  F                      G  Gsus4  G
To make the eagle soar,
 C                          E/G♯     Am
To bring the newborn cry __ of life,
   F         C                D  Dsus4  D
The hope of ev - 'ry spring:
C/G                    F/A       Dm7          G7sus4
These treasures are __ the pleasures of ___ the King.
```

Interlude | C Csus4 | C Csus4 | C Csus4 | C Csus4 |

Verse 2

```
   C           Csus4        C
To see His peo - ple flour - ish,
   Dm/C                  C  C/B
To live in light of day,
   Am                         Em
To watch His children grow to know
    F                    G  Gsus4  G
The wonders of His way,
   C                 E/G♯           Am
To feel the joys of ran - somed hearts
    F           C           D  Dsus4  D
And all His mer - cies bring:
C/G                F/A      Dm7        G7sus4     Am  Am/G
These treasures are __ the pleasures of __ the King.
Fmaj7              Dm7    G7sus4
These treasures are __ the pleasures of the King.
```

Interlude | C Csus4 | C Csus4 | C | A♭/C |

Verse 3

```
   D♭
To heal a broken body,
   E♭m/D♭               D♭  D♭/C
To mend a broken heart,
   B♭m                 Fm7
To knit together health - y homes
     G♭              A♭7  A♭7sus4  A♭7
That once lay torn a-part,
   D♭               F/A
To glory in the prais - es
    B♭m    G♭         D♭          E♭  E♭sus4  E♭
That __ His grateful chil - dren sing:
D♭/A♭              G♭/B♭  E♭m7      A♭7sus4     B♭m  D♭/A♭
These treasures are __ the pleasures of __ the King.
G♭maj7             E♭m7   A♭7sus4             D♭  D♭/C
These treasures are __ the pleasures of the King.
```

Bridge

```
           B♭m         E♭/G        A♭
But of all __ His re  -  gal plea - sures,

     D♭        G♭sus4       G♭           D♭/A♭
One __ does stand above __ the rest:

     Amaj7      B/A     E/G♯       Asus2    F♯m11
The Son He gave __ to serve and save

   Amaj7/E          E♭m7  A♭7sus4  A♭7
In perfect holiness.
```

Verse 4

```
   D♭   D♭sus4         D♭
Ex-isting pure and fault - less,

   E♭m/D♭             D♭
Em-bodiment of truth,

D♭6                D♭maj7
Guardian of right  -  eousness

     G♭maj7            A♭7   A♭7sus4  A♭7
With name beyond re-proof,

    D♭                     F/A       B♭m
His words uphold the u  -  niverse

  G♭      D♭       E♭  E♭sus4  E♭
In love un-wavering.

D♭/A♭          G♭/B♭    E♭m7       A♭7sus4     B♭m7  D♭/A♭
Jesus, You are __ the treasure of __ the King.

G♭maj7        E♭m7    A♭7sus4               D♭
Jesus, You are __ the pleasure of the King.

B♭m            E♭m7
Jesus, You are, __ You are

G♭maj7              A♭7sus4  A♭7
    The pleasure of ___            the King.
```

Outro

| D♭ G♭/D♭ | D♭ G♭/D♭ | D♭ G♭/D♭ |

D♭ G♭/D♭
The pleasure of __ the King.

| D♭ G♭/D♭ | D♭ G♭/D♭ | D♭ G♭/D♭ |

D♭ G♭/D♭
Je - sus, You are,

| D♭ G♭/D♭ | D♭ G♭/D♭ | D♭ G♭/D♭ |

D♭ G♭/D♭
You're the hope of ev - 'ry spring.

| D♭ G♭/D♭ | D♭ G♭/D♭ |

D♭ G♭/D♭
Je - sus, You are,

| D♭ G♭/D♭ | D♭ G♭/D♭ | D♭ G♭/D♭ |

D♭ G♭/D♭
Je - sus, You are,

| D♭ G♭/D♭ | D♭ G♭/D♭ | D♭ G♭/D♭ | D♭ G♭/D♭ |

D♭ G♭/D♭ D♭sus2
The pleasure of the King.

Pray

Words and Music by Rebecca St. James,
Michael Quinlan and Tedd Tjornhom

Tune down 1/2 step:
(low to high) E♭–A♭–D♭–G♭–B♭–E♭

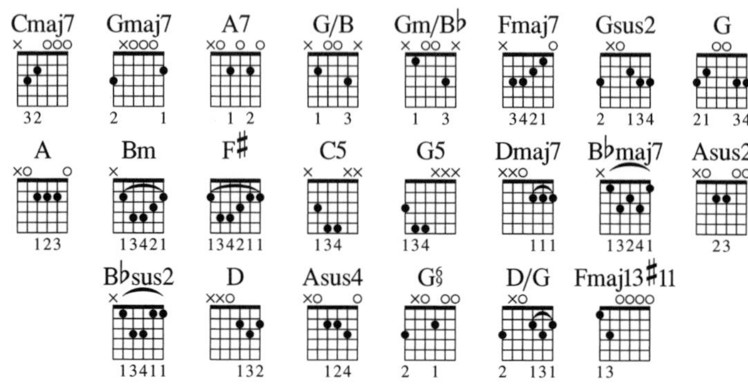

Intro

Cmaj7	Gmaj7	A7	G/B
Gm/B♭	Fmaj7	Gsus2	

Verse 1

```
G                     A
Je - sus, I am broken now.
       Bm        G
Before __ You I fall.
              A
I lay me down.
         Bm          G
All I want __ is You, my all.
                   A
I cry out from the ash - es,
       Bm                G
Burned __ with sin and shame;

I ask You, Lord,
         F♯
To make __ me whole again.
```

```
                C5                G5                Dmaj7
Chorus 1   For You say __ if I will come __ and will pray __ to You

                  C5                 G5                    B♭maj7
           There's forgive - ness when I turn __ from me and pray.

           G              C5               G5                 Asus2  Bm
              For you say __ if I will come __ and will pray __ to  You,

                     B♭sus2          Fmaj7
           You hear __ me and heal __ me when I     pray.

                                                         And Your

           G5
Verse 2      Ways

                              A
           Are not my own,

                     Bm                   Gsus2
           But I long __ for them to be,

                                      A
           So this is what I pray:

                           Bm
           One with You __ You'll make me.

           Gsus2                         F♯
             Melt me away till only You __ remain.

                C5                G5                Dmaj7
Chorus 2   For You say __ if I will come __ and will pray __ to You

                  C5                 G5                  B♭maj7     G
           There's forgive - ness when I turn __ to You and pray.

                C5                G5                Asus2 Bm
           For You say __ if I will come __ and will pray __ to  You,

                     B♭sus2          Fmaj7
           You hear __ me and heal __ me when I pray.

Interlude  | Bm      |         | Gsus2   |         |
           | D       |         | Asus4   | A       |
           | Bm      |         |
           | G6/9    |         |         |         |
```

Bridge

N.C.
Je - sus,

I am broken now before You.

F♯
Take me, I am Yours,

Chorus 3

C5 G5 Dmaj7
For You say __ if I will come __ and will pray __ to You

C5 G5 B♭maj7
There's forgive - ness when I turn __ from me and pray.

G C5 G5 Asus2 Bm
For you say __ if I will come __ and will pray __ to You,

B♭sus2 Fmaj7
You hear __ me and heal __ me.

Chorus 4

C5 G5 Dmaj7
For You say __ if I will come __ and will pray __ to You

C5 G5 B♭maj7
There's forgive - ness when I turn __ to You and pray.

G C5 G5 Asus2 Bm
For you say __ if I will come __ and will pray __ to You,

B♭sus2 Fmaj7
You hear __ me and heal __ me.

Outro

D/G D
When I pray, __ when I pray,

A
When I pray,

G/B D
When I pray,

A G/B
When I pray.

Fmaj13♯11
When I pray.

Revive Us, O Lord

Words and Music by Carman and Steve Camp

Melody:

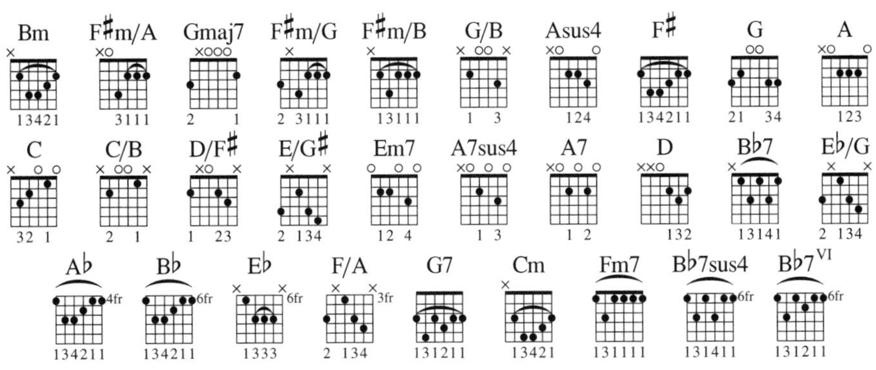

Intro

| Bm F♯m/A | Gmaj7 | Bm F♯m/A | F♯m/G |
| Bm F♯m/B | F♯m/G Gmaj7 | Bm F♯m/B | F♯m/G |

Verse 1

Bm F♯m/B Bm F♯m/B
We've turned from Your ways.

G/B Asus4 Bm F♯m/B
Lord, Your fruit we've ceased __ to bear.

F♯ Bm
We like the power

G Asus4
We once knew in our prayers.

Verse 2

Bm F♯m/B Bm F♯m/B
That gentle voice __ from heav-en

Gmaj7 A Bm F♯m/B
We cease to hear and know,

F♯ Bm
The fact that He __ has risen

G C C/B A
No longer stirs our souls.

Chorus 1

```
   D/F# G      A
Re-vive  us, O Lord,

   D/F# G      A
Re-vive  us, O Lord,

    D          G              E/G#   A
And cleanse us from our im-puri - ties,

    F#        Bm           G
And make us holy, hear our cry,

Em7    A7sus4 A7
And re-vive     us.

 D
O __ Lord.

| Bm   F#m/B   | F#m/G Gmaj7 | Bm   F#m/B      | F#m/G     |
```

Verse 3

```
Bm        F#m/B          Bm   F#m/B
  Though we've been un-faith-ful

Gmaj7       A              Bm    F#m/B
  We've nev - er been dis-owned.

F#                          Bm
  The Spirit that raised __ Christ from the dead

    G              C      C/B   A
Com-pels us to His throne.
```

Chorus 2

```
   D/F# G     A
Re-vive  us, O Lord,

   D/F#  G     A
Re-vive  us, O Lord,

    D           G              E/G#  A
And cleanse us from our im-puri - ties,

    F#        Bm            G
And make us holy, hear our cry,

Em7   A7sus4 Bb7
And re-vive     us.
```

Chorus 3

```
   Eb/G  Ab    Bb
Re-vive   us, O Lord,

   Eb/G  Ab    Bb
Re-vive   us, O Lord,

    Eb          Ab             F/A   Bb
And cleanse us from our im-puri - ties,

    G7      Cm
And make us holy,

         Ab
Hear our cry,

Fm7   Bb7sus4 Bb7 VI
And re-vive      us.
```

Chorus 4

Repeat Chorus 3 till fade

Run to You

Words and Music by Twila Paris

Tune down 1/2 step:
(low to high) E♭–A♭–D♭–G♭–B♭–E♭

Melody:

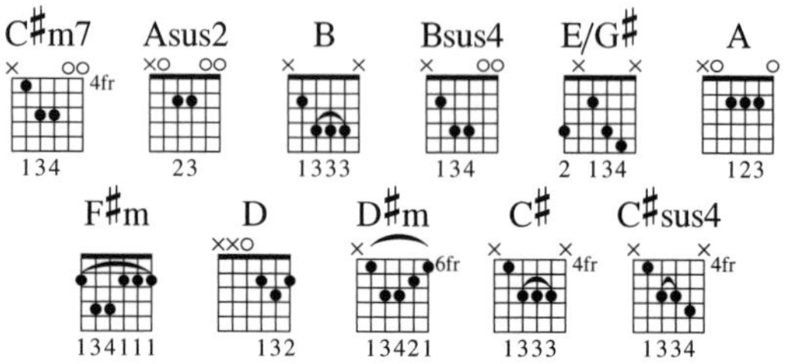

C♯m7 Asus2 B Bsus4 E/G♯ A

F♯m D D♯m C♯ C♯sus4

Intro ‖: C♯m7 | Asus2 | B | :‖

Verse 1

```
C♯m7                Asus2   Bsus4
Faster now than ev - er,      I run to You.
C♯m7                    Asus2  Bsus4
Now I know You bet - ter,      I run to You.
 C♯m7               Asus2       Bsus4                  E/G♯
I __ am a little old - er now,     You know it's true.
    C♯m7              Asus2
May - be a little wis - er, too.
Bsus4           E/G♯
  I run to You.
                   A                B
And I can see __  (I can see.)
      E/G♯                      A
Deep - er than I did before.
                                B
I do believe, (I believe.)
    E/G♯                        A
Nev - er have I been so sure
                F♯m                           D
That I need __ You ev'ry minute, ev'ry day,
                F♯m                                Bsus4   B
That I need __ You more than I could ever say.
```

```
           D♯m   B   C♯            D♯m
*Chorus 1* Ooh,          I run to You.

                B    C♯
           Ooh, ___ what else would I do?

                         D♯m     B
           I run to You.

                 C♯              D♯m
           Ooh, ___I run to You.

                B    C♯   C♯sus4
           Ooh.

           | D♯m       |          |          | C♯sus4    |

           C♯m7            Asus2      Bsus4
*Verse 2*  Even on the sad __ days,       I run to You.

           C♯m7              Asus2            Bsus4
           Even on the good __ days, too,       I run to You.

             C♯m7               A          B                      E/G♯
           E  -  ven before all else fails,     You know it's true.

               C♯m7                       Asus2     B                  E/G♯
           You __ are the wind in my __ sails,        I run to You.

                          A                B
           And I can see __   (I can see.)

                E/G♯                     A
           Deep  -  er than I did before.

                                       B
           I do believe, (I believe.)

              E/G♯                        A
           Nev  -  er have I been so sure

                       F♯m                              D
           That I need __ You ev'ry footstep, all the way,

                       F♯m                                        Bsus4    B
           That I need __ You so much more than I can say.
```

Chorus 2

```
D♯m  B  C♯           D♯m
Ooh,        I run to You.

     B   C♯
Ooh, ___ what else would I do?

             D♯m   B
I run to You.

    C♯              D♯m
Ooh, ___I run to You.

     B   C♯  C♯sus4
Ooh.
```

Guitar Solo

```
| C♯m7    | Asus2    | Bsus4    |          |
| C♯m7    | Asus2    | Bsus4    |          |
| C♯m7    | Asus2    | B        | E/G♯     |
| C♯m7    | Asus2    | B        |          |
```

Chorus 3

```
D♯m  B  C♯           D♯m
Ooh,        I run to You.

     B   C♯
Ooh, ___ what else would I do?

             D♯m    B
I run to You.    Ooh.

C♯            D♯m
   I run to You.

     B   C♯
Ooh.
```

Chorus 4 *Repeat Chorus 3 till fade*

Shepherd of My Heart

Words and Music by
Dick Tunney and Mark Baldwin

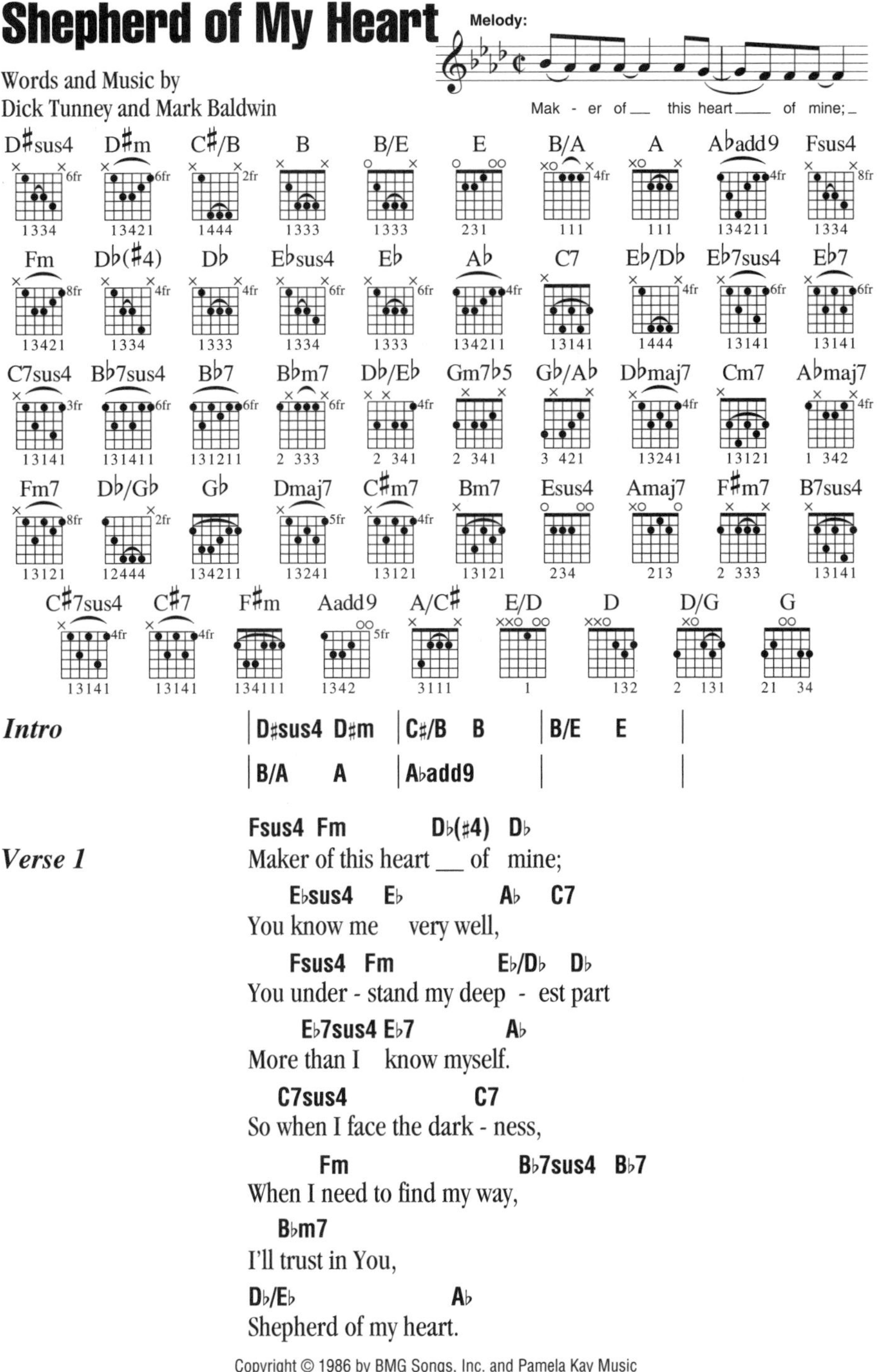

Intro

| D♯sus4 D♯m | C♯/B B | B/E E |
| B/A A | A♭add9 | |

Verse 1

Fsus4 Fm D♭(♯4) D♭
Maker of this heart __ of mine;
E♭sus4 E♭ A♭ C7
You know me very well,
Fsus4 Fm E♭/D♭ D♭
You under - stand my deep - est part
E♭7sus4 E♭7 A♭
More than I know myself.
C7sus4 C7
So when I face the dark - ness,
Fm B♭7sus4 B♭7
When I need to find my way,
B♭m7
I'll trust in You,
D♭/E♭ A♭
Shepherd of my heart.

Verse 2

```
Fsus4  Fm          D♭(♯4)   D♭
Keeper of this heart __ of  mine;
     E♭sus4   E♭              A♭   C7
Your patience    has no end,
          Fsus4   Fm       E♭/D♭    D♭
You've loved me back into __ Your arms
E♭7sus4  E♭7        A♭
Time and time again.
   C7sus4        C7
So if I start to wan - der
       Fm                           B♭7sus4  B♭7
Like a lamb that's gone astray,
   B♭m7
I'll trust in You,
D♭/E♭                  A♭
Shepherd of my heart.
```

Chorus 1

```
             D♭maj7      Cm7
You're the beacon of my __ nights,
             B♭m7   D♭/E♭     A♭maj7
You're the sunlight of my days,
      D♭maj7               Cm7   Fm7
I can rest within Your arms,
      B♭7sus4    B♭7            E♭7sus4  E♭
I can know Your __ loving ways.
   C7sus4                C7
So let the cold winds blow,
             Fm                       B♭7sus4  B♭7
And let the storms rage all around,
   B♭m7
I'll trust in You,
D♭/E♭
Shepherd of my heart.
| Fsus4  Fm  | D♭(♯4)  D♭  | D♭/G♭  G♭  | E♭sus4  |
```

Verse 3

```
Fsus4 Fm        D♭(♯4)  D♭
Giver  of this life ___   in me;
        E♭sus4   E♭          A♭   C7
You're what I'm    living for,
   Fsus4  Fm          E♭/D♭  D♭
For all my deepest grat  -  i - tude,
    E♭7sus4              A♭
You love me even more.
  C7sus4                 C7
So as I walk through val  -  leys
          Fm                 B♭7sus4   B♭7
List'ning for the Master's call,
   B♭m7
I'll trust in You,
D♭/E♭                    A♭      G♭/A♭
Shepherd of my heart.
```

Chorus 2

```
               Dmaj7       C♯m7
You're the beacon of my ___ nights,
               Bm7      Esus4        Amaj7
You're the sunlight of ___ my days,
       Dmaj7                C♯m7   F♯m7
I can rest within Your arms,
               B7sus4   B                Esus4     E
I can know ___ Your ___ loving ways.
   C♯7sus4               C♯7
So as I walk through val  -  leys
          F♯m                B7sus4   B
List'ning for the Master's call,
   B♭m7
I'll trust in You,
Esus4                     Aadd9      F♯m7
Shepherd of my heart.
   Dmaj7 A/C♯
I'll trust in ___ You,
Bm7               F♯m7      E/D     D
Shepherd of my                 heart.

| D/G     G     | Aadd9        |
```

Serve the Lord

Words and Music by Carman

Intro

| Bm D/F♯ G | | B7 Em | |
| Bm D/F♯ G | B7 Em | Asus4 | A |

Verse 1

```
              D
I believe __ in God the Father,
          A/C♯                 F♯7♯5   F♯7
Jesus Christ His only Son
             Bm       F♯m/A      G
And the blessed Holy Spir - it
      E/G♯                Asus4   A
Dis-tinct, yet Three in One.
       D/F♯
I be-lieve there is forgiveness
        A/C♯                F♯7♯5   F♯7
For everything we've done.
           G              Em
That is why all the more
A7sus4 D
I will      serve Him.
| Bm   D/F♯ G |          | A
```

Verse 2

```
          D
I believe __ the Son of God was

       A/C♯                 F♯7♯5  F♯7
Cruci-fied upon the tree

          Bm      F♯m/A       G
And laid within a borrowed tomb

     E/G♯              Asus4   A
Not far from Calva-ry.

      D/F♯
I be-lieve He rose up from the dead,

  A/C♯            F♯7♯5  F♯7
A-live for all to see.

         G             Em7
That is why all the more

A7sus4 D
I will     serve Him.
```

Chorus 1

```
         Asus4           A
I have made my deci - sion,

        G          D
I have staked my claim.

        G                D/F♯
I have drawn the line in the sand

      C          A
And I'll not be a-shamed.

With the world behind me

           G          D      F♯
And the cross be-fore,

         Bm           F♯m/A
By the grace of God

G      A          D            B♭7sus4   B♭7
I will serve the Lord.
```

Verse 3

```
           E♭
I believe __ you must be born again.

        B♭                G7♯5  G7
John three-sixteen is true.

      Cm       E♭/B♭     A♭
The old life      can be washed away,

F/A                       B♭7sus4
Ev'rything made new.

      B♭   E♭/G                  Cm
And I be-lieve the love of God

                  Dm7♭5              G7♯5
Can somehow find its way to you.

G7         A♭           B♭7sus4
   That is why all the more

        E♭           A♭
I will serve Him.
```

Chorus 2

```
E♭     B♭
I have made my decision,

         A♭              D
I have staked my claim.

         A♭             E♭/G
I have drawn the line in the sand

          Fm7          B♭
And I'll __ not be a-shamed.

With the world behind me

           A♭            E♭  B♭/D
And the cross before,

          Cm            E♭/B♭
By the grace of God

Fm7  B♭        E♭
I will serve the Lord.
```

Bridge

```
        B♭7sus4             B♭
And I know when Satan and __ his minions

A♭
Come to torment me,

            B♭7sus4             B♭
When I in-voke the name of Je - sus,

        B♭7sus4
Ev'ry demon has to flee.

                                B♭
I know the time will come

                 B♭7sus4
When Christ re-turns again someday.

          D♭
Till then, __ there's just one name on earth

          B♭7sus4                B♭
Where-by men can be saved.
```

Verse 4

```
         E♭
I believe __ there is a right and wrong,

   B♭/D           G7♯5  G7
A time to live and die.

         Cm   E♭/B♭    A♭
And the Bible      is the blueprint

F/A                     B♭7sus4
That all men should live by.

B♭7  E♭/G           Cm
I be-lieve I'm not alone

         Dm7♭5          G7♯5  G7
With my faith in Jesus Christ.

            A♭          B♭7sus4
That is why __ all the more

         E♭        Fm/E♭   E♭   Fm/E♭   E♭
We will serve Him.
```

Chorus 3

```
           B♭
We have made our decisions,

           A♭          E♭
We have staked our claim.

           A♭             E♭
We have drawn the line in the sand

     D♭                      B♭
And we won't be ashamed.


With the world behind us

         A♭            E♭
And the cross before __ us,

         Cm       E♭/B♭ A♭
By the grace of God   we will serve,
```

Outro

```
        Dm          Am
By the grace of God __

     B♭♮           B♭/C         F
We __ will serve __ the Lord.

      C
I have made my decision,

        B♭♮        F
I have staked my claim.

     B♭♮          F/A
I've drawn a line in the sand

     Gm                    C7sus4
And I won't be ashamed.

          C
With the world behind me

         B♭♮         F  C
And the cross before,

        Dm          Am
By the grace of God

B♭♮        C7sus4      F     F/A
I will serve __ the Lord.

        B♭          F/A
By the grace of God

Gm        A/C♯        Dm      F
I will serve __ the Lord.

        B♭          F/A
By the grace of God

Gm  C7sus4  F
I will serve the Lord.

| Dm    Am   B♭♮ |              |        D/F♯ Gm |
|                |      B♭/C  C | F              |
```

Shine on Us

Words and Music by
Michael W. Smith and Debbie Smith

Melody:

Lord, ___ let Your light,

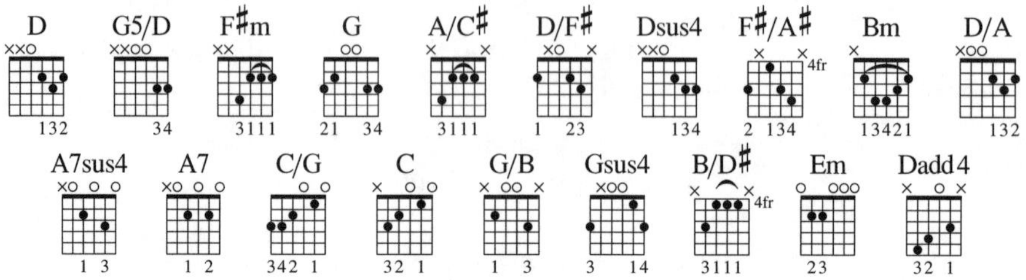

D G5/D F#m G A/C# D/F# Dsus4 F#/A# Bm D/A

A7sus4 A7 C/G C G/B Gsus4 B/D# Em Dadd4

Intro

| D | G5/D | D | F♯m |
| G | A/C♯ | D | |

Verse 1

D G5/D D
Lord, let Your light,

F♯m G A/C♯ D
Light of Your face shine on us.

G5/D D
Lord, let Your light,

F♯m G A/C♯ D
Light of Your face shine on us

Chorus 1

D/F♯ G A/C♯ D
That we may be saved,

D/F♯ G A/C♯ Dsus4 D
That we may have life

D/F♯ G
To find our way

F♯/A♯ Bm G
In the darkest night.

D/A A7sus4 A7
Let Your light __ shine on us.

Interlude | D | G5/D | D | F♯m |
| G | A/C♯ | D | |

Verse 2

```
D    G5/D    D
Lord, let Your grace,
        F♯m        G          A/C♯ D
Grace from Your hand fall on     us.
      G5/D    D
Lord, let Your grace,
       F♯m         G           A/C♯ D
Grace from Your hand fall on     us
```

Chorus 2

```
D/F♯ G  A/C♯    D
That  we may be saved,
D/F♯ G  A/C♯        Dsus4 D
That  we may have life
   D/F♯      G
To find our way
       F♯/A♯   Bm   G
In the darkest night.
                  D/A        A7sus4 A7    D
Let Your light __ shine on                us.
```

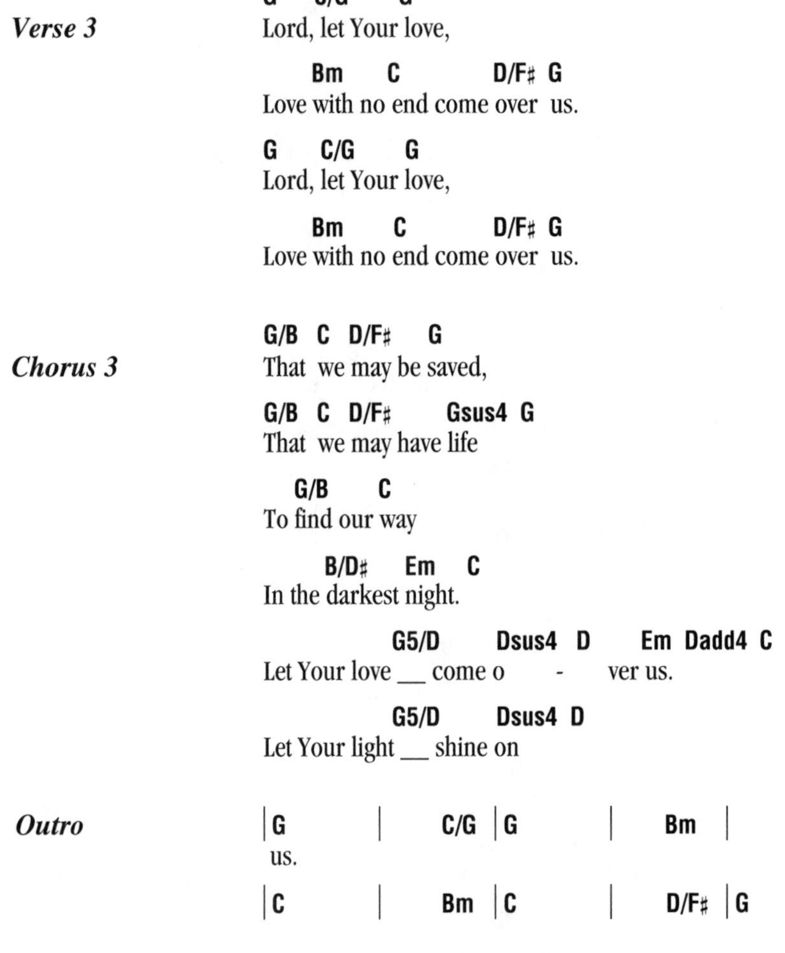

Verse 3

G C/G G
Lord, let Your love,

Bm C D/F♯ G
Love with no end come over us.

G C/G G
Lord, let Your love,

Bm C D/F♯ G
Love with no end come over us.

Chorus 3

G/B C D/F♯ G
That we may be saved,

G/B C D/F♯ Gsus4 G
That we may have life

G/B C
To find our way

B/D♯ Em C
In the darkest night.

G5/D Dsus4 D Em Dadd4 C
Let Your love __ come o - ver us.

G5/D Dsus4 D
Let Your light __ shine on

Outro

| G | C/G | G | Bm |
us.

| C | Bm | C | D/F♯ | G

Sing Your Praise to the Lord

Words and Music by Richard Mullins

Tune up 1/2 step:
(low to high) F–B♭–E♭–A♭–C–F

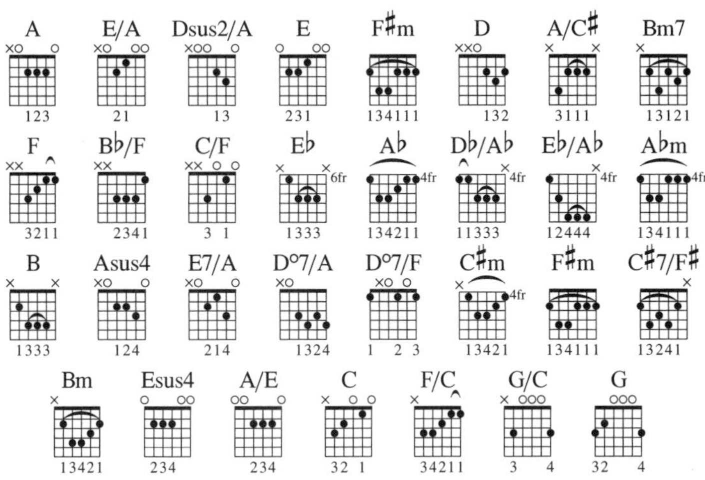

Intro ‖: A E/A Dsus2/A | A E/A Dsus2/A :‖

Verse 1

A E F♯m
Sing your praise to the Lord,

E
Come on ev'ry-body,

D A/C♯ Bm7 E
Stand up and sing one more hallelu - jah.

A E F♯m
Sing your praise to the Lord,

E
I can never tell you

D A/C♯ Bm7 E
Just how much good that it's gonna do __ you

F B♭/F C/F B♭/F
Just to sing a-new the song your heart learned to sing

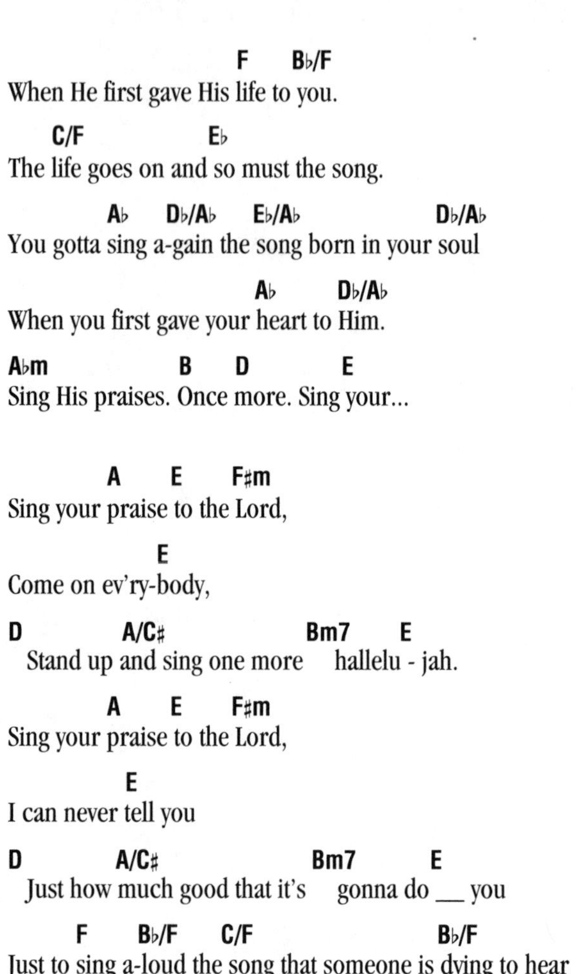

F   B♭/F
When He first gave His life to you.

C/F   E♭
The life goes on and so must the song.

A♭   D♭/A♭   E♭/A♭   D♭/A♭
You gotta sing a-gain the song born in your soul

A♭   D♭/A♭
When you first gave your heart to Him.

A♭m   B   D   E
Sing His praises. Once more. Sing your...

Verse 2

A   E   F♯m
Sing your praise to the Lord,

E
Come on ev'ry-body,

D   A/C♯   Bm7   E
Stand up and sing one more   hallelu - jah.

A   E   F♯m
Sing your praise to the Lord,

E
I can never tell you

D   A/C♯   Bm7   E
Just how much good that it's   gonna do ___ you

F   B♭/F   C/F   B♭/F
Just to sing a-loud the song that someone is dying to hear

F   B♭/F
Down in the madd'ning crowd,

C/F   E♭
As you once were before you heard the song.

A♭   D♭/A♭   E♭/A♭
You gotta let them know the truth is alive

D♭/A♭
To shine upon the way, so maybe

A♭   D♭/A♭   A♭m   B   D
They can go.   Sing His praises once more.

```
                A     E     F#m
Verse 3  Sing your praise to the Lord,

                    E
         Come on ev'ry-body,

         D          A/C#                Bm7     E
           Stand up and sing one more    hallelu - jah.

                A     E     F#m
         Sing your praise to the Lord,

                    E
         I can never tell you

         D          A/C#                 Bm7      E
           Just how much good that it's   gonna do __ you just to

         A E/A Dsus2/A                   A   E/A   Dsus2/A
         Sing              your praises to the Lord.

                  A   E/A   Dsus2/A                  A   E/A   Dsus2/A
         And ev'rybody sing           your praises to the Lord.
```

Interlude 1

| Asus4 | A | Asus4 E7/A | A |

```
Asus4           E7/A            A
   From the ris - ing of the sun

            D°7/A      A
To the place __ where it __ sets,

D°7/A              A
   The name of the __ Lord

D°7/A      A
   Is to be __ praised.

D°7/A            A
   The Lord is ex-alted

D°7/A             A
   Over all the na - tions,

D°7/A  A   D°7/A D°7/F          A
   His glory                 above the heav-
```

Bridge

```
C#m                  F#m          C#7/F#   F#m    C#7/F#
   ens. Who is like the Lord our God,

Bm                D                 Esus4     E
   The One who sits enthroned on __ high,

C#m                        F#m        C#7/F#   F#m    C#7/F#
   He who stoops to look down upon,

Bm           D                   A/E   Esus4 E
   Down up-on this earth and it's skies?
```

That is what you've gotta

Interlude 2

```
||: A  E/A  Dsus2/A    | A  E/A  Dsus2/A   :||
   sing.
```

```
                   A    E    F♯m
Verse 4   Sing your praise to the Lord,

                    E
          Come on ev'ry-body,

          D        A/C♯              Bm7    E
            Stand up and sing one more   hallelu - jah.

                   A    E    F♯m
          Sing your praise to the Lord,

                 E
          I can never tell you

          D       A/C♯               Bm7      E
            Just how much good that it's   gonna do __ you just to

          C     F/C             G/C           F/C
          Let the name of the Lord __ be praised,

          G           C   F/C          G/C
          Both for now __ and evermore.

                 E
          Praise Him, oh you servants.

                   A    E    F♯m
          Sing your praise to the Lord,

                    E
          Come on ev'ry-body,

          D        A/C♯              Bm7    E
            Stand up and sing one more   hallelu - jah.

                   A    E    F♯m
          Sing your praise to the Lord,

                 E
          I can never tell you

          D       A/C♯               Bm7      E
            Just how much good that it's   gonna do __ you just to

          A  E/A Dsus2/A                 A   E/A  Dsus2/A
          Sing          your praises to the Lord.

                      A   E/A  Dsus2/A
          And ev'rybody  sing

                          A   E/A  D°7/A    A
          Your praises to the Lord.
```

Sometimes He Calms the Storm

Words and Music by
Kevin Stokes and Tony Wood

Tune down 1/2 step:
(low to high) E♭–A♭–D♭–G♭–B♭–E♭

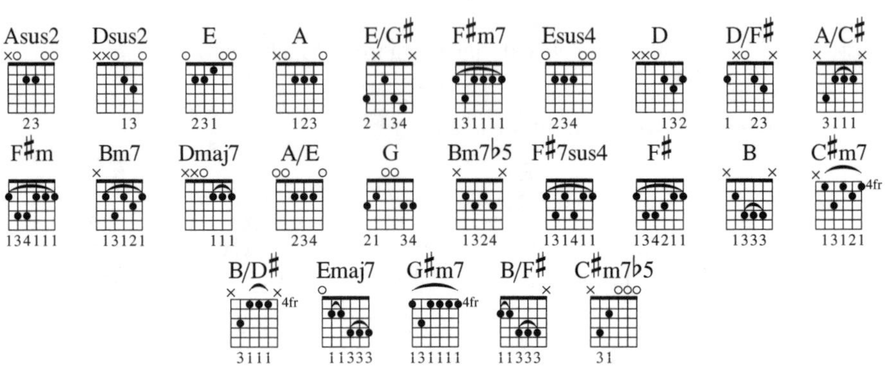

Intro

| **Asus2** | | | |
|: **Dsus2 E** | | :| *Play 4 times*

Verse 1

```
A                    E/G♯      F♯m7
   All who sail the sea __ of faith

     Dsus2        A    Dsus2
Find out before too long

A                              E/G♯     F♯m7
   How quickly blue skies can __ grow __ dark

     Dsus2               Esus4       E
And gentle winds grow __ strong.

     D                A
And suddenly fear is like white water

D/F♯              E/G♯
Pounding on the soul,

          A/C♯
And still __ we sail on,

      Dsus2          F♯m              Esus4    E
Know - ing that our Lord is in control.
```

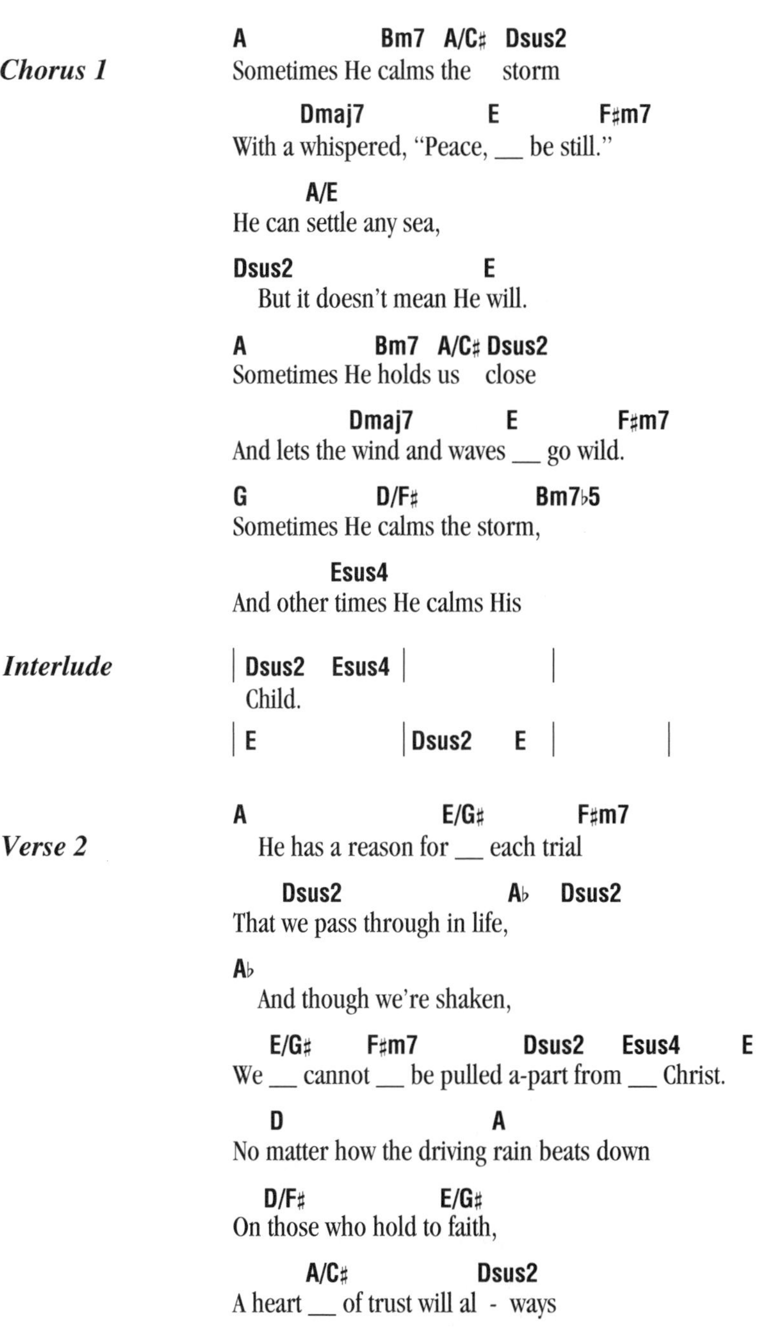

Chorus 1

A Bm7 A/C♯ Dsus2
Sometimes He calms the storm

Dmaj7 E F♯m7
With a whispered, "Peace, __ be still."

A/E
He can settle any sea,

Dsus2 E
But it doesn't mean He will.

A Bm7 A/C♯ Dsus2
Sometimes He holds us close

Dmaj7 E F♯m7
And lets the wind and waves __ go wild.

G D/F♯ Bm7♭5
Sometimes He calms the storm,

Esus4
And other times He calms His

Interlude

| **Dsus2 Esus4** | |
Child.

| **E** | **Dsus2 E** | | |

Verse 2

A E/G♯ F♯m7
He has a reason for __ each trial

Dsus2 A♭ Dsus2
That we pass through in life,

A♭
And though we're shaken,

E/G♯ F♯m7 Dsus2 Esus4 E
We __ cannot __ be pulled a-part from __ Christ.

D A
No matter how the driving rain beats down

D/F♯ E/G♯
On those who hold to faith,

A/C♯ Dsus2
A heart __ of trust will al - ways

F♯m Esus4 E
Be a quiet, peaceful place.

Chorus 2

```
A                 Bm7   A/C♯   Dsus2
Sometimes He calms the     storm

        Dmaj7              E           F♯m7
With a whispered, "Peace, __ be still."

        A/E
He can settle any sea,

Dsus2                          E
   But it doesn't mean He will.

A                Bm7   A/C♯ Dsus2
Sometimes He holds us    close

             Dmaj7              E           F♯m7
And lets the wind and waves __ go wild.

G                D/F♯               Esus4
Sometimes He calms the storm,

                                   F♯m7    A/E
And other times He calms His child,

           D        F♯7sus4   F♯
Oh, whoa.
```

Chorus 3

```
B                C♯m7  B/D♯  E
Sometimes He calms the    storm

        Emaj7             F♯          G♯m7
With a whispered, "Peace, __ be still."

        B/F♯          E
He can settle any sea,

                          F♯
But it doesn't mean He will.

B                C♯m7   B/D♯  E
Sometimes He holds  us      close

             Emaj7              F♯          G♯m7
And lets the wind and waves __ go wild.

A                E/G♯               C♯m7♭5
Sometimes He calms the storm,

           F♯7sus4
And other times He calms His...
```

Song of Love

Words and Music by Rebecca St. James,
Matt Bronleewe and Jeremy Ash

Tune down 1/2 step:
(low to high) E♭–A♭–D♭–G♭–B♭–E♭

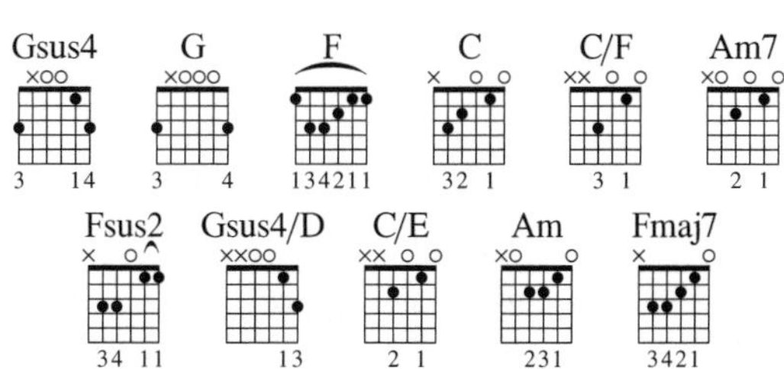

Intro

| **Gsus4 G** | **F C** |
| **Gsus4 G** | **C/F** |

Verse 1

C
Jesus, King of my heart.
Am7
Father, my peace and my light.
Fsus2 G C
Spirit, the joy of my soul You are.

Verse 2

C
Jesus, to You none compare.
Am7
Father, I rest in Your care.
Fsus2 G C
Spirit, the hope for my heart You are.

Chorus 1

```
     Gsus4  G        F                C
The heav - ens de-clare You are God,
              Gsus4  G                  F   C
And the moun - tains rejoice.
       Gsus4 G                F      C
The o    -    ceans cry "Allelu-ia"
         Gsus4/D   C/E                Fsus2
As we wor    -    ship You, Lord,
                                    C
For this is our song of love.
```

Verse 3

```
C
Jesus, You saved my soul.
    Am7
I'll thank You forevermore.
Fsus2     G                          C
Jesus, the love of my life You are.
```

Chorus 2 *Repeat Chorus 1*

Bridge

```
Gsus4  Am  G
Je    -    sus, I am in awe of the
Fmaj7    C
Love that You have shown.
Gsus4  Am         G                                Fsus2
Je    -    sus, how precious You are to me,

To me.
```

Chorus 3

```
       Gsus4  G       F              C
The heav - ens de-clare You are God,
             Gsus4  G              F   C
And the moun - tains rejoice.
       Gsus4 G             F      C
The o   -   ceans cry "Allelu-ia"
         Gsus4/D  C/E             Fsus2
As we wor   -   ship You, Lord.
       Gsus4  G       F              C
The heav - ens de-clare You are God,
             Gsus4  G              F    C
And the moun - tains rejoice.
       Gsus4  G            F      C
The o   -   ceans cry "Allelu-ia"
          Gsus4/D C/E             Fsus2
As we wor   -   ship You, Lord.
          Gsus4/D C/E             Fsus2
As we wor   -   ship You, Lord.
                               C
For this is our song of love.
```

Outro

```
    C                  Am7
||:    Our song of love,
                   Fsus2
Our song of love;
G                     C
This is our song of love.   :||
```

Repeat and fade

Speechless

Words and Music by
Steven Curtis Chapman and Geoff Moore

Melody:

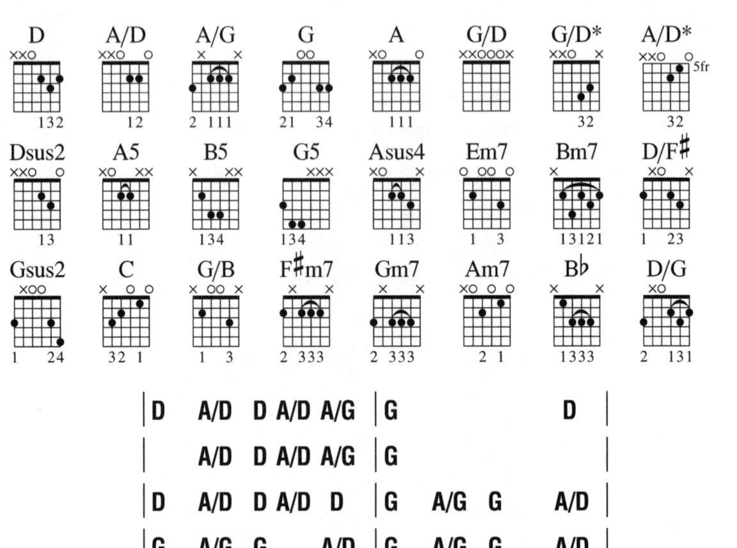

Intro

D A/D D A/D A/G	**G D**
A/D D A/D A/G	**G**
D A/D D A/D D	**G A/G G A/D**
G A/G G A/D	**G A/G G A/D**
G A/G G N.C.	**D A G**
G/D A/D G/D* A/D* G/D* A/D
D A G	

Verse 1

Dsus2 A5
Words fall like drops __ of rain;
B5 G5 Asus4
My lips are like clouds.
A5
I say so __ many things,
B5 G5 G
Trying to figure You out.
D A5
But as mercy o - pens my eyes
B5 G5
And my words are stolen a-way
B5 G
With this breathtaking view of Your grace.

```
                    D
Chorus 1      And I am speechless;
                   Em7
              I'm aston  -  ished and amazed.
                 Bm7              G
              I am silenced by Your wondrous grace.
                    D
              You have saved me;
                    Bm7                  G
              You have raised me from the grave.
              G/D  A/D  G/D*  A/D*  G/D* A/D  D
                                    And I     am   speechless
                 Em7
              In Your presence now;
                  Bm7              G
              I'm a-stounded as I con-sider how
                    Em7   D/F#
              You have shown us
                     G     A  D     A G
              A love that leaves us speech  -  less.
              | G/D  A/D  G/D* A/D* G/D*  A/D | D  A  G  |      |

              Dsus2                 Asus4
Verse 2          So what kind of love __ could this be
                     Bm7                        G
              That would trade heaven's throne for a cross?
              Dsus2                 Asus4
                 And to think You still __ celebrate
                  Bm7                     G
              Over finding just one who was lost.
              Dsus2                 Asus4
                 And to know You re-joice over us,
                Bm7                      G
              The God of this whole universe,
                  Bm7                    G            N.C.
              It's a story that's too great for __ words.
```

Chorus 2

```
             D
And I am speechless;
             Em7
I'm aston  -  ished and amazed.
        Bm7               G
I am silenced by Your wondrous grace.
             D
You have saved me;
             Bm7                 G
You have raised me from the grave.
G/D  A/D  G/D*  A/D*      G/D* A/D   D
                           And I     am    speechless
           Em7
In Your presence now;
          Bm7                  G
I'm a-stounded as I con-sider how
             Em7    D/F#
You have shown us
              G       A
A love that leaves us
Bm7              Em7   D/F#   G    A
Speechless.
           Bm7          Em7  D/F#  G  A
We are speechless.                 Oh, how
```

Bridge

```
Gsus2
Great is the love
                                  Bm7
The Father has lavished up-on us,
        Em7                    D/F#
That we should be called
      G                             C    G/B
The sons and the daughters of God?
| Em7 F#m7 G  A  Bm7 A | Gm7 Am7 Bb  C  Dsus2 A  |
```

Interlude

```
Dsus2                       Em7
We stand in awe of Your grace.
Bm7                         G
We stand in awe of Your mercy.
Dsus2                       Bm7
We stand in awe of Your love.
G                   A/G  G    A/G  G  A/G
We are speech   -   less.
```

Outro

```
          Dsus2                Em7
We are speechless in Your presence now.
           Bm7                  G
We're a-stounded as we con-sider how
            Em7  D/F#          G        A
You have shown us a love that leaves us
Dsus2                      Em7
Speechless.
We stand in awe of Your grace.
Bm7                        G
We stand in awe of Your mercy.
D                          Bm7
We stand in awe of Your love.
G                A/G  G   A/G  G  A/G
We are speech   -   less.
D                          Em7
We stand in awe of Your cross.
Bm7                        G
We stand in awe of Your power.
Em7 D/F#  G      A
We   are   speech-less.
Dsus2                      Em7
We stand in awe of Your grace.
Bm7                        G
We stand in awe of Your mercy.
D                          Bm7
We stand in awe of Your love.
G                A/G  G   A/G  G  A/G
We are speech   -   less.
D                          Em7
We stand in awe of Your cross.
Bm7                        G
We stand in awe of Your power.
Em7 D/F#  G      A
We   are   speech-less.
```

Testify to Love

Words and Music by Paul Field, Henk Pool,
Ralph Van Manen and Robert Riekerk

Tune down 1/2 step:
(low to high) E♭–A♭–D♭–G♭–B♭–E♭

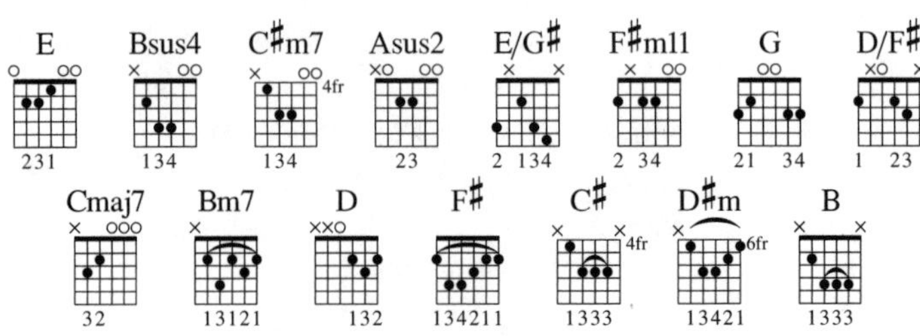

Intro

E	Bsus4	C♯m7	Asus2
E/G♯	Bsus4	C♯m7	Asus2

Verse 1

```
E/G♯                       Bsus4
  All the colors of the rain - bow,
C♯m7                 Asus2
  All the voices of the wind,
E/G♯                              Bsus4
  Ev'ry dream that reaches out,
     C♯m7                                  Asus2
That reaches out to find where love be-gins,
                  Bsus4
Ev'ry word of ev - 'ry story,
C♯m7                 Asus2
  Ev'ry star in ev'ry sky,
F♯m11    E/G♯           Asus2 Bsus4      E
  Ev'ry cor - ner of cre-ation   lives to testi-fy.
```

Chorus 1

```
E                           Bsus4
   For as long as I shall live,
                    C♯m7
I will testify to love.
                            Asus2
I'll be a witness in the si - lences
              Bsus4             E
When words __ are not enough.
                    Bsus4
With ev'ry breath I take,
                                  C♯m7
I will give thanks to God above,
                         Asus2
For as long as I shall live,
      Bsus4         E
I will testify to love.
```

Verse 2

```
E/G♯                                Bsus4
   From the mountains to the val - leys,
C♯m7                     Asus2
   From the rivers to the sea,
E/G♯                           Bsus4
   Ev'ry hand that reaches out,
      C♯m7                          Asus2
Ev'ry hand that reaches out to offer peace,
                  Bsus4
Ev'ry simple act __ of mercy,
C♯m7                     Asus2
   Ev'ry step to kingdom come,
F♯m11         E/G♯          Asus2
   All the hope __ in ev'ry heart
     Bsus4              E
Will speak what love has done.
```

Chorus 2 *Repeat Chorus 1*

Bridge

```
E
Colors of the rainbow, voices of the wind,
G                                   D/F#
Dream that reaches out where love __ begins,
Cmaj7
Word of ev'ry story, star in ev'ry sky,
Bm7                   D
Corner of creation tes - tify.
E
Mountains to the valleys, rivers to the sea,
G                             D/F#
Hand that reaches out to of - fer peace,
  Cmaj7
A simple act of mercy, kingdom come,
Bm7                               D
Ev'ry heart will speak what love __ has done.
E
Colors of the rainbow, voices of the wind,
G                                   D/F#
Dream that reaches out where love __ begins,
Cmaj7
Word of ev'ry story, star in ev'ry sky,
Bm7                   D      E
Corner of creation tes - tify.
```

Chorus 3

```
E                         Bsus4
   For as long as I shall live,
                     C#m7
I will testify to love.
                          Asus2
I'll be a witness in the si - lences
              Bsus4              E
When words __ are not enough.
                     Bsus4
With ev'ry breath I take,
                                  C#m7
I will give thanks to God above,
                        Asus2
For as long as I shall live,
       Bsus4
I will testify.
```

```
              F#                         C#
Chorus 4         For as long as I shall live,

                                 D#m
              I will testify to love.

                                      B
              I'll be a witness in the si - lences

                          C#                   F#
              When words __ are not enough.

                                C#
              With ev'ry breath I take,

                                           D#m
              I will give thanks to God above,

                                   B
              For as long as I shall live,

                    C#           F#
              I will testify to love.


Chorus 5      Repeat Chorus 4


              F#             C#
Outro         Ev'ry breath I take,

                               D#m
              Give thanks and testify, testify.

                  B             C#
              All __ my life, I'll testify.

              F#              C#
              For as long as I shall live,

                 D#m
              I'll testify, testify.

              B               C#       F#
              All my life, I'll testify.
```

Thank You

Words and Music by Ray Boltz

Melody:

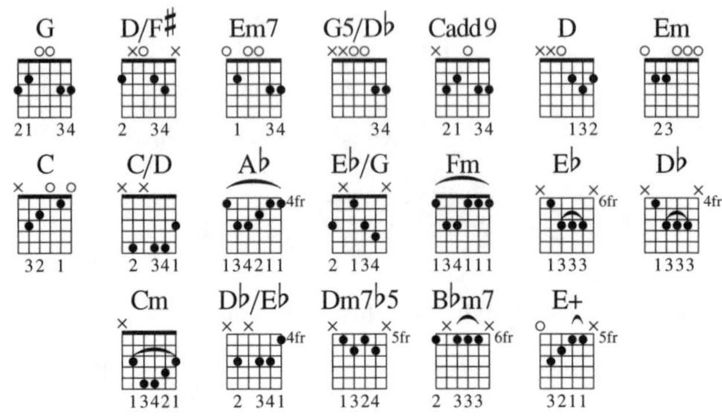

Verse 1

G **D/F♯**
I dreamed I went to heav-en,

Em7 **G5/D**
And you were there with me.

Cadd9 **G5/D**
We walked upon the streets __ of gold

Cadd9 **G5/D**
Beside the crystal sea.

G **D/F♯**
We heard the angels sing-ing,

Em7 **G5/D**
Then someone called your name.

Cadd9 **G5/D**
You turned and saw this young __ man,

Cadd9 **D** **G**
And he was smiling as he came.

```
                                G
Verse 2          And he said, "Friend,

                             D/F#
                 You may not know me now."

                 Em                          D
                       Then he said, "But wait!"

                 C                             D
                    You used to teach my Sun-day School

                 C                        D
                    When I was only eight.

                 G                                       D/F#
                    And ev'ry week you would say a prayer

                     Em                        D
                 Be-fore the class would start.

                 C                          D
                    And one day, when you said that prayer,

                            C      D       G
                 I asked Jesus,      in my heart.


                 G      D/F#     Em
Chorus 1         Thank you for giving to the Lord.

                 C               C/D                    G      C/D
                       I am a life __ that was changed.

                 G      D/F#     Em
                 Thank you for giving to the Lord.

                 C           C/D            G
                       I am so __ glad you gave.
```

Verse 3

```
          G                  D/F#
Then an-other man stood be-fore you;
Em                              D
    He said, "Remember the time
C                     D
  A missionary came __ to your church,
        C                  D
And his pictures made you cry?
G                               D/F#
  You didn't have much mon-ey,
        Em          D
But you gave it anyway.
C             D
  Jesus took the gift you gave,
        C       D      G
That's why I'm here to-day.
```

Chorus 2 *Repeat Chorus 1*

Verse 4

```
Ab                          Eb/G
    One by one they came, __
Fm                          Eb
  Far as the eye could see,
Db                               Eb
  Each life somehow touched
        Db        Eb
By your generosity.
Ab                        Eb/G
  Little things that you had done,
Fm
Sacrifices made,
Db                          Eb
  Unnoticed on the earth,
   Db      Eb       Ab
In heaven now pro-claimed.
```

```
          D♭
Bridge      And I know up in heaven

               A♭
          You're not supposed to cry,

          D♭
            But I am almost sure

                     A♭              E♭/G
          There were tears __ in your eyes.

             Fm
          As Jesus took your hand,

               Cm
          You stood before the Lord;

                    D♭
          He said, "My child, look around you,

               D♭          E♭
          For great is your re-ward!"


          A♭   E♭/G  Fm
Chorus 3  Thank you for giving to the Lord.

          D♭          D♭/E♭            A♭   D♭/E♭
              I am a life __ that was changed.

          A♭   E♭/G  Fm
          Thank you for giving to the Lord.

          D♭       D♭/E♭    A♭   D♭/E♭
              I am so __ glad you gave."

          A♭   E♭/G  Fm
          Thank you for giving to the Lord.

          D♭          D♭/E♭            A♭    D♭/E♭
              I am a life __ that was changed.

          A♭   E♭/G  Fm
          Thank you for giving to the Lord.

          D♭       D♭/E♭  E♭    Fm  E♭  Dm7♭5
              I am so __ glad __ you gave.

          B♭m7  D♭/E♭   A♭
              I am so glad you gave.

          | E♭/G    | Fm      | E+      | A♭
```

Thankful Heart

Words and Music by Bob Hartman,
John Elefante and Dino Elefante

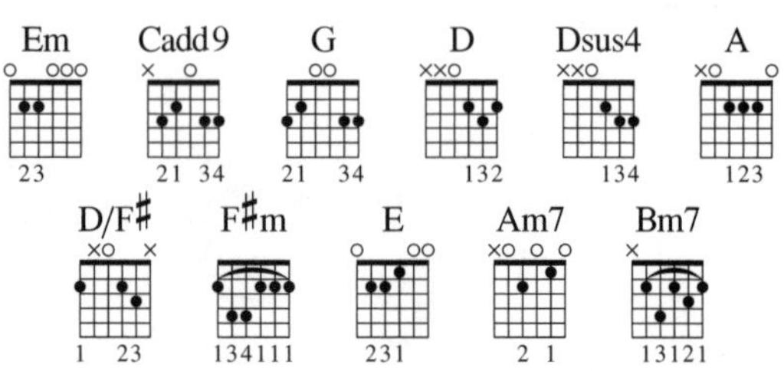

Intro

N.C.
I have a thankful heart

That You have given me.

And it can only come from You.

Verse 1

Em Cadd9 G
There is no way __ to begin

D Dsus4 D Em
To tell You how I feel;

Cadd9 G
There are no words __ to express

D Dsus4 D Em
How You've be-come so real.

Cadd9
Jesus, You've giv - en me

Em Cadd9
So much I can't __ repay.

Em A
I have no of - fering.

```
                      Cadd9     G
Chorus 1    I have a thank  -  ful heart
                           Cadd9    D
            That You have giv  -  en me.
                     Em         D/F#          Cadd9
            And it can on  -  ly come __ from You.

            Em                Cadd9      G
Verse 2        There is no way __ to begin
              D       Dsus4 D
            To tell You how    I feel.
            Em                      Cadd9      G
               There's nothing more __ I can say
               D       Dsus4  D     Em
            And no way to        repay
                              Cadd9
            Your warming touch
            Em                   Cadd9
               That melts my heart __ of stone.
            Em                   Cadd9
               Your steadfast love,
            Em           A
               I'll never be __ alone.
```

Chorus 2 *Repeat Chorus 1*

Chorus 3

```
            Cadd9      G
I have a thank - ful heart,
                     C   D
Word's don't come eas - ily.
            Em            D/F♯
But I am sure __ You can see
              Cadd9
My thankful heart.
```

Bridge

```
F♯m      E   Am7   Bm7
Help me be a man of God,
  F♯m        E    Am7     Bm7
A man who's after Your own heart.
F♯m     E         Am7  Bm7
Help me show my grati - tude,
     F♯m    E    Am7    Bm7
And keep in me a thankful heart.
```

Interlude

```
| Cadd9  | G      | Cadd9  | D      |
| Em     | D/F♯   | Cadd9  |        |
```

Chorus 4 *Repeat Chorus 1*

This I Know

Words and Music by
Margaret Becker

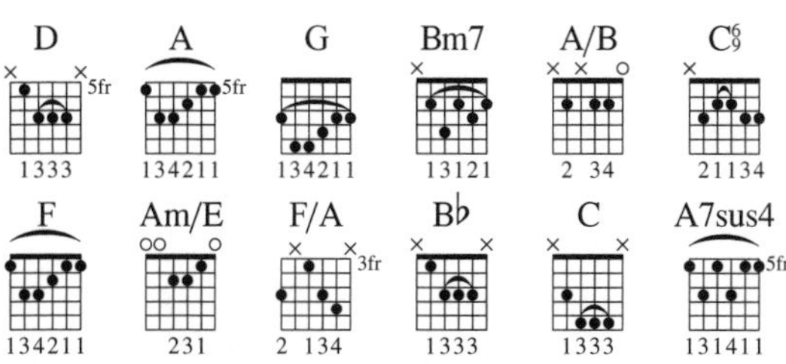

Intro

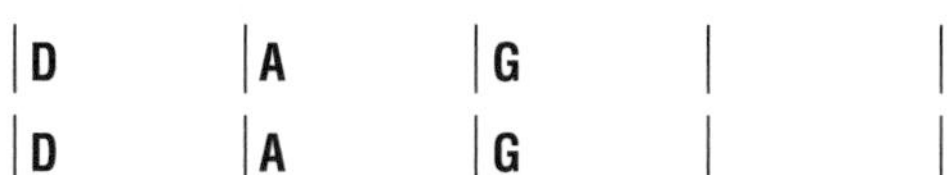

Verse 1

```
                D                    A
Oh Lord, (Oh Lord.) won't You hold my hand
     G
And help me to find a new place to stand?
                 D      A
All these chang-es that I've been through
      G
Have left me with only one absolute:
```

Chorus 1

```
D                    A
This I know, only this I know
           G
That Your love never changes as I go.
     D                 A
Only this I know, only this I know
           Bm7                    G
That Your love never changes as I go.
| N.C.   |        |
```

Verse 2

```
              D                    A
Oh Lord, (Oh Lord.) I've crossed mercy lines
   G
For what seems to be at least a thousand times.
           D                A
Instead (In-stead.) it's Your love that I see
G
Long, high, wide and deep a reachin' out to catch me.
```

Chorus 2

```
D                  A
This I know, only this I know:
G
(Love never changes.)

Never change, never change, no, not ever.
D                  A
This I know, only this I know:
          Bm7                  G
That Your love never changes as I go.
```

```
                A
Bridge          It was love that first drew me,

                   A/B                          G
                It is love that will keep me here.

                         A/B
                Now I see love burning brightly

                     Bm7               C6/9
                When ev'rything else isn't clear.

Interlude       | F        | Am/E     | F/A      | B♭   C          |
                | F        | Am/E     | F/A      | B♭   C  A7sus4  |

                D               A
Chorus 3        This I know, only this I know

                         G
                That Your love never changes as I go.

                   D               A
                Only this I know, only this I know

                         Bm7            G
                That Your love never changes as I go.

Chorus 4        Repeat Chorus 3 till fade
```

There Is a Redeemer

Words and Music by Melody Green

G Am7 G/B C D7 C/D D

21 34 | 2 1 | 1 3 | 32 1 | 213 | 1 | 132

Intro

| G Am7 G/B | C G/B | Am7 D7 | G C/D D |

Verse 1

G D G C G
There is a re-deem-er,

Am7 G/B C D G D
Je - sus, God's own Son.

G Am7 G/B C G/B
Precious Lamb of God, Mes-siah,

Am7 D7 G C/D D
Ho - ly One.

Verse 2

G D G C G
Jesus, my re-deem-er,

Am7 G/B C D G D
Name a - bove all names.

G Am7 G/B C G/B
Precious Lamb of God, Mes-siah,

Am7 D7 G C D
Oh for sinners slain.

Chorus 1

G G/B C G
Thank You, oh my Fa-ther,

C G D7
For giving us Your Son,

G Am7 G/B C
And leav-ing Your spirit

G/B Am7 D7 G C/D D
Till the work on earth is done.

Verse 3

```
G       D     G C  G
When I stand in glo-ry,

Am7 G/B  C   D   G      D
I        will see His face,

     G          Am7  G/B  C         G/B
And there I'll serve my  King for-ever

Am7   D7   G      C  D
In that holy place.
```

Chorus 2

```
G            G/B    C  G
Thank You, oh my Fa-ther,

    C                G      D7
For giving us Your Son,

     G    Am7 G/B  C
And leav-ing   Your spirit

G/B     Am7      D7       G      C/D  D
Till the work on earth is done.
```

Verse 4

Repeat Verse 1

Chorus 3

```
G            G/B    C  G
Thank You, oh my Fa-ther,

    C                G      D7
For giving us Your Son,

     G    Am7 G/B  C
And leav-ing  Your spirit

G/B     Am7      D7       G      C/D  D
Till the work on earth is done.

     G    Am7 G/B  C     G/B
And leav-ing  Your spirit till the

Am7      D7      G      D  G  C    G
Work on earth is done.
```

This Is Your Time

Words and Music by
Michael W. Smith and Wes King

Melody:

(Capo 3rd fret)

Em D C G/B D/F♯ Am B7

G Em7 Cadd9 Am7 Dsus4 G/C D/G

Intro

```
|Em    D    |C    G/B   |D/F# Em   |
|Am    D    |Am   B7    |
```

Verse 1

```
Em           D                   C               G/B
It was a test __ we could all __ hope to pass,
      D/F#               Em           Am   D   Am   B
But none of us would __ want to take.
Em                       D           C                G/B
Faced with the choice __ to deny __ God and live,
      D/F#                 Em          Am       D     Am
For her there was one __ choice to make.
```

Chorus 1

```
                              G                        D/F#
This was her time, __ this was her dance,
                             Em7                     Cadd9
She lived ev'ry mo  -  ment, left nothin' to chance.
                                G                       D/F#
She swam in the sea, __ drank of the deep,
                              Em7               Cadd9
Embraced the mys  -  tery of all she could be;

This was her time.
```

Interlude | Em D | C G/B | D/F♯ Em |
| Am D | Am B7 |

Verse 2

```
Em                          D                C              G/B
Though you are mourn - ing and griev - ing your loss,
D/F♯               Em          Am   D   Am   B7
Death died a long __ time a-go.
Em                  D              C              G/B
Swallowed in life, __ so her life __ carries on,
D/F♯              Em     Am     D     Am
Still, it's so hard __ to let go.
```

Chorus 2

```
                       G                        D/F♯
This was her time, __ this was her dance,
                       Em7                      Cadd9
She lived ev'ry mo  -  ment, left nothin' to chance.
                          G                      D/F♯
She swam in the sea, __ drank of the deep,
                       Em7                      Cadd9
Embraced the mys  -  tery of all she could be;
                  G                          D/F♯
What if tomor - row, and what if today
                        Em7                        Cadd9
Faced with the ques  -  tion, oh, what would you say?
```

Interlude | Am7 G | Dsus4 D | G G/B | Cadd9 |
| Am7 G | D/F♯ | | |

Chorus 3

```
                   G                         D/F#
This is your time, __ this is your dance,

              Em7                       Cadd9
Live ev'ry mo  -  ment, leave nothin' to chance.

                      G                      D/F#
To swim in the sea, __ drink of the deep,

                    D/F#                           G/C    C
And fall on the mer  -  cy and hear yourself pray - ing,

             G     D/G
"Won't You save me?

           G/C  D/G
Won't You save me?"
```

Chorus 4

```
                   G                         D/F#
This is your time, __ this is your dance,

              Em7                       Cadd9
Live ev'ry mo  -  ment, leave nothin' to chance.

                 G                        D/F#
Swim in the sea, __ drink of the deep,

                  Em7                        Cadd9
Embrace the mys  -  tery of all you can be.

                   G                         D/F#
This is your time, __ this is your dance,

              Em7                       Cadd9
Live ev'ry mo  -  ment, leave nothin' to chance.

                 G                        D/F#
Swim in the sea, __ drink of the deep,

                  Em7                  Cadd9
Embrace the mys  -  tery of all you can be. This is...
```

Outro

```
||: G          |               :||  Repeat and fade
  Your time.
```

Undivided

Words and Music by
Melodie Tunney

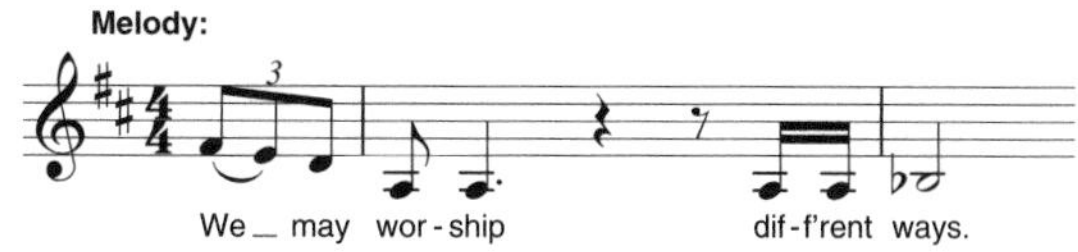

(Capo 3rd fret)

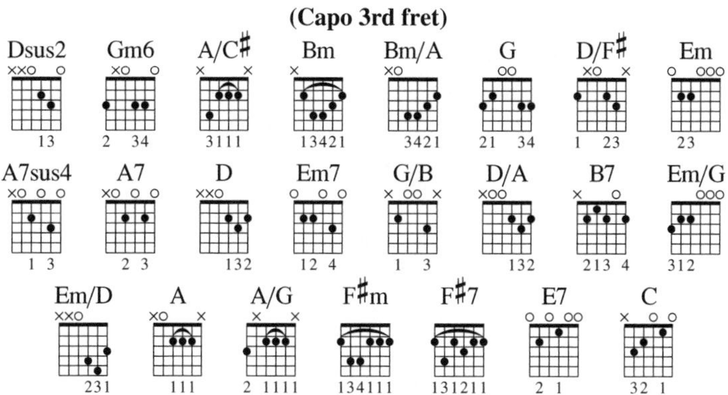

Intro | Dsus2 | Gm6 | Dsus2 | Gm6 |

Verse 1

```
        Dsus2           Gm6
We may worship diff'rent ways.
        Dsus2
We may praise Him,
A/C♯    Bm   Bm/A    G
  And yet spend all of our days
D/F♯        Em      A7sus4
Living life di-vided,       divided.
A7              Dsus2              Gm6
  But when we seek Him with open hearts,
      D         A/C♯        Bm
He re-moves the walls we've built
  Bm/A     G
To keep us a-part.
  D/F♯            Em7      A7sus4
We trust Him to u-nite us.
```

Chorus 1

```
   A7  D                    A/C♯
In our hearts we're undi-vided,
G/B                 D/A          A7sus4
Worshipping one Savior, one Lord.
   A7  D                    A/C♯
In our hearts we're undi-vided,
B7             Em    D/F♯     Em/G
Bound by His spirit forever more,
A7sus4  A7  Em/D  D
Un    -    di -  vid  -  ed.
```

Verse 2

```
A7sus4       Dsus2
   It doesn't matter
          Gm6
If we a-gree.
         Dsus2  A/C♯
All He asks is that
    Bm     Bm/A              G
We serve        Him faithfully
     D/F♯              Em7          A7sus4   A7
And love as He first loved us.
```

Bridge

```
Bm                  Em7
   He made us in His image

    A          A/G          F♯m   F♯7
And in His eyes we are all the same.

Bm                           Em7
   Though our methods may be diff'rent,

E7                           C          A7sus4
Jesus is the bond that will re-main.
```

Chorus 2

```
  A7  D                 A/C♯
In our hearts we're undi-vided,

G/B              D/A        A7sus4
Worshipping one Savior, one Lord.

  A7  D                 A/C♯
In our hearts we're undi-vided,

B7             Em   D/F♯    Em/G
Bound by His spirit forever more,

A7sus4  A7  Em/D   D
Un   -    di - vid  -  ed.

D/F♯   Em/G    A7sus4       A7 Em/D  D
In our hearts          we're un - di - vid  -  ed.
```

This Love

Words and Music by Margaret Becker,
Charlie Peacock and Kip Summers

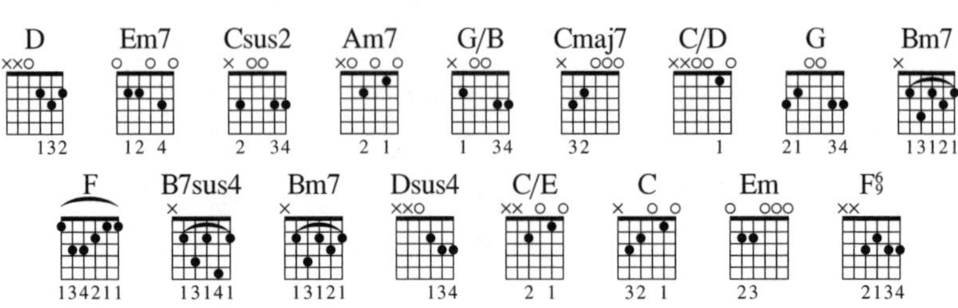

Intro ||: D Em7 | Csus2 | :|| *Play 4 times*

Verse 1

```
D             Em7              Csus2
   Not much heart left to break
D              Em7             Csus2
   When Your love came my way.
D                Em7             Csus2
   I wrapped my-self in walls of steel
D                  Em7            Csus2
   And begged my heart not to feel.
Am7       G/B
   But as if it knew,
Csus2          G/B
   It ran straight to You.
Am7
   Jumped right into Your arms;
               Cmaj7              C/D
There was nothing I could do.
```

Chorus 1

```
G       Bm7         F
   This love, this love,
Am7
Oh, the healing.
G       Bm7         F
   This love, this love.
Am7
Tell me, tell me.
G                 G/B
   Where would I go,
                Cmaj7
What would I do
      B7sus4  Bm7
With-out _______ Your love?
|Em7  Cmaj7|        |C/D       |        |Cmaj7    |        |
```

Verse 2

```
D           Em7        Csus2
   Not much reason to cry
D          Em7            Csus2
   Now that there's You and I.
D                Em7        Csus2
   I wrapped my dreams up in You
D                 Em7                 Csus2
   And there they'll stay 'til time is through.
Am7             G/B
   'Cause I can't let go,
Csus2        G/B
   No, I won't break free
Am7
   Of this loving hold that
Cmaj7              C/D
You have over me.
```

```
            G       Bm7          F
Chorus 2       This love, this love,

            Am7
            Oh, the healing.

            G       Bm7          F
               This love, this love.

            Am7
            Tell me, tell me.

            G                  G/B
               Where would I go,

                               Cmaj7
            What would I do

                  B7sus4   Bm7
            With-out ______ Your love?
            | Em7   Cmaj7 |       | C/D     |        |

Bridge      | Em7       |          | Dsus4     |

                                Em7
             Where would I go?

                                  Dsus4
            How could I live?

                             Em7
            What would I do?

                                Dsus4
            Tell me, tell me.

                               Cmaj7
            Where would I          go?
```

Chorus 3

```
G       Bm7          F
   This love, this love,

C/E          C/D
   Oh, the heal  -  ing.

G       Bm7          F
   This love, this love,

Am7
Tell me, tell me.

G                 G/B
   Where would I __ go,

                C
What would I do

      B7sus4 Bm7           Em7   C
With-out _______ Your love?

Am7    G   F        Em  C/D
Tell me, __ tell me, yeah.

G       Bm7          F
   This love, this love,

C/E          C/D
   Oh, the heal  -  ing.

G       Bm7          F
   This love, this love,

Am7
Tell me, tell me.

G                 G/B
   Where would I __ go,

                C
What would I do

      B7sus4  Bm7         Em7   C
With-out _______ Your love?

|Am7   G   F6/9  |           |
```

Thy Word

Words and Music by
Michael W. Smith and Amy Grant

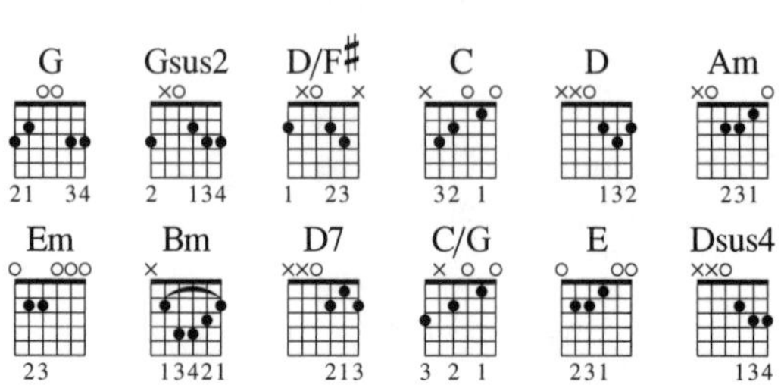

Intro | G | Gsus2 |

Chorus 1

```
G              D/F♯        G
Thy Word is a lamp unto my feet
      C        D     G
And a light un-to my path.
               D/F♯        G
Thy Word is a lamp unto my feet
      C        D     G
And a light un-to my path.
```

Verse 1

```
D              Am
When I feel a-fraid,
      Em                 Bm
And I think I've lost my way,
C           D7            C/G  G
Still You're there right be-side me.
D              Am
Nothing will I fear
    Em             Bm
As long as You are near.
C          D        E          Dsus4   D
Please be near me to the end.
```

Chorus 2 *Repeat Chorus 1*

Verse 2

```
D           Am
I will not for-get
     Em              Bm
Your love for me and yet
    C          D7    C/G    G
My heart for-ever is wander-ing.
D            Am
Jesus, be my guide
    Em               Bm
And hold me to Your side,
    C    D      E          Dsus4  D
And I will love You to the end.
```

Chorus 3

```
G              D/F#          G
Thy Word is a lamp unto my feet
      C       D    G
And a light un-to my path.
               D/F#          G
Thy Word is a lamp unto my feet
      C       D    G
And a light un-to my path,
      C       D    G
And a light un-to my path.
           C       D    G     Gsus2
You're the light un-to my path.
```

To Know You

Words and Music by
Nichole Nordeman and Mark Hammond

(Capo 1st fret)

Em Asus4 A C A/E Bsus4 B

Cmaj7 G D Am G/B D/A C

Intro | **Em** | **Asus4 A** |

Verse 1

Em
It's well past midnight

Asus4 A
And I'm awake with ques - tions that won't

Em
Wait for daylight,

Asus4 A C
Separating fact __ from my imag - inary fiction

Em A/E
On this shelf of my convic - tion.

Asus4 A
I need to find a place __ where

Bsus4 B
You and I __ come face __ to face.

Verse 2

```
Em
   Thomas needed
Asus4               A
Proof that You had really risen
Em
   Undefeated.
Asus4                A
When he placed his fingers
             Cmaj7
Where the nails once broke Your skin,
          Em               A/E
Did his faith fin'lly be-gin?
     Asus4             A                            Bsus4
I've lied if I've denied __ the common ground
               B
I've shared __ with him.
```

Chorus 1

```
         C                             G
And I, __ I really want to know __ You.
  D                                         Am
I want to make each day a diff'rent way
                          G/B     C
That I can show You __ how
                          G
I really want to love __ You.
    D
Be patient with my doubt;
           Am                   G/B    C
I'm just tryin' to figure out Your ___ will,
                          D
And I really want to know You
| Em          | D/A    A     |
  Still.
```

Verse 3

```
Em
  Nicodemus
Asus4          A
Could not under-stand how You could
Em
  Truly free us.
   Asus4            A
He struggled with the image of a
Cmaj7
Grown man born again.
   Em                   A/E
We might have been good friends,
    Asus4          A
'Cuz sometimes I still question, too,
     Bsus4    B
How easily we come to You
```

Chorus 2

```
      C                      G
But I, __ I really want to know __ You.
 D                                  Am
I want to make each day a diff'rent way
                  G/B     C
That I can show You __ how
                  G
I really want to love __You.
   D
Be patient with my doubt;
       Am               G/B      C
I'm just tryin' to figure out Your ___ will,
                  D         E
And I really want to know You still.
```

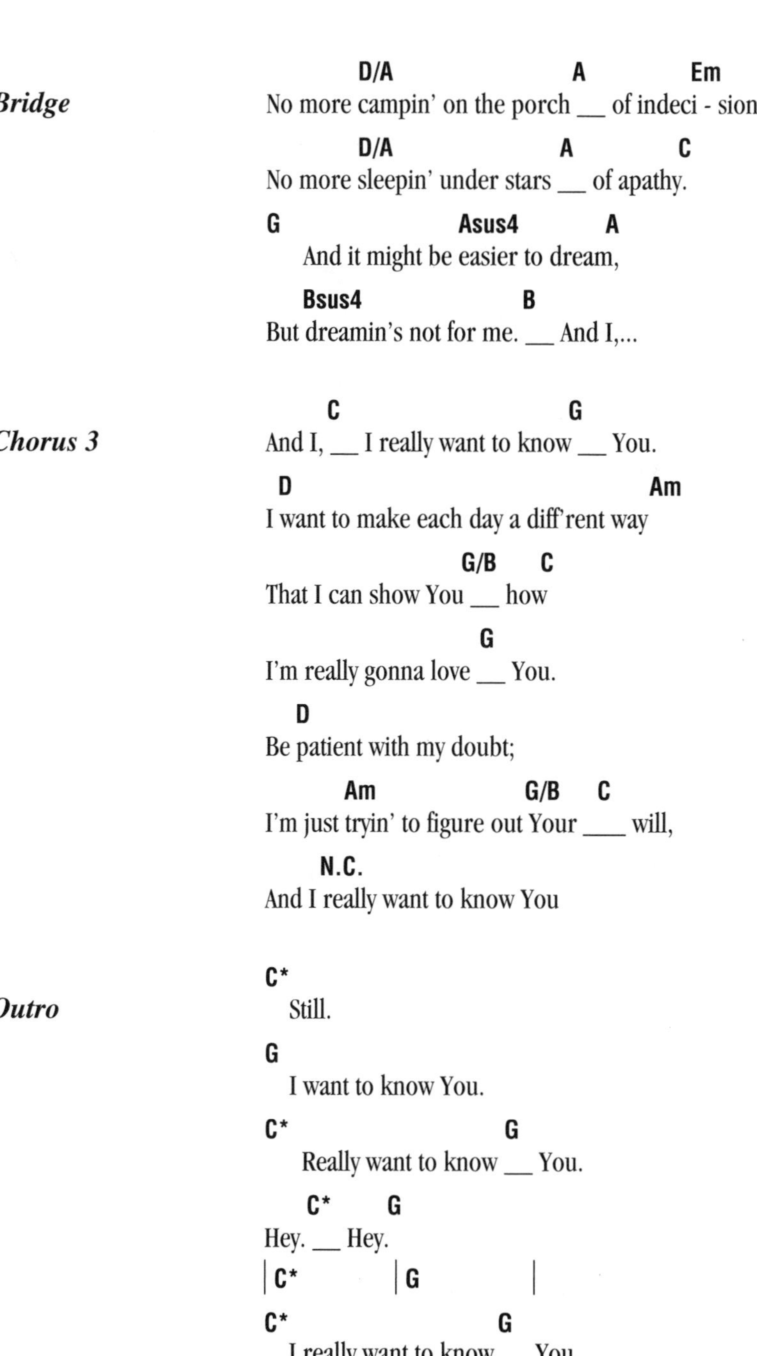

Bridge

D/A A Em
No more campin' on the porch __ of indeci - sion,

D/A A C
No more sleepin' under stars __ of apathy.

G Asus4 A
And it might be easier to dream,

Bsus4 B
But dreamin's not for me. __ And I,...

Chorus 3

C G
And I, __ I really want to know __ You.

D Am
I want to make each day a diff'rent way

G/B C
That I can show You __ how

G
I'm really gonna love __ You.

D
Be patient with my doubt;

Am G/B C
I'm just tryin' to figure out Your ___ will,

N.C.
And I really want to know You

Outro

C*
Still.

G
I want to know You.

C* G
Really want to know __ You.

C* G
Hey. __ Hey.

| C* | G |

C* G
I really want to know __ You.

C* G
I really want to know __ You.

| C* | G | C* | G | C* | G |

Undo Me

Words and Music by
Jennifer Knapp

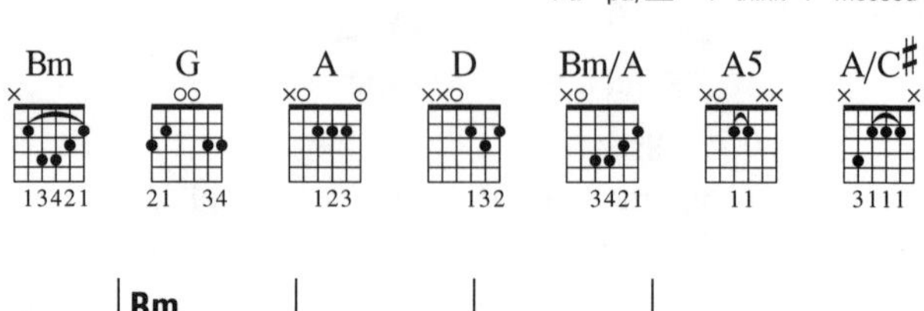

Intro | Bm | | |

Verse 1

```
Bm                G              A
   Papa, I think I messed up again.
       Bm                                G       A
Was it somethin' I did or was it some - thin' I __ said?
Bm                  G               A
   I don't mean to do __ you wrong;
                 Bm                     G      A
It's just the way __ of human nature.
Bm                  G                A
   Sister, I know I      let you down;
     Bm                              G          A
I can tell by the fact you'll never    come a  -  round.
Bm                            G         A
   You don't have to say __ a thing;
         Bm                     G                 A
I can tell __ by your eyes exact-ly what you mean:
```

Chorus 1

```
              G                   D                        A
That it's     time to get down __ on my knees and pray,
 D      A    Bm A
"Lord, un - do  me.
G                        D                     A
   Put away my flesh __ and bone till You __ own
      D   A Bm      A
This spir-it through me.
G          A
Lord, undo __ me."
| Bm        | G    A     | Bm    A Bm |          |
```

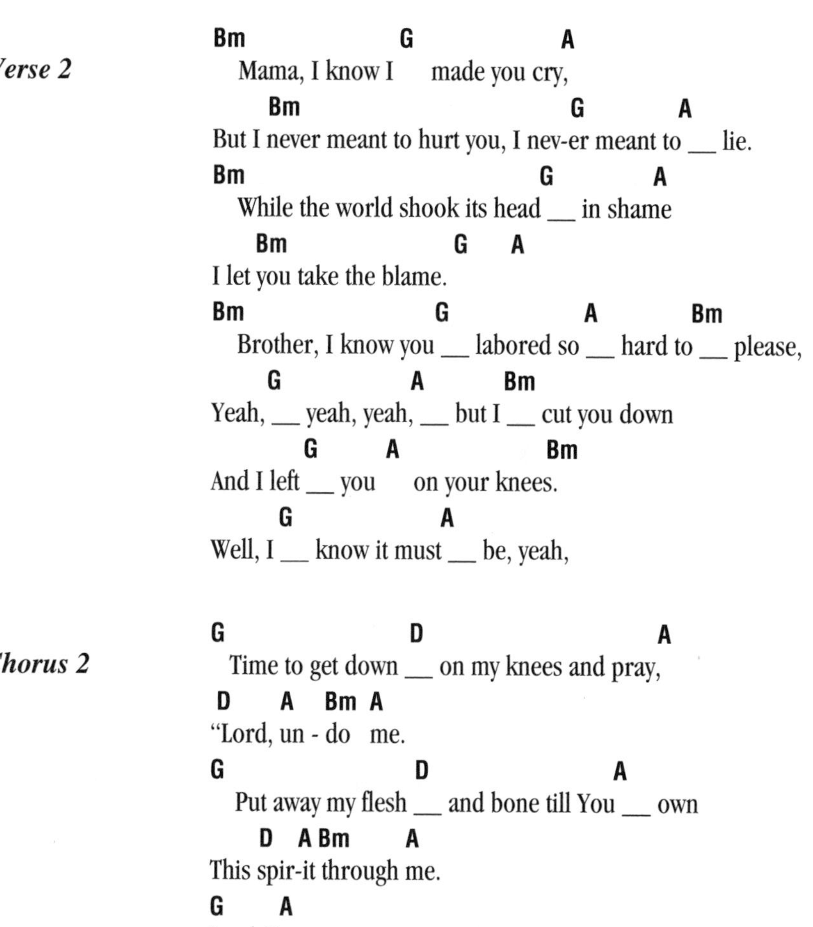
Verse 2
Bm G A
Mama, I know I made you cry,
Bm G A
But I never meant to hurt you, I nev-er meant to __ lie.
Bm G A
While the world shook its head __ in shame
Bm G A
I let you take the blame.
Bm G A Bm
Brother, I know you __ labored so __ hard to __ please,
G A Bm
Yeah, __ yeah, yeah, __ but I __ cut you down
G A Bm
And I left __ you on your knees.
G A
Well, I __ know it must __ be, yeah,
Chorus 2
G D A
Time to get down __ on my knees and pray,
D A Bm A
"Lord, un - do me.
G D A
Put away my flesh __ and bone till You __ own
D A Bm A
This spir-it through me.
G A
Lord, I

```
                Bm       Bm/A
Bridge          Am wanting, needing,
                G        A
                Guilty and greedy,
                Bm          Bm/A
                Un-righteous, un-holy.
                G       A
                Un-do me, undo __ me."

                Bm                       G       A
Verse 3           Abba Father, You must    wonder why
                Bm                          G       A
                More times than Peter I have __ denied.
                Bm                      G         A
                  Three nails and a cross __ to prove I
                Bm                G         A
                Owe __ my life eter-nally to You.

                            G               D                        A
Chorus 3        Well, it's time __ to get down __ on my knees and pray,
                D    A   Bm A
                "Lord, un - do me.
                G                  D                    A
                  Put away my flesh __ and bone till You __ own
                   D   A Bm     A
                This spir-it through me.
                G        A   N.C.
                Lord. Undo          me."

Outro           ||: Bm              | G         A          :|| Play 3 times
                | Bm       A5   N.C. | Bm   A/C# N.C.   | Bm       A5
```

Via Dolorosa

Words and Music by
Billy Sprague and Niles Borop

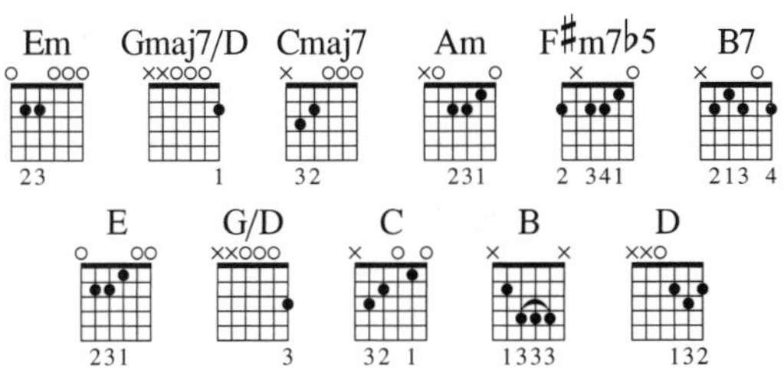

Intro

| Em | Gmaj7/D | Cmaj7 | | |
| Em | Gmaj7/D | Cmaj7 |

Verse 1

```
                Em          Gmaj7/D
Down the Vi - a Doloro - sa
        Cmaj7
In Je-rusalem that day,
      Em                         Gmaj7/D        Fmaj7
The soldiers tried to clear __ the narrow street,
                 Am                    Em
But the crowd __ pressed in to see
      F♯m7♭5                  B7          Em    Gmaj7/D   Cmaj7
The man condemned to die __ on Calva-ry.
```

Verse 2

```
            Em                     Gmaj7/D
He was bleeding from a beat  -  ing
                Cmaj7
There were stripes upon His back,
            Em                          Gmaj7/D      Cmaj7
And He wore a crown of thorns __ upon His head;
                Am                   Em
And he bore __ with ev'ry step
        F♯m7♭5                      B7                Em       E
The scorn of those who cried __ out for His death.
```

Chorus 1

```
              Am          B7
Down the Via Dolo  -  rosa,
                Em                G/D
Called "The Way of Suffering,"
                C                        B7
Like a lamb __ came the Messi  -  ah,
              Em       E
Christ the King.
          Am                         B7
But He chose to walk that road
               Em       Gmaj7/D Cmaj7
Out of His love for you and  me;
                Em            Cmaj7
Down the Vi  -  a Doloro  -  sa,
          Cmaj7 B7            Em    Gmaj7/D   Cmaj7
All the way          to Calva-ry.
```

Bridge

```
              B
The blood __ that would cleanse
              Cmaj7
The hearts __ of all men
           D                         B7
Made its way through the heart
       Em         E
Of Je-rusalem.
```

Chorus 2

```
             Am        B7
Down the Via Dolo  -  rosa,
               Em                  G/D
Called "The Way of Suffering,"
               C                      B7
Like a lamb __ came the Messi  -  ah,
             Em      E
Christ the King.
          Am                         B7
But He chose to walk that road
              Em       Gmaj7/D Cmaj7
Out of His love for you and  me;
               Em           Cmaj7
Down the Vi  -  a Doloro  -  sa,
        Cmaj7 B7           Em    Gmaj7/D   Cmaj7
All the way          to Calva-ry.
| F♯m7♭5  B7      | Em         |
```

Wait for Me

Words and Music by
Rebecca St. James

Tune down 1/2 step:
(low to high) E♭–A♭–D♭–G♭–B♭–E♭

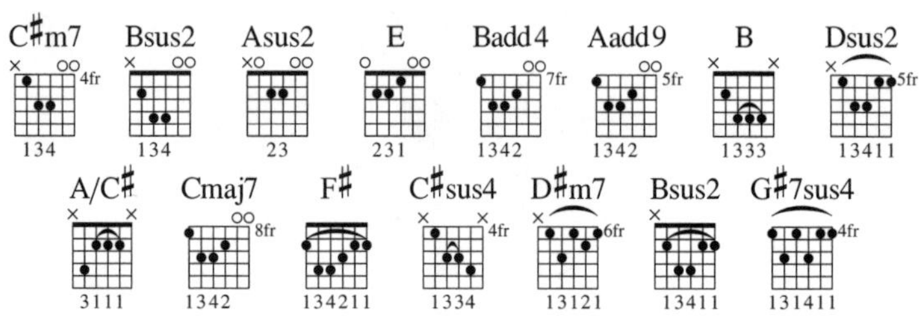

Intro ‖: C♯m7 | Bsus4 | Asus2 | Bsus4 :‖

Verse 1

```
E                                              Badd4
Darling, did you know that I, I dream about __ you?
                                  C♯m7
Waiting for the look in your eyes
               Badd4
When we meet __ for the first time.
E                                            Badd4
Darling, did you know that I, I pray about __ you?
                                Aadd9
Praying that you will hold on.
            Bsus4               B
Keep your loving eyes only for me.
```

Chorus 1

```
            E                             Badd4
'Cause I am waiting for, praying for you, dar-ling.

            C♯m7
Wait for me, __ too.

              Asus2          Bsus4
Wait for me as __ I wait for you.

            E                             Badd4
'Cause I am waiting for, praying for you, dar-ling.

            C♯m7
Wait for me, __ too.

              Asus2          Bsus4
Wait for me as __ I wait for you.

        C♯m7  Badd4
Darling wait;

        Aadd9   B
Darling wait.
```

Verse 2

```
E                                        Badd4
Darling, did you know I dream about life to-gether,

                   Aadd9
Knowing it will be for  -  ever?

           Badd4
I'll be yours __ and you'll be mine.

    E                                Badd4
And darling, when I say, "'Til death do us part,"

                      C♯m7
I'll mean it with all of my heart.

               Bsus4
Now and always faithful to you.
```

Chorus 2

```
              E                            Badd4
'Cause I am waiting for, praying for you, dar-ling.

              C♯m7
Wait for me, __ too.

                Asus2           Bsus4
Wait for me as __ I wait for you.

              E                            Badd4
'Cause I am waiting for, praying for you, dar-ling.

              C♯m7
Wait for me, __ too.

                Asus2           Bsus4
Wait for me as __ I wait for you.
```

Bridge

```
              Dsus2  A/C♯
Darling, wait.

              Cmaj7  Badd4
Darling wait.

Dsus2                                  A/C♯
Now, I know you may have made mistakes,

                   Asus2
But there's forgive - ness and a second chance.

   Bsus4            Asus2
So wait for me, darling, __ wait for me.

Bsus4        Asus2
Wait for me, wait for me.
```

Chorus 3

F♯ C♯add4
'Cause I am waiting for, praying for you, dar-ling.

D♯m7
Wait for me, __ too.

Bsus2 C♯sus4
Wait for me as __ I wait for you.

F♯ C♯add4
'Cause I am waiting for, praying for you, dar-ling.

D♯m7
Wait for me, __ too.

Bsus2 C♯sus4
Wait for me as __ I wait for you.

Chorus 4

Repeat Chorus 3

Outro

D♯m7 C♯sus4
Darling, wait.

Bsus2 C♯sus4
Darling, wait.

D♯m7 C♯sus4
Wait for __ me;

Bsus2 G♯7sus4
Darling, wait.

D♯m7 C♯sus4
'Cause I'm wait - ing for you.

Bsus2 C♯sus4
'Cause I'm wait - ing for you.

D♯m7 C♯sus4
So wait for __ me.

Bsus2 G♯7sus4
Darling wait;

D♯m7
Wait for ___me.

The Warrior Is a Child

Words and Music by Twila Paris

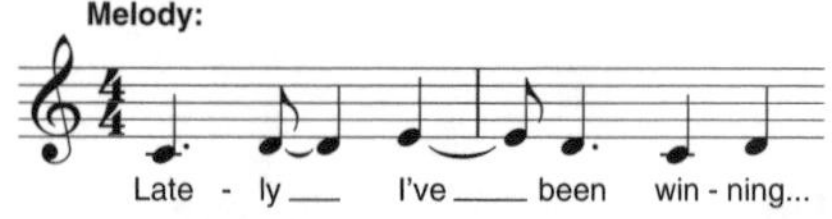

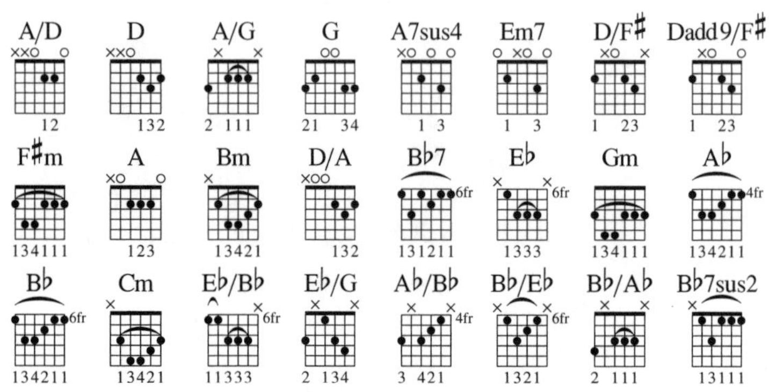

Intro

| A/D D A/D | D A/D D | A/G G A7sus4 | |
| A/D D A/D | D A/D D | A/G G A7sus4 | |

Verse 1

A/D D A/D D A/D D A/G G A7sus4
Late - ly I've been win-ning bat - tles left and right.
A/D D A/D D A/D D A/G G
But e - ven win-ners can get wound-ed in the fight.
Em7 D/F♯ G D/F♯
People say that I'm amazing, strong beyond my years.
Em7 D/F♯ G A7sus4
But they don't see in-side of me I'm hiding all the tears.

Chorus 1

D F♯m G A
They don't know that I go running home __ when I fall down.
D F♯m G A
They don't know who picks me up when no __ one is around.
Bm D/A G Dadd9/F♯
I drop my sword and cry __ for just a while,
Em7 D/F♯ G
'Cause deep inside this ar - mor
A7sus4
The warrior is a child.

Interlude

| A/D D A/D | D A/D D | A/G G A7sus4 | |
| A/D D A/D | D A/D D | A/G G A7sus4 | |

Verse 2

A/D D A/D D A/D D A/G G A7sus4
Un - a - fraid be-cause His ar - mor is the best.

A/D D A/D D A/D D A/G G
But e - ven sol - diers need a qui - et place to rest.

Em7 D/F♯ G Dadd9/F♯
People say that I'm amazing, never face re-treat.

Em7 D/F♯ G A7sus4
But they don't see the enemies that lay me at His feet.

Chorus 2

D F♯m G A
They don't know that I go running home __ when I fall down.

D F♯m G A
They don't know who picks me up when no __ one is around.

Bm D/A G Dadd9/F♯
I drop my sword and cry __ for just a while,

Em7 D/F♯ G
'Cause deep inside this ar - mor

A7sus4 D B♭7
The warrior is a child.

```
                   E♭          Gm                        A♭                          B♭
Chorus 3   They don't know that I go running home __ when I fall down.

                          E♭         Gm                           A♭                     B♭
           They don't know __ who picks me up when no __ one is around.

             Cm                      E♭/B♭                A♭       E♭/G
           I drop my sword and look up for a smile,

                   A♭                     E♭/G        A♭
           'Cause deep inside this ar  -  mor,

                          A♭/B♭                   E♭/G
           Deep inside, deep inside this ar  -  mor,

                                 A♭         A♭/B♭                    E♭/G
           Deep inside this ar - mor, deep inside this ar   -   mor,

                                 A♭           A♭/B♭
           Deep inside this ar - mor, the warrior is a child.

Outro      | B♭/E♭ E♭  B♭/E♭ |  E♭  B♭/E♭ E♭ | B♭/A♭ A♭  A♭/B♭ |              |

               B♭/E♭      E♭  B♭/E♭          E♭   B♭/E♭  E♭
           ||: La, la, la, la, la, la,     la, la, la,

           B♭/A♭ A♭  B♭7sus2
           La,    la,  la.               :||  Play 3 times

                                      E♭
           The warrior is a child.
```

Whatever You Ask

Melody:

Words and Music by
Phill McHugh and Michele Wagner

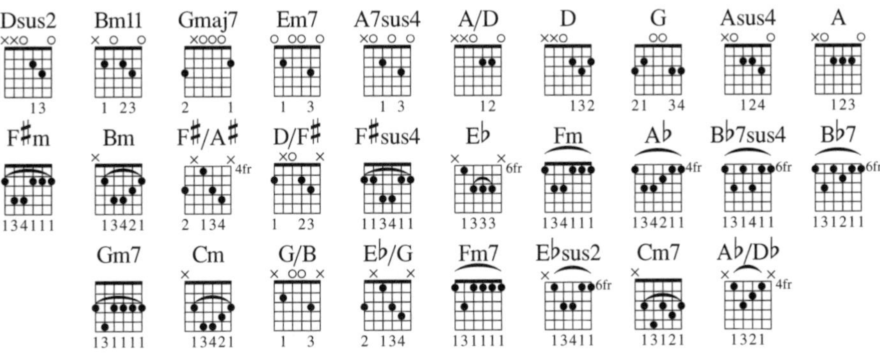

Intro | Dsus2 | | Bm11 |
| | Gmaj7 | Em7 A7sus4 |

Verse 1

```
Dsus2
Lord, I see the things You ask of me:
Bm11
   Faithfulness, holiness, and purity.
Gmaj7
   I love Your truth;
                              Dsus2
I long to show it to the world for You.

So, Lord, I need Your help to understand
Bm11
   The other person that I sometimes am.
Gmaj7
   I never want to live a day
    A/D     D     A7sus4
That I can't say to __ You,
```

Chorus 1

```
                D              Em7
"Lord, what-ever You ask,
  G               Asus4   A
I want to obey __ You,
   F#m              Bm         G                  A7sus4
To let my life beat __ with a servant's heart."
              D          Em7
Lord, what-ever You ask,
        G          F#/A#            Bm
I know __ that You can give me wisdom
           G          D/F#          Em7
And cour - age to equal the task.
       A7sus4       Dsus2
What-ever You ask.
```

Verse 2

```
  Dsus2
I face so much, it steals away:
Bm11
   The will to make the time to serve or pray.
     Gmaj7
And there are days I don't
                                  Dsus2
Take up Your cross and follow You.

But I have learned that I can talk with You.
Bm11
   You know ev'rything that I'm goin' through.
  Gmaj7                                  A7sus4
If I'll just ask, I find that You're right there,
        A/D D                          A7sus4
Provid  -  ing me with the strength __ I need.
```

Chorus 2

```
               D          Em7
Lord, what-ever You ask,

 G          Asus4  A
I want to o-bey You,

  F♯m          Bm      G             A7sus4
To let my life beat __ with a servant's heart.

               D        Em7  D/F♯
Lord, what-ever You ask,

        G        F♯/A♯          Bm
I know __ that You can give me wisdom

          G       D/F♯           Em7
And cour - age to equal the task.

      A7sus4           D    Em7  G
Lord, what-ever You ask.

| F♯m   Bm    | G     A     | F♯sus4  N.C.
```

Chorus 3

```
               E♭        Fm
Lord, what-ever You ask,

 A♭           B♭7sus4 B♭7
I want to obey __ You,

  Gm7         Cm7       A♭            B♭7sus4
To let my life beat __ with a servant's heart.

               E♭        Fm
Lord, what-ever You ask,

        A♭      G/B            Cm
I know __ that You can give me wisdom

          A♭     E♭/G           Fm7
And cour - age to equal the task.

      E♭/G    A♭      E♭/G          Fm7
Give me cour - age to equal the task,

                B♭7sus4
Lord, whatev  -  er You ask.
```

Outro

```
| E♭sus2     |            | Cm7        |            |
| A♭         | Fm7  A♭/D♭ | E♭sus2
```

We Trust in the Name of the Lord Our God

Melody:

Some trust_ in char - i - ots;

Words and Music by Steven Curtis Chapman

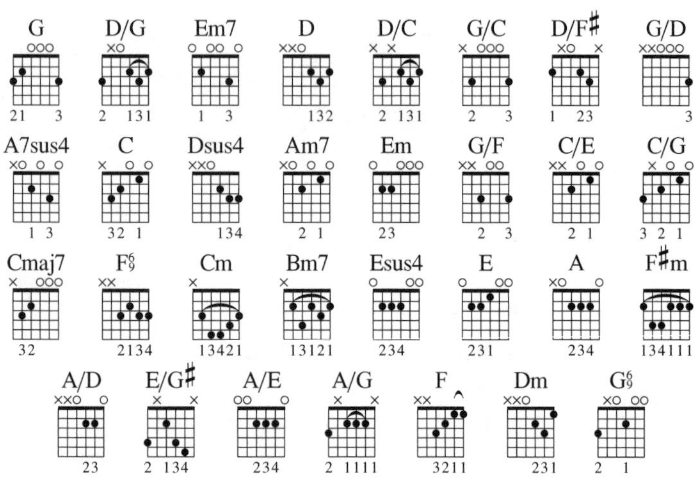

Intro ‖: G D/G Em7 D | D/C G/C D :‖

Verse 1

G D/F♯ Em7 G/D
Some trust __ in chariots;

G/C D G
We trust in the name of the Lord our God.

D/F♯ Em7 G/D
Some trust __ in horses;

G/C A7sus4 D G
We trust in the name of the Lord our God.

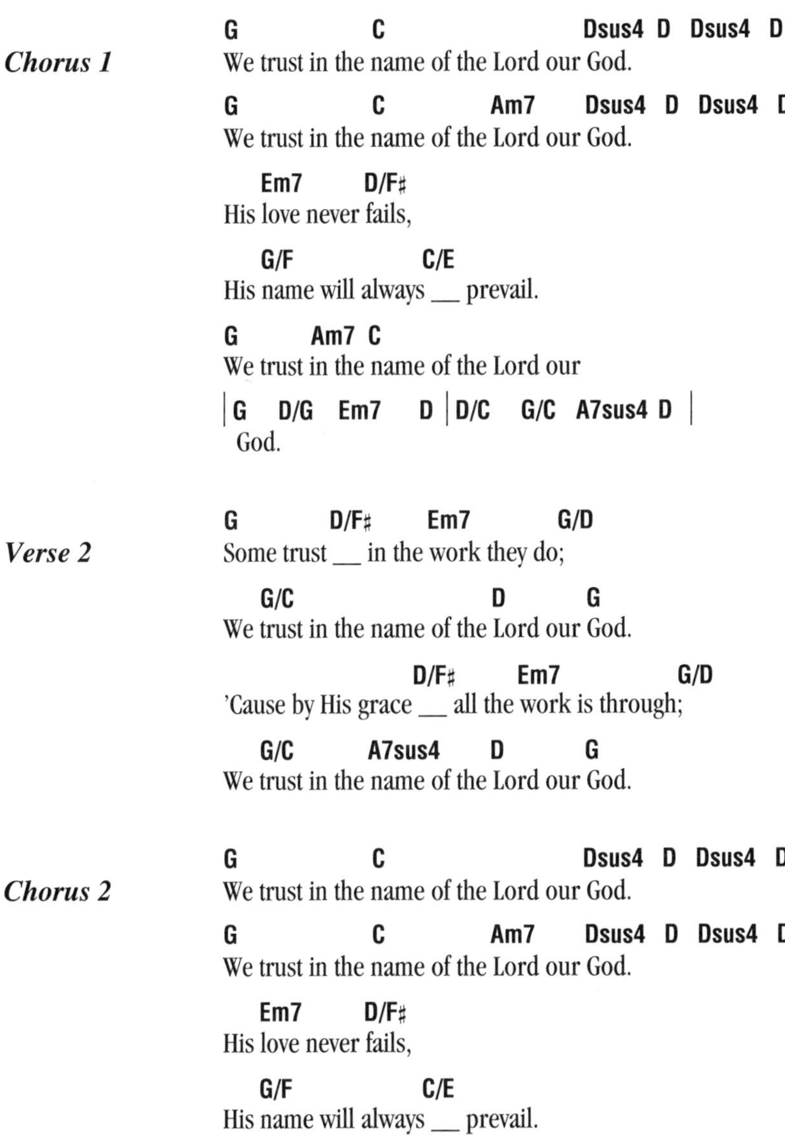
G C Dsus4 D Dsus4 D
Chorus 1
We trust in the name of the Lord our God.
G C Am7 Dsus4 D Dsus4 D
We trust in the name of the Lord our God.
Em7 D/F♯
His love never fails,
G/F C/E
His name will always __ prevail.
G Am7 C
We trust in the name of the Lord our
| G D/G Em7 D | D/C G/C A7sus4 D |
God.
G D/F♯ Em7 G/D
Verse 2
Some trust __ in the work they do;
G/C D G
We trust in the name of the Lord our God.
D/F♯ Em7 G/D
'Cause by His grace __ all the work is through;
G/C A7sus4 D G
We trust in the name of the Lord our God.
G C Dsus4 D Dsus4 D
Chorus 2
We trust in the name of the Lord our God.
G C Am7 Dsus4 D Dsus4 D
We trust in the name of the Lord our God.
Em7 D/F♯
His love never fails,
G/F C/E
His name will always __ prevail.
G Am7 C G C/G G
We trust in the name of the Lord our God.

Bridge

```
   D/F# C       G
Oh, glo  -  ry to the name,

   C   G/B Am7  Cmaj7 D
The name of  our sal-va  -  tion.

   F§       C            Cm
Oh, glory to the name above all names,

   G          Bm7    Esus4   E
The name of the Lord our God.
```

Verse 3

```
A              F#m
Some trust in the wealth of things;

  A/D                   E      A
We trust in the name of the Lord our God.

               E/G#     F#m    A/E
The name worth more than anything;

  D         Bm7         E      A
We trust in the name of the Lord our God.
```

Chorus 3

```
A           D                 Esus4 E  Esus4 E
We trust in the name of the Lord our God.
A           D                 Esus4  E  Esus4  E
We trust in the name of the Lord our God.

  F#m     E/G#
His love never fails,

  A/G          D/F#
His name will always __ prevail.

A     Bm7  D          Esus4   F#m Esus4
We trust in the name of the Lord our God.

|D   E   F  G  C  D|
```

A   D   Esus4 E Esus4 E
Chorus 4 We trust in the name of the Lord our God.

A   D   Esus4 E Esus4 E
We trust in the name of the Lord our God.

F♯m   E/G♯
His love never fails,

A/G   D/F♯
His name will always __ prevail.

A   D   Esus4
We trust in the name of the Lord our,

A   D   Dm
We trust in the name of the Lord our,

A   D   Esus4
We trust in the name of the Lord our

G6/9
Outro God. Trust in the name, trust in the name, trust in the name.

Bm7
Ah, __ trust in the name, trust in the name, trust in the name.

G6/9
Trust in the name, trust in the name, trust in the name.

Bm7
Ah, __ trust in the name, trust in the name, trust in the name.

G6/9
Trust in the name, trust in the name, trust in the name.

Bm7
Ah, __ trust in the name, trust in the name, trust in the name.

G6/9
Trust in the name, trust in the name, trust in the name.

Bm7   G6/9
Ah, __ trust in the name, trust in the name, trust in the name, name!

When It's Time to Go

Words and Music by Jeff Silvey and Billy Simon

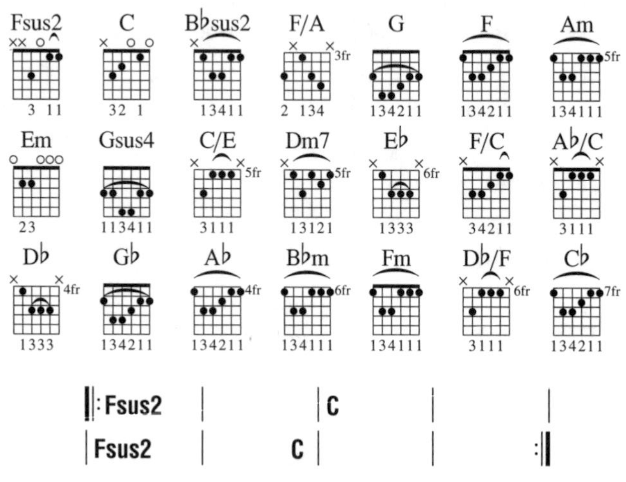

Intro

||: Fsus2 | | C | | |
| Fsus2 | C | | :||

Verse 1

C
Nothing new in this old town,

Fsus2
The sun comes up and heads back down.

B♭sus2 F/A C
Working hard from dawn __ to dusk again.

Seventeen and a heart for a change,

Fsus2
The byways calling out his name

B♭sus2 F/A C
But not yet; there's too much goin' on.

G
'Cause daddy needs a hand

F G
And mama's tender heart might

F G Am
Crumble to the ground.

G
Though they'd understand, he felt like saying:

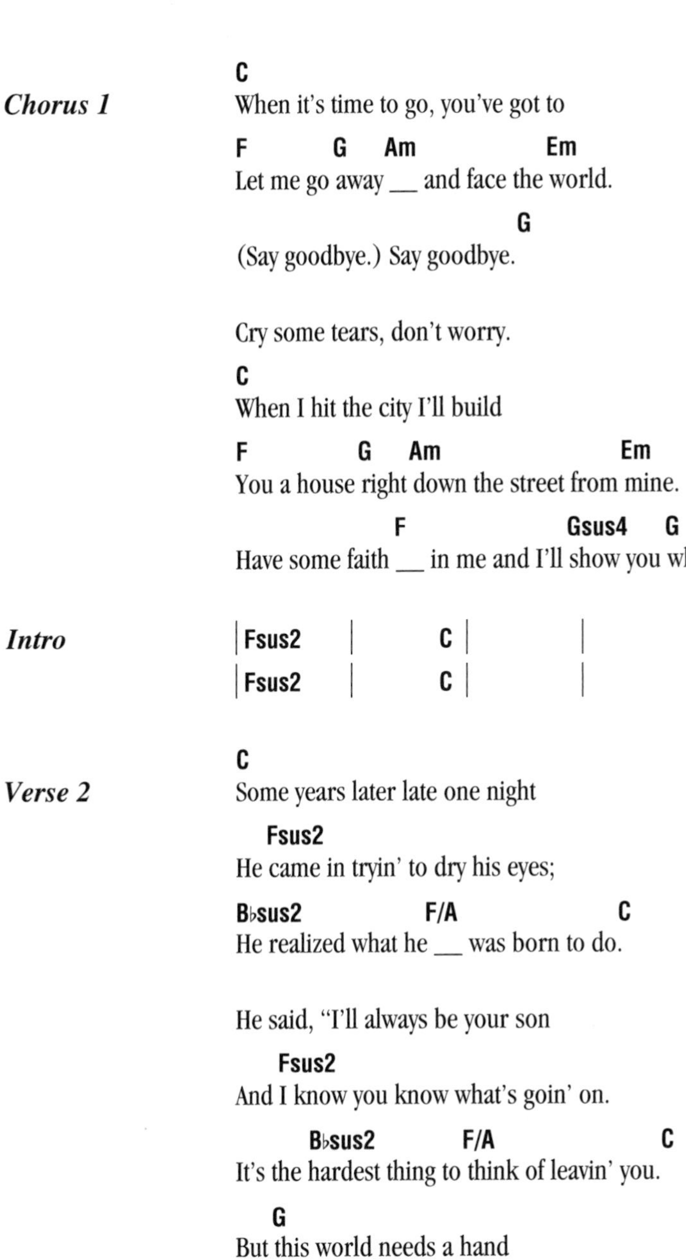

Chorus 1

C
When it's time to go, you've got to

F G Am Em
Let me go away __ and face the world.

G
(Say goodbye.) Say goodbye.

Cry some tears, don't worry.

C
When I hit the city I'll build

F G Am Em
You a house right down the street from mine.

F Gsus4 G
Have some faith __ in me and I'll show you why.

Intro

| Fsus2 | C | | |
| Fsus2 | C | | |

Verse 2

C
Some years later late one night

Fsus2
He came in tryin' to dry his eyes;

B♭sus2 F/A C
He realized what he __ was born to do.

He said, "I'll always be your son

Fsus2
And I know you know what's goin' on.

B♭sus2 F/A C
It's the hardest thing to think of leavin' you.

G
But this world needs a hand

F G
And I've got just the thing they

F G Am
Need to make it through.

G
It's so clear to me though I know what's coming.

Chorus 2 *Repeat Chorus 1*

Bridge

```
                Am  G   F     C/E Dm7  G        C
And as they tore His flesh like an    -    imals,
                Am  G F       C/E  E♭  F/C A♭/C
There were those I know who felt Him say:
```

Chorus 3

```
D♭
When it's time to go, you've got to
G♭          A♭   B♭m                Fm
Let me go away __ and save the world.
                                A♭
(Say goodbye.) Say goodbye.

Cry some tears, don't worry.
D♭
When I hit the city I'll build
G♭            A♭   B♭m                  Fm
You a house right down the street from mine.
                    G♭                  A♭
Oh, have some faith __ in me and I'll show you why.
```

Chorus 4 *Repeat Chorus 3*

Chorus 5 *Repeat Chorus 3*

Outro

```
| B♭m   A♭   | G♭    D♭/F  | C♭
```

When You Are a Soldier

Words and Music by Steven Curtis Chapman

(Capo 3rd fret)

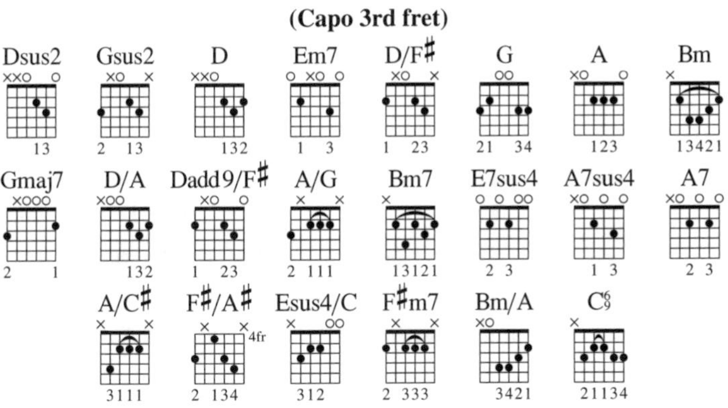

Intro | Dsus2 | | Gsus2 | |

Verse 1

D Em7 D/F♯ G D/F♯
When you are __ a sol - dier, I will be your shield.

G A Bm Gmaj7 D/A A
I will go with you into __ the battle-field.

Bm Gmaj7 A
And when the ar - rows start to fly,

D/F♯ G
Take my hand and hold on tight.

A/G D/F♯
I will be __ your shield,

Bm7 E7sus4
'Cause I know how it feels

A7sus4 A7 Dsus2 Gsus2
When you are a soldier.

Verse 2

```
D                    Em7          D/F#     G                   D/F#
When you're tired __ from run  -  ning, I will cheer you on.

G             A   Bm            Gmaj7        D/A  A
Look beside you and you'll see, __ you're not a-lone.

                          Bm    Gmaj7      A
And when your strength __ is all but gone,

          Dadd9/F#       G
I'll carry you until you're strong.

             A/G            D/F#
And I will be __ your shield,

       Bm7               E7sus4
'Cause I know how it feels

       A7sus4    A7
When you're a sol - dier.
```

Bridge

```
G   D/F#            A                 Bm
    I will be the one __ you can cry __ your song to.

    D/F#                      A    Bm7   A/C#
My eyes will share your tears.

G               D/F#              A    F#/A#     Bm
    I'll be your friend if you win __ or if you're __ defeated.

       Em7                 Esus4/C  A
When-ever you need me, I will be here.
```

Verse 3

```
Dsus2          Em7        D/F#      G                 D/F#
When you're lost __ in dark  -  ness, I will hold the light.

G          A    Bm            G   A
I will help you find your way __ through the night.

          Bm      Gmaj7     A
I'll remind __ you of the truth

                    D/F#        G
And keep the flame __ alive in you.

    G     F#m7  Em7 Dadd9/F#
And I will be      your shield,

       Bm7                Em7
'Cause I know how it feels

A7sus4      A7    Bm      Bm/A
When you are __ a soldier.

    G      A             D/F#
And I will be __ your shield,

       Bm7               Em7
'Cause I know how it feels

A7sus4        A7      Dsus2
When you are          a soldier.
```

Outro

```
|Dsus2    |        |Gsus2    |        |
|Dsus2    |        |Gsus2    |   C6/9 |        |Dsus2
```

Wisdom

Words and Music by Twila Paris

Tune down 1/2 step:
(low to high) E♭–A♭–D♭–G♭–B♭–E♭

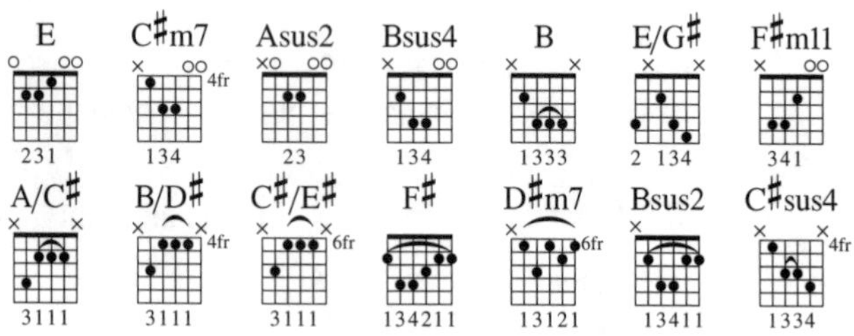

Intro ‖: E | C♯m7 | Asus2 | Bsus4 :‖

Verse 1

```
 Asus2                  Bsus4
   I see a multitude of peo - ple,
 E                            Asus2
   Some far away and some close by.
                          B
 They weave together new reli - gion
            Asus2                  E/G♯
 From tiny rem  -  nants they have found,
           Asus2       B
 A bit of truth, __ a greater lie.
 F♯m11                             B
   And all the prophets stand and sing __ a pleasant song,
 F♯m11                            B
   A million cords that bind the spir - it growing strong.
           Asus2           Bsus4
 My heart is breaking, I must re-mind them:
```

```
                E
Chorus 1   You are the only way,

                  C#m7
           You are the only voice,

                  Asus2
           You are the only hope,

                    Bsus4
           You are the only choice.

                     E
           You are the one true God,

                   C#m7
           No matter what we say.

                     Asus2
           You are the breath of life,

                  Bsus4
           You are the only way.

                  A/C#    B/D#
           Give us wis - dom.

                  A/C#    B/D#   Bsus4
           Give us wis - dom.


           Asus2                 Bsus4
Verse 2       There is a moment of deci - sion,

           E/G#                   Asus2
              But all the days go rushing by,

                                B
           An undercurrent of confu - sion

                    Asus2          E/G#
           To threaten all __ that we believe

                   Asus2          B
           With little time __ to wonder why.

           F#m11                              B
              And all the prophets sing the same __ familiar song;

           F#m11                     B
              Even the chosen can be led __ to sing along.

                      Asus2               Bsus4
           These hearts are breaking, will You re-mind us?
```

Chorus 2

```
                          E
You are the only way,
                            C♯m7
You are the only voice,
                           Asus2
You are the only hope,
                             Bsus4
You are the only choice.
                            E
You are the one true God,
                             C♯m7
No matter what we say.
                               Asus2
You are the breath of life,
                          Bsus4
You are the only way.
              A/C♯      B/D♯
Give us wis  -  dom.
              A/C#      B/D#
Give us wis  -  dom.
```

Bridge

```
A/C♯                  Bsus4       B     E/G♯              B
   You chose the sim  -  ple things __ to overcome the wise.
A/C♯              B              E/G♯         Asus2   B
Wisdom is grant - ed in the name __ of Jesus Christ.
              E           A/C♯    B/D♯
In the name __ of Jesus Christ.
```

Chorus 3

```
                          F♯
You are the only way,
                              D♯m7
You are the only voice,
                             Bsus2
You are the only hope,
                               C♯sus4
You are the only choice.
                             F♯
You are the one true God,
                               D♯m7
No matter what we say.
                                 Bsus2
You are the breath of life,
                                  C♯sus4
We need You here today.
                          F♯
You are the only way,
                              D♯m7
You are the only voice,
                             Bsus2
You are the only hope,
                               C♯sus4
You are the only choice.
                             F♯
You are the one true God,
                               D♯m7
No matter what we say.
                                 Bsus2
You are the breath of life,
                            C♯sus4
You are the only way.
               B/D♯      C♯/E♯
Give us wis  -  dom.
               B/D♯      C♯/E♯
Give us wis  -  dom.
```

Outro

```
‖: F♯       | D♯m7       | Bsus2       | C♯sus4   :‖
```

Repeat and fade

Where There Is Faith

Words and Music by Billy Simon

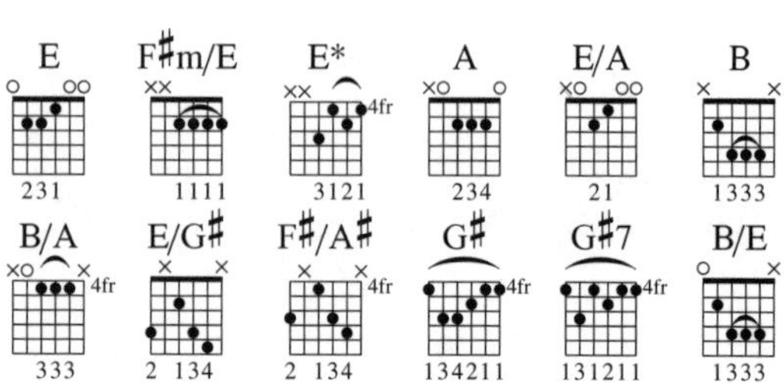

Intro | E | F♯m/E E* | E | F♯m/E E* |

Verse 1

```
E          F♯m/E  E*          E
    I believe __ in  faithfulness,
        F♯m/E  E*        A
I believe __ in giving of __ myself
E/A   A          E         F♯m/E   E*
  For someone else.
E          F♯m/E   E*             E
    I believe __ in   peace and love,
        F♯m/E  E*      A
I believe __ in  honesty __ and trust.
E/A        A     E         F♯m/E  E*
  But it's not e-nough;
        B                B/A
For all __ that I believe __
                    E            A
May never change __ the way it is
          E/G♯                       B
Unless I __ believe that Jesus lives.
```

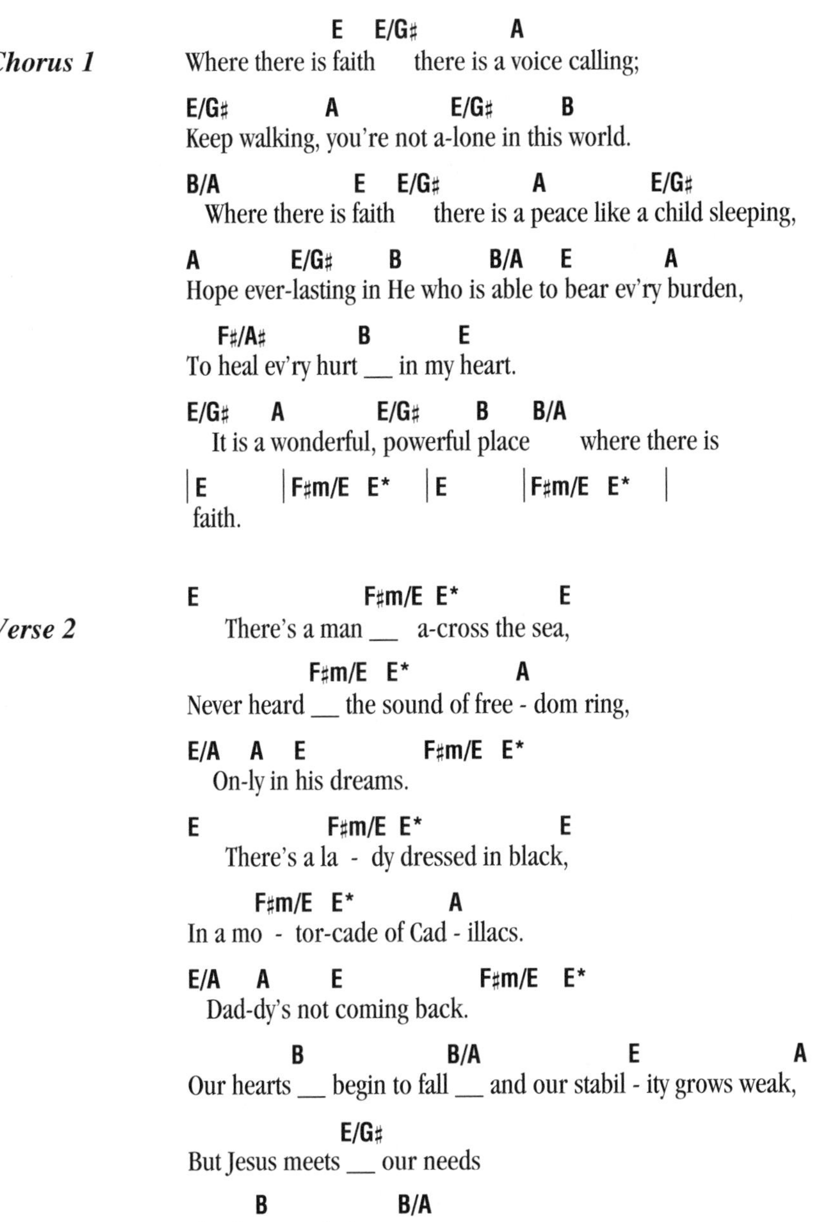

Chorus 1

```
                 E    E/G♯          A
Where there is faith    there is a voice calling;

E/G♯          A             E/G♯        B
Keep walking, you're not a-lone in this world.

B/A                E    E/G♯           A            E/G♯
   Where there is faith    there is a peace like a child sleeping,

A          E/G♯      B          B/A    E          A
Hope ever-lasting in He who is able to bear ev'ry burden,

   F♯/A♯          B          E
To heal ev'ry hurt __ in my heart.

E/G♯    A           E/G♯       B     B/A
   It is a wonderful, powerful place       where there is

|E        |F♯m/E  E*   |E        |F♯m/E  E*    |
 faith.
```

Verse 2

```
E                   F♯m/E  E*           E
     There's a man __    a-cross the sea,

             F♯m/E  E*             A
Never heard __ the sound of free - dom ring,

E/A   A   E              F♯m/E  E*
   On-ly in his dreams.

E               F♯m/E  E*                E
     There's a la  -  dy dressed in black,

        F♯m/E  E*            A
In a mo  -  tor-cade of Cad - illacs.

E/A    A      E               F♯m/E   E*
  Dad-dy's not coming back.

              B                 B/A                E                 A
Our hearts __ begin to fall __ and our stabil - ity grows weak,

                  E/G♯
But Jesus meets __ our needs

        B             B/A
If only __ we believe.
```

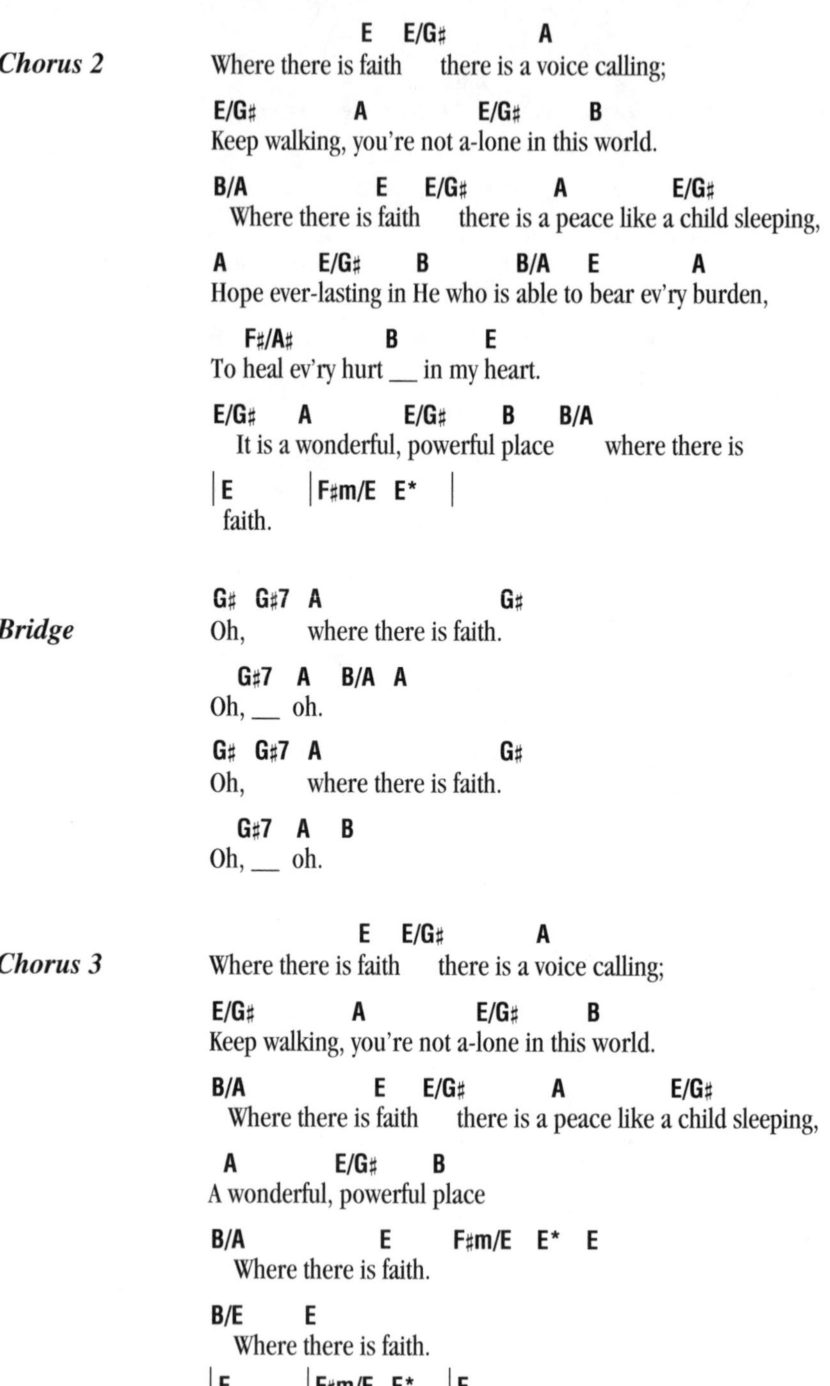

Chorus 2

E E/G♯ A
Where there is faith there is a voice calling;

E/G♯ A E/G♯ B
Keep walking, you're not a-lone in this world.

B/A E E/G♯ A E/G♯
Where there is faith there is a peace like a child sleeping,

A E/G♯ B B/A E A
Hope ever-lasting in He who is able to bear ev'ry burden,

F♯/A♯ B E
To heal ev'ry hurt __ in my heart.

E/G♯ A E/G♯ B B/A
It is a wonderful, powerful place where there is

| E | F♯m/E E* |
faith.

Bridge

G♯ G♯7 A G♯
Oh, where there is faith.

G♯7 A B/A A
Oh, __ oh.

G♯ G♯7 A G♯
Oh, where there is faith.

G♯7 A B
Oh, __ oh.

Chorus 3

E E/G♯ A
Where there is faith there is a voice calling;

E/G♯ A E/G♯ B
Keep walking, you're not a-lone in this world.

B/A E E/G♯ A E/G♯
Where there is faith there is a peace like a child sleeping,

A E/G♯ B
A wonderful, powerful place

B/A E F♯m/E E* E
Where there is faith.

B/E E
Where there is faith.

| E | F♯m/E E* | E

Guitar Chord Songbook

Each book includes complete lyrics, chord symbols, and guitar chord diagrams.

Children's Songs

A great resource for over 70 songs for kids, complete with the chords and lyrics for each. Songs include: Alphabet Song • Any Dream Will Do • The Brady Bunch • The Candy Man • Do-Re-Mi • Edelweiss • Eensy Weensy Spider • Home on the Range • It's a Small World • Old MacDonald • On Top of Spaghetti • Puff the Magic Dragon • The Rainbow Connection • Sing • Supercalifragilisticexpialidocious • Take Me Out to the Ball Game • Twinkle, Twinkle Little Star • and more!

00699539 ....$12.95

Christmas Carols

A convenient reference of 80 Christmas carols for the player who just needs the lyrics and chords. Songs include: Angels We Have Heard on High • Away in a Manger • Deck the Hall • Good King Wenceslas • The Holly and the Ivy • I Heard the Bells on Christmas Day • Jingle Bells • Joy to the World • O Holy Night • Silent Night • Up on the Housetop • We Wish You a Merry Christmas • Welsh Carol • What Child Is This? • and more.

00699536 ....$12.95

Christmas Songs

A great resource of the chords and lyrics for 80 Christmas favorites, including: Baby, It's Cold Outside • The Chipmunk Song • The Christmas Shoes • The Christmas Song (Chestnuts Roasting on an Open Fire) • Feliz Navidad • Frosty the Snow Man • Grandma Got Run Over by a Reindeer • Happy Holiday • (There's No Place Like) Home for the Holidays • I've Got My Love to Keep Me Warm • It Must Have Been the Mistletoe (Our First Christmas) • Merry Christmas, Darling • Miss You Most at Christmas Time • Rudolph the Red-Nosed Reindeer • Silver Bells • We Need a Little Christmas • What Are You Doing New Year's Eve? • and more.

00699537 ....$12.95

Contemporary Christian

A great, easy-to-use collection of just the chords and lyrics to 80 hits from today's top CCM artists. Includes: Abba (Father) • Alive • Awesome God • Don't Look at Me • El Shaddai • Find Us Faithful • Friends • The Great Divide • He Will Carry You • His Strength Is Perfect • I Will Be Here • Just One • Live Out Loud • Love Will Be Our Home • A Maze of Grace • Oh Lord, You're Beautiful • Pray • Run to You • Speechless • Testify to Love • Via Dolorosa • and more.

00699564 ....$14.95

Country

80 country standards, including: Abilene • Always on • Amazed • Blue • Boot Scootin' Boogie • Breathe • Have This Dance • Crazy • Folsom Prison Blues • F Low Places • Hey, Good Lookin' • I Feel Lucky • I H Dance • Sixteen Tons • Your Cheatin' Heart • and m

00699534 ....

Folksongs

80 folk favorites, including: Aura Lee • Camptown Deep River • Git Along, Little Dogies • Home on the Hush, Little Baby • I've Been Working on the Railro Got Peace Like a River • Man of Constant Sorrow • Knows the Trouble I've Seen • Scarborough Fair • W Saints Go Marching In • and more.

00699541 ....

Pop/Rock

The chords and lyrics to 80 chart hits, including: All Do • Closer to Free • Come Sail Away • Drops of Jupi Me) • Every Breath You Take • Give a Little Bit • H Tonight • Hurts So Good • I Want You to Want Me Remember You • Imagine • More Than Words • Mr. Smooth • Summer of '69 • Superman (It's Not Easy) After Time • What I Like About You • Wheel in th Wonderful Tonight • and more.

00699538 ....

Rock 'n' Roll

80 rock 'n' roll classics in one convenient collection: A Up • At the Hop • Blue Suede Shoes • Chantilly Lace of Earl • Great Balls of Fire • It's My Party • La Bam Loco-Motion • My Boyfriend's Back • Peggy Sue Around the Clock • Stand by Me • Surfin' U.S.A. • an

00699535 ....

FOR MORE INFORMATION, SEE YOUR LOCAL MUSIC DEALER, OR WRITE TO:

HAL•LEONARD® CORPORATION

7777 W. BLUEMOUND RD. P.O. BOX 13819 MILWAUKEE, WI 53213

Visit Hal Leonard online at **www.halleonard**

Prices, contents, and availability subject to change withou